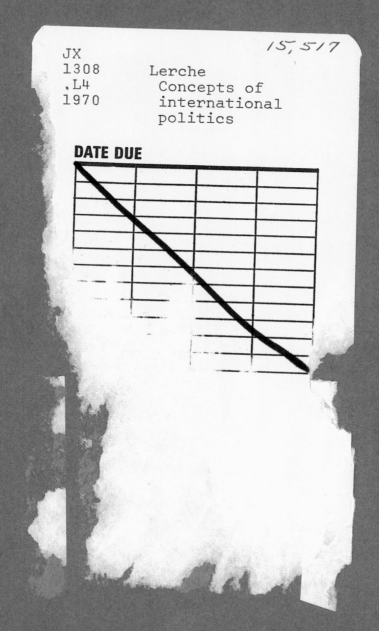

CONCEPTS OF
INTERNATIONAL
POLITICS

CHARLES O. LERCHE, Jr.

ABDUL A. SAID

School of International Service
The American University

CONCEPTS OF INTERNATIONAL POLITICS

2nd edition

PRENTICE-HALL, INC., Englewood Cliffs, N. J.

13–166041–1

Library of Congress Catalog Card Number: 76–86518

Current printing (last digit):

10   9   8   7   6   5   4   3   2   1

Prentice-Hall International, Inc., *London*
Prentice-Hall of Australia Pty. Ltd., *Sydney*
Prentice-Hall of Canada Ltd., *Toronto*
Prentice-Hall of India Private Ltd., *New Delhi*
Prentice-Hall of Japan, Inc., *Tokyo*

Printed in the United States of America

Preface
to the First Edition

This book is an experiment. It is an attempt to present in a convenient and reasonably systematic form a conceptual framework for the study and the comprehension of international politics. This academic field, with no methodology uniquely its own and with no long history of illustrious scholarly pioneering, in recent years has exploded in a "conceptual revolution." An army of scholars using a broad variety of techniques of analysis and synthesis, has made a massive and many-sided effort to organize the familiar data of international affairs into an intellectually responsible discipline. It is out of this ferment that the present volume grows.

Contemporary students of international politics are often informally classified as "theorists" or "policy scientists," depending on whether their primary interests lie in the development of valid and broadly applicable generalizations or in the solution of particular problems of state relationships in the real world. This book leans to the first category in that its emphasis throughout is general and theoretical, with its goal one of contributing to a deeper understanding of the entire international political process on the part of its readers. The authors, however, must openly confess a bias: they feel that a sound theoretical grounding is as vital to the policy-oriented specialist as it is to the system-oriented generalist.

In this book, therefore, the authors attempt to develop a sufficiently useful—that is, teachable—view of the international political system and process to provide the student either with a base for more advanced theoretical studies or with the capacity to deal in a more sophisticated and competent manner with the data of ongoing international political relations. This is a formidable task, and the authors are as aware as their readers will be of the extent to which their aim was perhaps over-ambitious. The ideas and the organizational framework presented here, however, have been tested in classroom use for several years with considerable numbers of students. The results have been encouraging to an extent to justify the opinion that this approach may have general applicability.

The table of contents suggests the major divisions of the book. Part I focuses upon the individual state and is devoted generally to an elaboration of the broad idea of "foreign policy." Part II develops the notion of "politics" as the crucial form of interstate relationship. Part III includes a discussion of five critical areas of political action in the contemporary world that promise to retain their relevance into the future. Parts I and II together are intended to provide a theoretical base for the moderately more specific discussions in Part III. The short reading lists that follow each chapter emphasize works that are conveniently and inexpensively available in paperback format.

ACKNOWLEDGMENTS

The familiar "debt of gratitude" that academic authors usually acknowledge to their students for "inspiring" or "provoking" a book in this case is to be taken literally; both the conceptual skeleton and the final shape of this book grew out of the day-by-day necessity both authors have experienced of confronting undergraduate students with basic yet meaningful materials in international politics.

Miss Thea Fund, Mr. Philip M. Burgess, and Mr. Bahram Farzanegan, while student assistants of the authors, gave of their time and enthusiasm to the preparation of this book far beyond the call of duty or the expectations of the authors.

Dr. Kenneth W. Thompson of the Rockefeller Foundation and Dr. William Olson of the Legislative Reference Service of the Library of Congress read the manuscript and contributed to the further education of the authors while sparing the readers many questionable generalizations and imprecisions of expression.

Mrs. Elizabeth Forrest, whose technical skill was matched by a fine editorial sense, prepared the final form of the manuscript with great speed, good humor, and finesse.

The authors, of course, recognize their ultimate responsibility for all errors of fact and inaccuracies of judgment, and express their hope that both categories of fault have been kept to a minimum.

C. O. L., Jr.
A. A. S.

Washington, D.C.
January, 1963

Preface
to the Second Edition

The untimely death of my late friend and coauthor, Charles O. Lerche, was a great personal loss to me and to the community of political science. Charles O. Lerche was a living witness to excellence. As a true academician with a searching mind, he was knowledgeable of the past, fully aware of the present, and actively probed the future. He was a courageously independent thinker of breadth and imagination who chose to direct his inquiry to the very center of things. His approach to the facts of our political life was equally direct, and his analysis and interpretations were incisive, meaningful, and straightforward. His works are not only stimulating in themselves, but also provide an example of what freedom, independence, and courage really mean in a free society. While his physical absence will deprive us of his keen analysis of mankind's problems and possibilities, his ideals and vision endure in this book as well as in his other works.

Almost a decade ago, when the first edition of this book was in the planning stage, we decided to analyze international politics on three levels: the individual political actor within the political system; the political system itself, including the social structure and the process of political action; and the substance of political action. Now, one edition and countless crises later, we are as convinced as ever of the utility and academic validity of this device. This edition, no less than its predecessor, seeks to analyze the interplay of the foreign policy process with the demands of international politics.

Otherwise, several differences in emphasis may be noted. New conditions in international politics have brought about a broader scope of consideration in Parts II and III of the book. Erosion of the bipolar world, the rise of revolution as an ideology, the dynamics of modernization, the changing nature of force and conflict, and recent approaches to international law and organization receive what we feel is their contemporary due.

As the second edition was being prepared, we were impressed—and to a considerable degree, discontented—with how many of the theoretical insights originally formulated in Part I of the book remain valid today. This is not to suggest a prescience or an insight beyond ordinary mortals on the part of the authors, but rather that problems of theorizing about international politics have proved as intractable to the best efforts of the political scientist as was suspected when the first edition was written. Nevertheless, the second edition includes a completely new introduction showing the development of the study of international relations, the present state of the discipline, and a statement of the intellectual base of our approach. The concise and brief nature of the first edition remains intact.

ACKNOWLEDGMENTS

In the preparation of this edition the author is indebted to Professors Samuel L. Sharp and James R. Jose of The American University and to Colonels Dana G. Mead and Anthony A. Smith, and Major William J. Taylor, of the United States Military Academy. Their impeccable academic judgment has improved this volume in countless ways.

Professors John R. Aidem, Leonard Corren, Bahram Farzanegan, and Herbert S. Graves read the proposed changes in the second edition and contributed to the further education of the author while sparing the readers many questionable generalities and imprecisions of expression.

Several of his student assistants, Cyrus Elahi, Harold Lippman, Keith Rosenberg, David Frame, Richard Eurich, Edward Feinberg, Wray Kunkle, and McKean Tredway, gave their time and enthusiasm to this book far beyond the call of duty. Miss Lois M. Gardner, whose technical skill was matched by patience, prepared the final form of the manuscript.

Mrs. Susanne MacVaugh prepared the initial form of the manuscript with skill, finesse, and good cheer. Finally, my family tolerated and sustained me with comfort while I prepared this book.

A. A. S.

Washington, D.C.
May, 1969

Contents

CONCEPTS OF INTERNATIONAL POLITICS

Introduction

The study of international relations has experienced a thoroughgoing revolution in the years since World War II. As taught in the interwar period (and it was taught only seldom before 1920), it was a highly emotionalized form of diplomatic history. Its purpose was clear—to learn why men had gone to war in the past, to appreciate the errors of their ways, to discover institutions that would make war illegal and irrational, and always to urge participation in the League of Nations. It was rationalist, moralist, legalistic, and optimistic. Its goal was utopia, its methodology a mixture of history and exhortation. More recent studies have, however, been characterized by the utilization of a broad spectrum of analytical approaches and research techniques.

DEVELOPMENT OF THE STUDY OF INTERNATIONAL RELATIONS

Four major trends can be discerned in the development of the study of international relations. Beginning shortly before World War I and continuing throughout the interwar years, attention was focused on diplomatic history. In the interwar years, another concentration was on the singular study of current events. At the same time, a trend premised on the assumption that international conflicts could be solved by a study of international law and organization became prominent. Since the beginning of World War II the study of international relations has been motivated by a "realist" viewpoint, stemming from an empirical orientation.

These trends should not be characterized as a linear progression, since they have often run parallel to each other, or have arisen in response to a preceding trend. Contemporary writing incorporates the ideas expressed in all of these trends; each one contributes in some degree to the advance of the discipline.

Scholarship during the period of concern with diplomatic history was characterized by meticulous attention to historical detail and historical method. The discipline was replete with lucid accounts of particular periods or significant diplomatic events. The diplomatic historian sought to explore fully a given historical event, utilizing a maximum quantity of documentary evidence. This historical orientation precluded the development of a theoretical or propositional core for the discipline.

The second trend, arising as a reaction to the diplomatic historian's lack of emphasis on current events, focused on current events to the virtual exclusion of the historical record. These essentially descriptive efforts, based almost exclusively on *The New York Times* and divorced from historical antecedents, were necessarily superficial and speculative. Again a theoretical inquiry was either disavowed or considered unfeasible.

The third trend, professing innovation and borrowing from the first two methods, turned to the problems of international law and international organization. Its exponents asserted that the task of the scholar was to work toward the transformation of society and the construction of international institutions. This activist position was largely inspired by the establishment of the League of Nations, the hopes associated with its inception, and the goal of communicating the ideas of the League to the world, with particular emphasis on the isolationist inclined United States. The single belief that attracted most of these scholars was that establishment of a strong international organization would cause the perplexing issues of international politics to disappear.

In general, the temper and scholarship of the early interwar period were characterized by a spirit of optimism. It was felt that, by resolving the technical and procedural problems of international organization, world government and hence peace would be within man's grasp. Consequently, research tended to deal, to the exclusion of other concerns, with international law and the constitutional and procedural difficulties of international institutions. However, by 1939 history and empirical realities over-took this optimistic approach. The political turmoil of Europe and the Far East in the 1930's, the rise of dictators, and the impotence of the League in the face of these events contributed to a feeling of despair and cynicism among scholars and the world at large.

In the great backwash of cynicism and disappointment that overtook the academic community, particularly in the United States, during World War II, the reformist approach to the study of international relations was ruthlessly jettisoned. The prevailing academic judgment then was that the faith of the reformers was misplaced; man was neither perfect nor perfectible, reason and morality had no role to play in the study or practice of international relations, institutions could never be reformed or war eliminated. Power—usually crudely identified as mobilized military strength—was the only absolute in the affairs of nations, and *Machtpolitik* was neither immoral nor irrational, only inevitable.

This sour verdict, compounded equally by dejection at the failure of interwar dreams and of the immediate exigencies of wartime, continued over the postwar period. It received intellectual underpinning with the appearance in 1947 of what might be the most important single book ever written on the theoretical approach to international relations: *Politics Among Nations,* by Professor Hans J. Morgenthau. International politics, according to Professor Morgenthau, is a struggle for power. All states are impelled by the urge to amass, protect, and manipulate power; power is the single "national interest" of everyone. He argued that this clue to the behavior of states would unlock the riddles of international politics and provide the scholar with the insight to understand the process and to give useful advice to the statesman.

This was (and is) widely advertised as the "realist" approach to international politics, as opposed to the "idealist" hypothesis of the interwar years. It swept the field for the first six years after its initial publication; the debate that rocked the academic community as Morgenthau was directly challenged by his critics did not begin until the early 1950's. When students took a second look at the doctrine, they came to appreciate that this type of "realism" was simply pessimism and cynicism about human motivations which ignored all the evidence that, although man was obviously no angel, neither was he a beast. If all men were insensate animals, unmoved either by reason or ethics, no destiny awaited the species in an atomic age except early and total destruction. "Realism," a term once identifying a neo-Machiavellian worship of blind force and an almost loving refutation of any claims to simple decency in the human race, has come to be recognized as Utopian (in a strange upside down way), as was the naïve do-goodism of the League of Nations group of an earlier era. Today the "realist-idealist" controversy is a good deal less significant, and even Professor Morgenthau is less insistent on the absolute sovereignty of the thrust for power as the ubiquitous end of state action.

But although Morgenthau's "realism" is no longer taken seriously, and the "power concept" is not so militantly urged, his real contribution to the field is greater than ever. In his pioneering work, he showed us how to think systematically about international politics; in other words, to think by means of *concepts* rather than in terms of institutions or events. The result of any such exercise is a set of generalizations about state behavior rather than a blueprint for a policy to deal with a particular contingency. Morgenthau started us thinking about the *causes* of state behavior in general and social science terms; his suggestion that the effective source of state action is a quest for power alerted students—especially those who rejected his particular thesis—to the necessity of discovering the true motivations of states. Morgenthau's sophisticated intelligence and broad education showed the profession—convinced for two generations that history, politics, law, and philosophy were the only sources of insight—that sociologists and psychologists had a great many interesting things to say about the phenomenon of international relations.

As the power concept lost its seductiveness and "realism" its appeal, the true Morgenthau influence began to be felt. Younger scholars, excited by the challenge, undertook to emulate Morgenthau and began to think systematically and conceptually. Certain universities—Princeton, Yale, Chicago, Northwestern—became centers of this enterprise that soon began calling itself, with considerable justification, the "scientific" study of international relations. Today the introductory course in international relations in any college or university (the most accurate indicator of the state of the field) is likely to be a theoretical course concerned with inculcating an understanding of the elements of the international political system and the establishment of a set of generalizations about the action and interaction of states in a political setting. No longer do students learn details about the foreign policy of France between 1958 and the present as end in itself; that sort of material is important only for illustrating a generalization or a broadly applicable rule.

PRESENT STATE OF THE DISCIPLINE

Today we are all theorists, analyzing the data that come before us not for their intrinsic interest or even their policy relevance, but rather in an attempt to develop a conceptual system (roughly defined as a workable scheme for classification of data) that will make it possible to deal with universals rather than particulars. Those of us who have become "policy-oriented" and are interested in the adoption of our action formulas by governments are obliged to take our stand on whatever theoretical and "scientific" insights we may possess at the moment, and to use them as a basis for ordering contemporary data. For an academic, it is a tremendously exciting field of study, alive with ideas, hypotheses, schemes, and theories; although there may not be as many theories as there are theorists, there is unquestionably a host of ideas wandering around seeking converts. Approving critics talk of a "healthy ferment" within the discipline; disapproving ones characterize the field as one of "unrelieved confusion."

Nevertheless, we may make certain loose generalizations about the present state of the discipline. It is a young field: young in the freshness of its approach and in the chronological age of its students. Only a few of the "old masters" of the profession are generally regarded as productive and provocative today. For most of its failures, as well as most of its successes, the discipline of international relations has the youth of its students to credit.

In the second place, contemporary study of international relations is oriented to a search for causal rather than normative factors. Value judgments are universally admitted to be relevant to the practice of foreign policy, but since they are postulated a priori, they do not lend themselves to rational and scientific analysis. The student, therefore, tends to concentrate on developing the rules that govern the cause-effect relationship in the affairs of states. This may be a weakness; if the serious scholars suspend normative judgment on events, the function of assigning value to policy choices falls to political leaders, journalists, and other manipulators of the mass psyche. In any case, in a self-conscious attempt to avoid the soft-headedness of the Utopians or the frozen cynicism of the neo-Machiavellians, modern authors usually beg the question of value judgments and seek to liberate themselves from the thrust of day-by-day crisis.

Third, modern students of international relations are by and large interdisciplinary in their orientation and background. Although political science and political understanding are, of course, crucial, so are a host of other kinds of knowledge and insights: economic, demographic, geographic, sociological, psychological, anthropological, linguistic, theological, and so on. Today there is something of a bias toward the so-called "behavioral" social sciences, especially cultural anthropology and social psychology; these disciplines are felt to offer the prospect of a total understanding of man, and thus to open the way for his prediction and control.

This Promethean urge is offset to some extent by a rising interest in what may be called the "philosophy of science." Sober reassessment of the nature of what we are about will inevitably return us to fundamentals and relieve us of many of our contemporary apprehensions about the potentialities of such intoxicating phrases as the "culture concept," the "iron law of oligarchy," and "small group dynamics." Sociologists and anthropologists have opened new horizons for students, but they are no more the panacea that will resolve our doubts than were their intellectual forerunners, the philosophers, the jurisprudents, and even the economists.

Finally, "IR" is an iconoclastic discipline today. Its students attack each other with abandon, and the academic scene is littered with the debris of repudiated conceptual systems. Many of the influential newer books in the field are a "wrecking operation"; their authors take on the most prestigious scholars, and leave little except wreckage.

This lack of consensus is reminiscent of the period of flux and controversy through which the science of astronomy passed after being liberated from the geocentric theory of Ptolemy. Dozens of students thronged the observatories and laboratories of the Western world, taking advantage of their new intellectual freedom to observe and classify to their hearts' content. Inevitably they began to hazard generalizations, many of which were proved wrong by their colleagues. Only out of such probing and checking can progress toward valid generalization be achieved in a discipline in which the data are not manipulable, but only observable and classifiable.

So much for generalizations about the field. What are contemporary scholars actually concerning themselves with as they try to organize a vast and constantly growing body of data into useful and valid categories? Recent thinking in international relations encompasses a five-fold classification of the intellectual enterprise.

We find first a concern with the nature of theory itself and just what theory will look like when it is completed and perfected. This area involves a good deal of interest in how "scientific" international relations may expect to become, particularly the question of whether we may reach the capacity to predict or must forever confine ourselves to the explanation of events after they happen.

A second major concern of conceptual thinking today is in the area of research techniques. In the past decade, scholars have been asking many new questions about the action and interaction of states, and out of this effort has come some appreciation of the data that must be acquired before any convincing answers can be given. The search for different sorts of information has led to the development of entirely new techniques of research, and the adaptation of others drawn from sister disciplines to the purposes of international relations study.

Initially, we may mention the entire field of *quantitative methods.* If the scientific method is inductive, and if true knowledge of the world can be acquired by the observation and classification of quantitative data, then international relations theory must in some way make use of quantification in its search for scientific truth. Some of us have fallen into the trap laid by the logical positivists, who contend that only that which can be counted, weighed, measured, or observed can be called "truth"; most of us, however, try to blend our quantitative work with qualitative analysis and "humanistic insights." The various researches of Karl Deutsch on the "social transactions" that occur across national frontiers (for example, in nationalism and social communication) are remarkable for both the ingenuity of his methods and the volume of his findings.

Certain other modern research techniques are also involved. *Content analysis,* borrowed from the scientific study of communications, has opened new vistas in such areas as threat-perception and communication of symbols. *Psychometrics*—the development of ways to measure psychic phenomena such as "friendliness" or "hostility" between states—has occasionally been very useful and stimulating. *Mathematical formulation* of internal relationships, growing out of the pioneering work of British mathematician Lewis F. Richardson, has recently come in for some searching re-examination. Effort has been invested in actual experimentation by means of various devices of "political gaming": the creation of a simplified "model" situation in the form of a game played by a limited number of human subjects whose actions and reactions are carefully observed and analyzed. This enterprise has been materially aided (at least in the universities wealthy enough to afford one) by the employment of electronic computers.

The third and fourth classifications of intellectual enterprise require some semantic clarification before their content is summarized. One of the troubles confronting students of international relations is the imprecise use of terminology. Descriptive terms that should be distinguishable are used as synonyms: "international relations," "world politics," "world affairs," "politics among nations," and "international politics" are only a few names given to the over-all field. These, incidentally, are all drawn from the titles of standard textbooks in the field (including our own), all of them presumably about the identical body of subject matter! Modern scholars, despairing of ever achieving semantic agreement through persuasion and conversion, have begun making their definitions operational by using one single term to refer to only one relationship, and then remaining true to that use. Thus, we may say analytically, that IR theory can encompass two kinds of theories: action theory, dealing with one state as it moves within the system, and interaction theory, dealing with the relations of states to each other. Action theory is the realm of foreign policy analysis, and interaction theory is that of international politics.

Thus the third contemporary concern is in the area of action theory—the way states and their decision-makers act as they analyze their situations, select their objectives, and decide upon and execute courses of action. Here some of the most important and interesting areas of inquiry are being explored: ends-means analysis, decision-making, capability analysis, and the influence of the structure and functioning of a society on the foreign policy of its government.

The fourth concern has been in the area of interaction theory: the sphere of *international politics* (politics rather than relations, because the "actors" are states and public organizations rather than individuals). Here there is much less agreement on definitions and premises than in action theory; much greater scattering and diffusion of effort is apparent. The range of speculation and hypothesizing runs from systematic models of the entire international system at one extreme to very detailed examinations of specific forms of interaction at the other. There is a further differentiation between attempts to generalize about the "patterns" of (or formed by) interaction, and those studies that concentrate upon the behavior of the actors while engaged in interaction. Areas of analysis in interaction theory include balance theory, equilibrium theory, value theory, game theory, "challenge and response" theory, "image" theory, and "expectation" theory.

The fifth major concern is what we may broadly call "systems analysis": the development of testable hypotheses about the international system itself, as distinct from separate states. By and large this has taken two major forms: an assault on the concept of "actor" in the international political sense, and a fresh look (or group of looks) at the role of environmental factors in the relations of states. One group grapples with the nature of the state today and the direction of its evolution, the changing concept of the individual and the social group as factors in international politics, and the evolving place of supranational entities like international organizations and "security communities" as self-energizing actors in the system. A second group concentrates on factors external to human actors, refining concepts like "environmental determinism," "the international social system," "social change," "order," and "community" as they are relevant to the behavior of states. Those concerned primarily with the changing concept of "actor" are considered action theorists; those dealing with environmental factors are known as interaction theorists.

A system can be most broadly defined as a whole made up of inter-related parts. Systems analysis is a conceptual device which utilizes this idea of systems and applies it to empirical reality for the purpose of categorizing and understanding different phenomena in our complex world.

Systems analysis in its broadest context can be viewed as consisting of four basic elements: the *system* itself, which can be repeatedly broken down into subsystems; its *environment,* or all of reality outside the system; *inputs*—those factors which influence the system and bring about changes in it; and *outputs* emanating from the system—the system's responses to inputs. In analyzing a system, the analyst first attempts to distinguish between the system and its environment. He then proceeds to study inputs fed into the system and the resulting outputs produced by it. In this way he can register how the system changes (i.e., maintains itself) and thus have a better understanding of how it operates.

With the possible exception of the Universe, no systems are per-petually self-maintaining. A mechanical system such as the automobile is in fact incapable of maintaining itself, in that it cannot produce out-puts on its own to meet the stresses and strains of inputs. However, there do exist systems that can respond on their own, to a limited extent, to inputs. The human organism is one of them. Minor wounds can be healed without medical attention; most maladies are overcome in a healthy body by means of body defense mechanisms; the general system of the body is constantly maintained by the continuing creation of new cells to replace the old. When the body can no longer handle inputs, the human system breaks down and life ceases.

Social and political systems function in much the same way as the human body. Social systems in general, and political systems in particular, are at least partially self-maintaining. A political system such as the na-tion-state responds to the demands of inputs by issuing outputs that will hopefully counteract stresses created by the inputs. Thus the decision-makers in Czarist Russia responded to domestic demands in 1905 by issuing a semiliberal constitution. The Israeli reaction to Arab threats in June 1967 illustrates response to external inputs.

Systems analysis has not been a completely useful tool for analyzing the behavior of the international system and its national subsystems. A prin-cipal difficulty is the inability of one to define explicitly the distinct com-ponents of the system and the environment. The problem of delineating the boundary of a system is especially acute when dealing with social systems. In viewing international relations, we must ask: What is and what is not to be regarded as political in human behavior on the inter-national level? If the political system is viewed as the aggregate of the political activities or roles of its members, where does one draw distinctions among political, social, religious, and economic activities?

Thus, while systems analysis is a fine theoretical tool, operationally it runs into great difficulties in meeting its first task—specifically defining just exactly what the system is supposed to deal with.

RECENT TRENDS IN THEORY OF
INTERNATIONAL RELATIONS

The direction in which this vast array of theoretical enterprise is taking the discipline of international relations can be appreciated best against the backdrop of the discipline's primary source, traditional political theory. Two logically related trends are discernible in the transition from traditional political theory to recent theories of international relations.

The first trend is the revision of the traditional image of political man, who, according to the prior image, is rational in either political, economic, or moral terms. Such classically-oriented theorists as Charles Beard, Hans J. Morgenthau, and Jacques Maritain retain this image of political man derived from Platonic, Thomist, or liberal sources.

Influenced to a greater or lesser degree by the behavioral sciences, such recent leading figures in international relations theory as Kenneth Boulding, Herbert Kelman, Harold Lasswell, David McClelland, and Charles Osgood have rejected for purposes of analysis the classical image of political man, and are attempting to understand him in terms of his psychological motivations or sociological conditionings. They speak of the images, cognitive structures, values, needs for achievement, and stereotypes which govern the behavior of political actors. Dismissing the doctrine of human reason, they assume that human consciousness is a function of fluid settings.

The second trend is revision of the image of political community held by traditional political theorists. The classical image was formalistic; traditional theorists dealt in such grandiose abstractions as national ethos, the state, realism, sovereignty, and the public philosophy. Such theorists as Raymond Aron, E. H. Carr, Louis Hartz, A. D. Lindsay, and Walter Lippmann continue to employ concepts gleaned from classical sources.

However, other recent theorists in international relations, such as Gabriel Almond, David Apter, Karl Deutsch, David Easton, and Richard Snyder, have discarded the classical image of political community in their attempt to reify the traditional abstractions. The state is considered a decision-making process, while sovereignty becomes no more than the state's situational capabilities. The public philosophy is simply those values which the political system allocates. They look for linkages among the social, economic, and cultural system of collectivities and the political systems. They employ indices, variables, and empirically-based concepts to analyze all political communities.

The new directions in theory of international relations have resulted in greater awareness of political reality. Empiricism has replaced the moralism and legalism that cloaked the substantive political collectivity from the traditional political theorists. Multilevel analyses of causation have replaced simplistic economic, power, political, and moral interpretations of political action. In a sense, recent theorists may feel pride for having liberated the discipline of international relations from the strictures of traditional political theory.

Nonetheless, the progress they have made has been purchased at a price. Only when the liabilities are counted can the value of recent directions in theory of international relations be assessed fully.

A primary weakness of recent theory is its failure to encompass human purposes as expressed in terms of values and ideologies. Perhaps recent theorists have overreacted to the traditional political analyses of such "isms" as constitutionalism, democracy, nationalism, communism, or imperialism. Yet, political theorists need to recognize the methodological significance of values and the substantive relevance of ideologies. That is, they must always explicate all the assumptions upon which their analyses are predicated, and recognize that ideological factors are crucial determinants of political realities. Louis Hartz and Hannah Arendt urged and demonstrated in their substantive works that theorists cannot ignore such ideational factors as liberalism, racism, and imperialism. Many theorists, however, seem to overlook the fact that the political world is not free of values.

Another weakness of recent theorists is their penchant for reductionism. A large number of them view politics as the interaction of tensions, conflicts, and diffuse pressures which stem from groups and subgroups. Many recent theorists of the behavioral persuasion have even discounted the individual. Each individual consists of a series of tensions and pressures, internal and external. Man as the real actor is abolished; only his interests, desires, frustrations, and pathological tendencies remain.

As a result of the reductionist trend, recent theory has developed with an uncertain world-view that lacks stability and boundaries. Such factors as childhood fantasies, swaddling practices, and mail flows are of doubtful political relevance. Of course, the problem today is that there is no commonly accepted criterion of what is germane to politics. Without certain assumptions, perhaps given only for ad hoc purposes of analysis, theorists cannot proceed from methodological to substantive concerns. This is not to say that theorists in international relations should return to the rationalistic and formalistic womb of traditional political theory. Nonetheless, every theoretically-inclined discipline has to include some constants, and the study of international politics is no exception.

The scattering of theorists' interests has resulted not only in new substantive insights, but also in methodological formalism. At times it seems that model building in the social sciences has become an end in itself. In refuting the accusation of "scholasticism," theorists argue that their approach is intrinsically antischolastic and antiformalistic, that it disdains universals and is concerned only with the real, specific things found in life.

This argument cannot be accepted. When recent theorists have proposed general theories, formalism of some type has crept in. Disorderly accumulation of data is another example of theoretical sterility which has yielded only statistical profiles and collections of empty stereotypes.

Methodological formalism has also led to a fragmentation of the discipline of international relations. Methodological cults do not communicate with one another because there is no common ground. For instance, many content analysts, systems theorists, and decision-making analysts speak in jargon that is unintelligible to all except the initiated. While some devotees of conceptual rigor premise that time will yield a new synthesis for analyzing international politics, the fruits of recent years do not imply this happy ending.

Finally, many of the approaches and methods of recent theorists have tended to distort political realities. Having invested so much effort in developing methodologies, theorists who turn subsequently to substantive analyses are often trapped. By subsuming all political realities within their theoretical models, they have confounded reality and the products of their own minds. Rather than confront reality, they often merely refine their techniques, retest their theorems one against the next, strengthen the logical coherence of their models, and close every possible gap or hole left in their systems. Their closed methodological systems preclude examination of many substantive factors of political relevance that the traditional, historical, institutional, or ideational approaches might have encompassed.

So we see that empiricism has often led to an examination of nonpolitical, even trivial, phenomena. Reductionism has tended to cloak political reality behind a behavioral metaphysics. Logical consistency has resulted at times in rigid formalism. Pretensions of value-free analysis generally have only disguised judgmental assumptions and resolved (and perhaps unresolvable) moral issues. These weaknesses, however, are not intrinsic to the theoretical study of international politics. The pitfalls can be overcome when theorists reconcile their methodological fervor with the imperatives of substantive analysis.

APPROACH OF THIS STUDY

Politics can usefully and instinctively be analyzed from any of three points of view. We can inquire into the motivations and tactics of the individual political actor as he moves within the political system. Second, we can examine the political system itself—the social structure within which the political actor moves—in order to understand the processes of political action and the opportunities and limitations affecting its members. Last, we can focus on the substance of political action to discover what it is that the actors are concerned with and what the social consequences of their political maneuvering might be.

In this book we shall look at international politics from each of these points of view. Part I is a discussion of the individual political actor (the state) and its foreign policy. This will include a study of the problem a state faces in relating the ends it seeks to the means at its disposal. The relationship is obviously two-way: ends without means add up to futility; means not related to relevant ends culminate in frustration. Both the attempts and generalizations about ends (via such notions as national interest and the calculus of ends) and the renewed interest in such concepts as strategy and ideology reveal the important relationships.

This study then examines how foreign policy decisions are made, and the environmental factors that influence the decisional unit. We turn next to the progressively subtle methodology of discovering the effective range of choice open to the policy-maker at any given time. The once sovereign word "power" as representing an analytically useful concept is challenged. "Power," in a sense, betrayed its advocates by being simultaneously too broad and too constricted. It concealed a fatal imprecision beneath a facade of great clarity. We substitute "capability" for the old idea of "power" and divide it into two more sharply defined terms: "influence," which refers to the ability of the state to gain consensus by persuasive devices short of force, and "coercion," the province of force pure and simple, as one state attempts to bend the other to its will. Finally, we study the various means employed by policy-makers to implement foreign policy decisions.

Part II centers on the international political system, both in theory and in practice. Our effort here is devoted to a study of the operating assumptions and patterns of interaction formed by the contacts that states have with each other. We begin by examining the concepts of sovereignty, independence, power politics, the balance of power, and regulating mechanisms of international politics. This book does not attempt to develop a rigid and over-all set of categories of interaction. We question the assumption that any one of these concepts is the central focus for the study of international politics.

"Balance of power," a phrase that refers to a condition, can easily become "balanced power," which refers to a relationship of interaction. *Equilibrium theory* seems a natural derivation from the notion of balance. Many theoretical and analytical excursions into the nature of power, control, and capability are motivated by an urge to learn more about what is balanced in an equilibrium, and what falls out of balance and creates disequilibrium, tension, and crisis. The very idea of deterrence clearly owes its intellectual birth to analysts thinking in the categories of balance-type interaction; mutual deterrence is a classic type of balance or unstable equilibrium.

Even among those who reject the balance as a useful interaction concept, there has been a thrust for what contemporary students call a "central" or "organizing focus," some architectonic interaction concept that will provide the framework for more elaborate analysis. This was the rationale of the original Morgenthau "power thesis." *Politics Among Nations* was more a study of interaction than of action, more an analysis of international politics than a study of the foreign policy of states. He postulated the search for power by all states primarily to provide the motivation necessary to set interaction patterns in motion. We argue that the central focus for this study of state interaction is properly *value theory*, since all politics is a struggle for the maximization of competing value systems. This, however, runs afoul of the antinormative orientation of contemporary conceptual disputation, and so far has relatively few takers among interaction theorists (although many more among analysts of the foreign policy process).

We examine next the barrage of exertive influences, changing conditions, and emerging directions in the present international system. The sources and changing nature of conflict, the relationship of force to conflict resolution, and the restraints upon conflict are analyzed.

Part III deals with the substance of international politics and is organized as a discussion of several major problems that grip the entire system and its members. The present problems of war, technology, ideology, trade, development, modernization, and organization are studied in detail.

The following pages will take you on a very rapid tour through the workshop of the international relations enterprise. You will be exposed to the barrage of concepts that are in daily use among academic students and practitioners of the discipline. You will be initiated into some of the operational hypotheses of the field, and have now been alerted to the impressive lack of consensus that exists among us. It is now very appropriate for you to inquire what relevance all of this abstract system-building has for you.

Every action that a man makes in the world is postulated upon a theory; every interpretation he makes of an event is grounded in certain operational (perhaps unconscious) generalizations about the world and his place in it. There is no more vicious (and effective) theorist than the man who smugly says: "I don't have any theory, I just let the facts speak for themselves," for he presents a simplistic explanation—which is, hence, very appealing. Of course, even the supremely "objective" facts of history must be interpreted anew to each generation. History itself teaches us nothing; historians, however, teach us a great deal—and even the most dedicated historical scholars have a theoretical base that governs the inclusion and exclusion of data in the history they write.

So we all base our actions on theory. There is no question about the role of generalization, hypothesis, and cause-and-effect relationship in human endeavor. The real questions are not whether responsible officials use theory in their judgments, but whether their theoretical foundations are explicit and self-conscious, or concealed, implicit, and often misunderstood. There is a second and equally important reason why practical men can benefit from theoretical discussion: in the process they may discover that the generalizations upon which they have proceeded in the past are inconsistent, incomplete, or perhaps even wrong. There is always the possibility, therefore, that a personal inventory of one's working concepts might result in their overhaul, or at least in their clarification, strengthening, or elaboration. What we are suggesting is that, since you will probably never be able to dispense with theoretical and conceptual considerations in your encounter with international relations, there is reason for you to became acquainted with the broad body of such discussion that is going on in the academic community and among serious students of all sorts.

We have attempted to point out the determination of most current thinking to fight shy of normative judgments and all questions along the "good-bad" and "right-wrong" axes. Speaking personally, this is a tendency we find utterly deplorable. It is only when the minds of students of international relations are turned to the problems that divide the world, and not the problems induced by one's own system, and they approach these problems not only with the tools of a laboratory but with human compassion, that the task of building a better world may begin, much less be completed.

The cause of scientific truth is no more advanced than that of human freedom if "frontier thinking" implies a suspension of moral judgment on the objects of inquiry. These are not mathematical symbols or hydrocarbon molecules that the scholars are studying; their subject matter consists of living, feeling men. It would be a melancholy comfort, if we were all blown into a cloud of radioactive dust, to realize that the scientific scholars knew exactly why this was happening. Men live by the things they cannot prove, and we lose much if, in our search for the reasons for human behavior, we forget the truth about man is not as important as the miracle that man exists at all.

As you deal with the problems of international relations, never forget that you are engaged in something that matters in the here and now, as well as in the awful scales of truth. Be logical, scientific, rigorous, objective, and honest; but above all, be compassionate. Think in terms of concepts, as we feel you must; but never forget to think like human beings.

REFERENCES

* Charlesworth, James C., ed., *Contemporary Political Analysis*. New York: The Free Press, 1967.
* Dahl, Robert A., and Deane E. Neubauer, eds., *Readings in Modern Political Analysis*. Englewood Cliffs, N.J.: Prentice-Hall, Inc., 1968.
* Deutsch, Karl W., *The Analysis of International Relations*. Englewood Cliffs, N.J.: Prentice-Hall, Inc., 1968.
Easton, David, *Framework for Political Analysis*. Englewood Cliffs, N.J.: Prentice-Hall, Inc., 1965.
* Eulau, Heinz, *Behavioral Persuasion in Politics*. New York: Random House, Inc., 1962.
* Farrell, R. Barry, ed., *Approaches to Comparative and International Politics*. Evanston, Ill.: Northwestern University Press, 1966.
Frohock, Fred M., *Nature of Political Inquiry*. Homewood, Ill.: Richard D. Irwin, Inc., and The Dorsey Press, 1967.
* Irish, Marian D., ed., *Political Science: Advance of the Discipline*. Englewood Cliffs, N.J.: Prentice-Hall, Inc., 1968.
* Kaplan, Morton, *System and Process in International Politics*. Science Ed's. New York: John Wiley & Sons, Inc., 1957.
———, *New Approaches to International Relations*. New York: St. Martin's Press, Inc., 1968.
* Kariel, Harry S., *The Promise of Politics*. Englewood Cliffs, N.J.: Prentice-Hall, Inc., 1966.

* Indicates paperback edition.

Knorr, Klaus, ed., *Contending Approaches to International Politics*. Princeton, N.J.: Princeton University Press, 1969.

* McClelland, Charles A., *Theory and the International System*. New York: The Macmillan Company, 1966.

Meehan, Eugene J., *Theory and Method of Political Analysis*. Homewood, Ill.: Richard D. Irwin, Inc., and The Dorsey Press, 1967.

Pool, Ithiel de Sola, ed., *Contemporary Political Science*. New York: McGraw-Hill Book Company, 1967.

* Said, Abdul A., ed., *Theories of International Relations: The Crisis of Relevance*. Englewood Cliffs, N.J.: Prentice-Hall, Inc., 1968.

* Scott, Andrew M., *The Functioning of the International Political System*. New York: The Macmillan Company, 1967.

* Sorauf, Frank J., *Perspectives on Political Science*. Columbus, Ohio: Charles E. Merrill Books, Inc., 1967.

* Van Dyke, Vernon, *Political Science: A Philosophical Analysis*. Stanford, California: Stanford University Press, 1950.

* Young, Oran R., *Systems of Political Science*. Englewood Cliffs, N.J.: Prentice-Hall, Inc., 1968.

* Indicates paperback edition.

part I

THE ACTORS: THE STATE IN INTERNATIONAL POLITICS

ONE

The Nature
of Foreign Policy

This book is a guide to the ideas used by men in the discussion, study, or practice of international politics. Our subject matter is first "international," dealing almost entirely with the relationships of different national groups ("states") with one another. It is also a "political" study; the kinds of relationships in which we are primarily interested are those that we shall define as political. There are many international relations other than political—e.g., economic, cultural, interpersonal—but we shall consider them less on their own merits than in terms of their impact on the political behavior of peoples, governments, and states.

POLITICS: THE STRUGGLE TO MAXIMIZE VALUES

"Politics" is a common word in the English language that refers to an equally familiar phenomenon. However, precise definition of the word is usually rather difficult. Individuals have strong emotional responses to the concept; any definition cannot help but reflect the definer's biases. Since the words "politics" and "political" will appear repeatedly throughout this book, it is important that we make our meaning explicit at the outset. Our first undertaking, therefore, is a definition of politics and a demonstration of how political concepts find their eventual international expression in a state's foreign policy.

The Nature of Politics

Politics consists of the organizational activity in which men engage to maximize their convictions about social values. By political action men attempt to realize their differing notions of the "public good." Thus politics is really a *process*—a means to a value-centered end—which is meaningless except in terms of the values that give rise to political action.

Such a definition of politics is broad in its applicability to the acts men perform in a political context. Indeed, it must be, since political acts include virtually the entire spectrum of human activity. The definition is, however, quite explicit in emphasizing social values as the roots of politics. Since these shared ideas of "the good" are what make political action unique, almost any human action can, with an appropriate value motivation and organizational setting, be termed *political*. Without the value drive or the organizational nexus, the same action is in the strict sense *apolitical*.

Human beings do not agree on any single inclusive set of social values. Struggles reflecting differing value judgments are integral to the political process. Achievement of a political goal is normally at the expense of other political actors who have their own goals and aspirations. Thus the range of political action may extend from agreement and cooperation between political actors to the various zones of partial agreement or total opposition and conflict. The experienced political practitioner has at his command strategies and tactics to help him attain the highest feasible level of value satisfaction.

These two ingredients of politics—the value-rooted ends of action and the political climate of struggle and disagreement—are as clearly demonstrated in international politics as they are in the more familiar environment of electoral politics in a democracy. Foreign policy consists of a society's attempt at realization on the international plane of what it conceives as good. It is the value root of foreign policy that makes nationalism so intense today, and makes resolution of conflict so difficult. That international politics takes place in a climate of disagreement and conflict would seem to require no demonstration. In its key aspects, then, international politics is the same sort of social process as politics at any level; with appropriate conceptual adjustments, insights derived from international politics are broadly applicable to internal political relations, and vice versa.

Within any political system, disagreement and conflict over value choices take place within a larger value consensus that helps hold the system together. Such an agreement on fundamentals gives rise to the system in the first place, and makes political action possible. We shall see later that the international system incorporates such a consensus (although only imperfectly grasped by many states), and that political action on the international plane is feasible only in its terms.

Social Values and Foreign Policy

Each society, especially when it deems itself a "nation" and is organized into a state, has a social code that contributes to its peculiar identity, and which activates and energizes all political action. If the prevailing concepts of "good" and "evil" could be rationalized within the boundaries of the society itself, they would have little or nothing to do with international affairs. However, ever since the Industrial Revolution and the dawn of modern nationalism, national value structures have impinged upon the world outside their borders; social values have come to relate intimately with questions of foreign policy.

Certain aspirations, needs, and wants are widely shared in any society. Many of these require governmental action to attain even partial fulfillment, and men look to their political leaders to act on their behalf. Obviously, one area of value preference in which only public agencies can act effectively is that of international relations. Individuals or subgroups of a society cannot function adequately in the interest of the entire group; only officials armed with the authority and sanctions of society at large can deal with extra-societal problems. Foreign policy, therefore, is the exclusive province of government, because only government can act on behalf of all the people individually and of the society collectively.

The content of governmental action in the international arena is determined by the set of social values controlling the society at large. Before the birth of political consciousness in the states of Europe, international politics consisted only of the relations of kings; mass attitudes and preferences had no foreign policy relevance. The rise of nationalism made foreign policy in one sense "democratic"; governments became obliged to structure their international efforts so as to reflect the mass value judgments of the people they represented. The analytical apparatus of statecraft is no more than a standardized technique for translating the value preferences of a society into a workable frame for governmental action.

The Value Content of Foreign Policy

From an analytical point of view, we must avoid becoming overly specific about the social values that underlie foreign policy. Values are seldom self-evident, and the concepts of good and evil that a government chooses to pursue always stem from a mixture of sources within the society. We can identify at least five differing versions of "good" that are usually combined in a single foreign policy.

1. The good of the individual citizen: primarily the wish to be secure in his person, beliefs, and property as they become threatened by forces outside his society.
2. The good of the society at large: collective values, normally including preservation of the social system, augmentation of its prestige, protection of its ideology, and so on.
3. The good of the state (the juristic personality) as such: the more common ingredients include self-preservation, security, well-being, and the "strength" of the political unit.
4. The good of "special interest groups" in the state/society: these tend to be included to the maximum extent possible within the operative notion of the general interest, and contribute largely to the shaping of public policy on specific issues.
5. The good of the government itself and of its personnel: values peculiar to membership in a public community that inescapably find expression in the actualities of policy.

Thus the values maximized by the state in foreign policy are varied in origin and substance. It is the task of officials charged with policy-making to shape this broad spectrum of needs and wants into some semblance of integrity, and to apply the resulting value synthesis to the phenomena of international politics. The statesman may compromise among competing values, accepting some at the cost of rejecting others, or he may find some other rationalizing device. He cannot, however, avoid the necessity of building his approach to world affairs on a foundation of value choices.

Foreign Policy and International Politics

The base of any foreign policy is a state's mission to maximize its value synthesis. Once it moves onto the international scene, however, it encounters other states, each seeking the accomplishment of its own value-derived goals. Thus international politics is at bottom an exercise in the prosecution of value differences, and grows less from objective environmental conditions than it does from the judgments men make about those conditions.

In this respect, international politics is not dissimilar to domestic politics, but there is a significant difference between the two that makes the international variety peculiarly perplexing and fascinating to its students. Although domestic politics—at least in a stabilized society—goes on within a well-understood set of rules that cover the range of permissible action and are enforced by social and governmental mechanisms, no such structure inhibits the practice of international politics. States are free to pursue their value purposes as far as their wishes and strength will permit; they are normally checked by the strength of other states and only occasionally by institutional mechanisms.

International politics, because of the highly internalized motivations of its practitioners and the lack of universal limitations on approved action, is ever on the verge of explosion. The values that go into foreign policy are deeply held and powerful; the restraints are relatively few and of imperfect effect. In many respects, therefore, international politics is a manifestation of the political process in its simplest form.

INTERESTS, GOALS, AND OBJECTIVES

Our discussion up to this point has established that foreign policy is purposeful and that value judgments are the bases upon which a state proceeds in international politics. The state, however, must act in the real world; it cannot function effectively on behalf of values that remain abstract, absolute, and undefined. No foreign policy can really achieve "freedom," "power," "justice," "honor," or even "peace"—to cite a few of the more common values of foreign policy—except in concrete terms and in relation to specific situations. The statesman must translate "values" into "objectives" before he can begin to act.

From "Social Values" to "National Interest"

The key concept used by a policy-maker in applying value judgments to the realities of political action is "national interest," a notion notoriously vague and difficult to define. It may be considered as the general, long-term, and continuing purpose which the state, the nation, and the government all see themselves as serving. It is rooted in the social consciousness and cultural identity of a people, and includes all the disparate ideas of the good that we have noted. In practice it is synthesized and given form by the official policy-makers themselves.

We cannot be more specific in defining the content of national interest, since both its value roots and the process of its synthesis are peculiar to the history and institutional makeup of a society. We can, however, be quite explicit about its function. As the overriding purpose governing the state's relations with the outside world, it serves two purposes: it gives policy a general orientation toward the external environment, and, more importantly, it serves as the controlling criterion of choice in immediate situations. The dominant view of national interest, in other words, dictates the nature of a state's long-term effort in foreign policy and governs what it does in a short-term context.

National interest thus flows from the application of a highly generalized value synthesis to the over-all situation in which a state is placed in world politics. It is, within the terms of its social origin, relatively slow to change, and change is evolutionary rather than revolutionary. National interest provides the necessary measure of consistency to national policy; a state, consciously adhering to its national interest in a rapidly changing situation, is more likely to maintain its balance and continue to progress toward its goals than it would if it changed its interest in adapting to each new situation.

Ends and Means in Foreign Policy

The development of national interest (which may remain an abstract concept) is the first step in formulating a foreign policy, even though it remains an abstract concept. Before the concept may actually serve as a guide to action, the statesman must grapple with a classic problem: reconciliation of ends and means.

The ends of state action in international politics—the national interest and such national goals as may be derived from it—are postulated a priori. Before policy can be made, the statesman must somehow mesh the facts of his problem, including whatever means he has at his disposal, with the conceptual system formed by his set of ends. In specific policy situations, one of the most difficult problems faced by policy-makers is determination of the most appropriate relationship between abstract ends and concrete means.

Ends, in theory, determine means; in a situation permitting several possible courses of action, the one chosen should most directly advance the national interest. In practice, however, there is always a temptation to allow means to determine ends, to decide that the objective which is the most feasible to attain is the one that the state should seek. Intermediate ends—ends that, if achieved, are intended only to serve as means to still further ends—tend also to acquire an absolute relevance in themselves as ends.

Any confusion in the ends-means relationships, any loss of appreciation of the value roots of policy, or any reluctance to remain firmly committed to long-range concepts of interest, cannot help but deprive a foreign policy of vigor, effectiveness, and flexibility. Governments that succumb to these dangers quickly find themselves thrust on the strategic defensive and, to a major extent, placed at the mercy of others who know more precisely what they are trying to accomplish. There is no substitute for a clearly rationalized and thoroughly understood purpose in foreign policy, especially in the contemporary period, which is an era of great change in the international milieu.

The Nature of an Objective

State action in foreign policy is always in pursuit of an "objective": that state of affairs which the state feels is most in its national interest. An objective may call for some change in the existing situation, or for the protection and preservation of an existing set of relationships judged desirable. It is crucial, however, that an objective be formulated in concrete terms appropriate both to the prevailing conditions and to the effective range of action enjoyed by the state.

An objective flows from the application of national interest to the generalized situation in which policy is being made. An intermediate value postulation antecedent to the choice of an objective is often made by the selection of a "goal," defined here as a quasi-Utopian formulation of what would be the most desirable future state of affairs of a particular issue. Adoption of a goal, rooted in the relatively fixed factors of the decisional milieu, assists materially in the evaluation of dynamic forces that will shape the particular objective selected.

Thus, within any single policy situation, the relations of the national interest, the postulated goal, and the selected objective are largely functions of different time spans of analysis. National interest has an implication of perpetuity or ultimacy; its interests will presumably keep the state involved in the problem forever, or at least as long as the political system endures. A goal is set in terms of the maximum time span that can be anticipated analytically. As long as the general shape of the situation remains constant, the postulated goal will be in effect; any drastic change, however, would require selection of a new goal more in harmony with the nature of the problem. An objective is immediate or short-range in its time component; the state of affairs that is the target of state action is attainable in terms of the forces operative at the moment of decision.

The ends-means relationship is central to the choice of an objective. While the goal represents the best conceivable state of affairs, the objective is actually the closest approximation to the goal that the decision-makers feel is feasible. The postulated end of state action in most situations does no more than point out the direction in which the state should move. The distance it actually goes along this figurative line depends on the means it has available for use in the situation.

It is essential that a policy-maker formulate his objective as precisely as possible, not only to give himself a means of concentrating his attention and effort on crucial issues, but also because he can better appraise degrees of success or failure if he is quite clear about his aims. An objective stated in abstract and nebulous terms can never be attained; much state effort is wasted and many decisions rendered pointless because the objective is couched in fuzzy, abstract, and absolute terms.

The Common Objectives of States

After arguing as we have that each state's set of interests, goals, and policy objectives is unique to itself, it may seem somewhat contradictory to suggest that it is possible and useful to discuss "the common objectives of states." The uniqueness of state purpose is confined to matters of detail, but the general problem of foreign policy presents itself to all states in the same fundamental terms. States are compelled by the logic of sovereignty and the inexorabilities of the political system in which they function to seek the same kinds of satisfaction. At least conceptually we may divide the objectives sought by any foreign policy into six categories, remembering that each state defines its purpose within each category in such specific language as suits its dominant interest:

1. Analytically, *self-preservation* must be considered an ubiquitous objective of state action. The "self," preservation of which is deemed a supreme good, is the collective entity of the state and its human and territorial manifestations. A state's desire for existence, if it wishes to remain a state, is self-evident. States normally act so as to maximize their chances of survival in the world; for most this is simultaneously the highest and most basic purpose of foreign policy.

2. Second in importance to self-preservation is the objective of *security*. Since the nature of the international political system is such that existence for any state is never certain, each is impelled to arrange its relations with the rest of the world so as to give itself the best possible opportunity for continued existence. This is usually called a "search for security," but real security is clearly unattainable under the prevailing conditions. What

the security objectives of states amount to is no more than the reduction of all visible and conceivable threats to a practical minimum. A measure of insecurity is really an inescapable cost of doing business in the state system.

3. Third in the list of common objectives of states is what we call *well-being*. After the higher-priority objectives of self-preservation and security have been satisfied to the maximum permitted by the state's situation, the state tries to improve the actual conditions of existence of its citizens. This well-being is both conceptually and practically the welfare of the collectivity rather than that of individuals; the unit of calcuation is "the economy," and the measures of prosperity tend today to be those familiar "macro-economic" concepts, "gross national product" and the "rate of economic growth." Of course there may be no real clash between collective well-being and the economic welfare of individuals, and even when such a conflict develops it is only seldom on an explicit "guns or butter" basis. In cases of unavoidable divergence of interest, however, the normal pattern of political value choices dictates the intrinsic superiority of collective well-being over any individual or group interests.

4. Another common objective of state action is *prestige*. States normally act so as to appear impressive to others, in order to receive deference and status concessions from them. The achievement of a satisfactory prestige level is one of the more frustrating problems of foreign policy: how much prestige and status is enough in a given context? It is obvious that any politically self-conscious people has a strong urge to be well thought of by others, and to wish concrete evidence of its prestige. One serious confusion that often complicates the search for prestige centers about the criteria of high status: a state may wish prestige in terms of certain aspects of its own ego-image, but may receive generous deference in other terms that do not meet its wants. A reputation for a high level of artistic achievement, for example, is of little significance to a state that wishes rank as a major military power. The difficulties implicit in any attempt to "win" prestige, however, have not served to deter states from the attempt.

5. Of somewhat less pervasiveness but of great importance to some states is the promotion and/or protection of ideology. The present century is, far more than any since the sixteenth, an age of total belief systems, and a number of states, both large and small, have made both the protection and promulgation of their ideologies a major element in foreign policy. Carrying within itself implications of proselytization and messianism, ideology as a foreign policy objective again raises questions of the explicitness and attainability of goals, and of the criteria of success and failure in foreign policy. There is, furthermore, some contemporary evidence that even the more militant ideologically-oriented states have

had some second thoughts about the practicability of seeking ideological vindication by the processes of international politics.

6. Finally, we must take note of *power* as a common objective of states. As we shall point out later (Chapter Three), power considerations belong more in a discussion of the means of foreign policy than in a catalogue of the ends of state action. Yet an indispensable preliminary step to the accomplishment of a goal may be the accumulation of additional increments of power, and for "reasons" of prestige or demands of security a state may overtly establish an increase in power as a major objective of policy. While it is a serious oversimplification to state flatly that all international politics is a struggle for power, and that every state's primary motivation is the urge to augment its store, it is undeniable that, for a broad variety of real or spurious reasons, many states legitimize power as an appropriate end of state action.

POLICY AND THE STRATEGIC DECISION

The tension between ends and means is never more acute than when a state's policy-makers are approaching a decision as to whether or not to act and, if action is to be taken, what steps should be taken first. An objective must be selected and a course (or courses) of action launched. Officials must serve the interests and goals already formulated and yet act in situations permitting only a limited range of means. The choices are often extremely difficult; policy decisions must be in the largest sense "strategic." Unable to accomplish everything they wish, states must weigh the competing claims on their resources and capabilities and decide not only what portion of their goals are susceptible of accomplishment at the moment, but also the priority system that governs the relative emphasis given to different areas of action.

The Meaning of "Policy"

A "policy" is here understood to be a course of action designed to attain an objective. Although we shall defer detailed analysis of policy-making until Chapter Two, certain larger aspects of the concept of policy are appropriately considered here.

We should first note a semantic difficulty. The "foreign policy" of a state usually refers to the general principles by which a state governs its reaction to the international environment; such catchwords as "isolationism," "balance of power," or "imperialism" are often, if somewhat inaccurately, used to characterize particular foreign policies. On the other hand, if a policy is a course of action oriented to a single objective, a state has as many policies as it has objectives. Thus "foreign policy" and "foreign policies" have completely different meanings. Probably the best way to avoid confusion is to keep in mind that foreign policy (singular) is usually phrased in terms of goals, whereas policies (plural) draw their relevance from objectives.

Second, a policy always involves both *decision* and *action*, with decision perhaps the more important ingredient. Action on behalf of an objective can result from policy only if the decision itself indicates clearly what the policy-maker had in mind both as to objective and procedure. As a result, the formalized decision (the "policy paper") normally includes at least three elements of clarification and guidance for anyone concerned with its implementation: (1) formulation of the objective in the most precise terms possible; (2) the nature of the action to be undertaken, stated with sufficient clarity to guide and direct the state's other officials; and (3) the forms and perhaps the amounts of national power to be applied in pursuit of the objective.

A third factor bearing on policy is reflected in the final point in this list. A policy decision normally calls for the commitment of resources, the assumption of a risk, or both. This is the cost/risk factor in policy-making, which we shall examine later. Here we need only keep in mind that, in foreign policy as in life, everything has its price. Often the most excruciating problem in policy determination is the decision about how much effort should be made in pursuit of an objective in view of competing claims of other goals and limitations in the state's resources.

The Need for Priorities

No state can accomplish everything it wishes in its foreign policy; almost by definition, a state's reach exceeds its grasp. Objectives and goals tend to formulation in absolute terms—a government speaks of "security," "peace," or "freedom," never of "partial security," "relative peace," or "a measure of freedom." The ends of policy are unlimited, but the means are sharply limited both in logic and in fact. States, even large and powerful ones, must budget their effort as carefully as a housewife allocates her available funds.

Thus every state must have an operative system of priorities that governs its policy choices. Some questions are simply more important than others in terms of the social values on which the nation's approach is built. Some, indeed, are literally absolute, such as self-preservation; unless the state exists, any other purposes are really beside the point. Others, while clearly critical, must take second place to those of the highest priority. As the scale of priorities is elaborated, each intermediate objective takes its place in relation to all others.

Priority ranking of interests, goals, and objectives is critical in determining the relative claim that each has on the state's resources, energy, and "worry time." Such a set of criteria of intrinsic importance is a major determinant of policy. A state, for example, is always willing to suffer a setback with respect to a low-priority end in order to gain ground on a higher-priority goal. Over-all strategies are established on a priority basis; long-term commitments of power can be made intelligently only on the principle of "first things first."

A state that attempts to conduct its foreign policy without priorities, or with its priority system vague and imprecise, rapidly discovers priorities imposed upon it by force of circumstance. With no real sense of the relative importance of different problems, all issues tend to become equally significant; in many cases, each problem is dealt with as if it were of absolute priority. Top priority thus tends to be assigned on the basis of recent occurrence rather than long-term criticality.

The "importance" of issues is determined in every case by the internalized values of the state. No one outside a state can state unequivocally what ought to be the priorities of its policy; even self-preservation has no more importance than a state chooses to give it, and cases can be found where states voluntarily chose to go out of existence in order to achieve certain other values. The priorities that a state applies are its own, peculiar to its *Weltanschauung* and appropriate to no other society.

Thus far we have been using "importance" as if it were an absolute, and as if priorities flow automatically from a single unified system of values. In practice, however, many kinds of concerns are important to a state, and determination of the appropriate criterion of priority is frequently a serious problem in policy-making.

One of the more common conflicts of policy is between a functional or procedural priority and a substantive priority. Priorities of means and priorities of ends, in other words, often apply in different ways and impose hard choices. A state may be vitally interested in preservation of the principle and practice of peaceful change in world affairs in general (a procedural priority), and yet may at the same time be under great pressure to use force to make an important gain in its level of security (a substantive priority). There is, unfortunately, no easy or simple answer to this dilemma; governments resolve it recurrently on an ad hoc basis.

In the dimension of time, priorities lend themselves to confusion. Every government finds itself in situations in which a particular move must be made immediately—even though the issue is intrinsically minor and the step will in some way hurt another enterprise of greater ultimate significance but of less immediate relevance. In most cases the officials concerned make every effort to avoid irreparable damage to their long-range and higher-priority concerns while dealing with immediate issues; only by accident or almost inexcusable carelessness will a government become so engrossed in its immediate problems as to permit more significant long-range issues to go by the board.

A final consequence of an unclear priority system should be noted. If a government faces a priority choice without being sure of its own criteria of importance, it may refuse to make any choice at all. Its policy effort will therefore be expended in an attempt to defer the necessity of decision, demonstrated most explicitly by maneuvering for the purchase of time. If the breathing space it wins is used to resolve its priority dilemma, it may deal effectively with the difficult choice when it arises again. If, however, the time bought is frittered away uselessly, the need for a decision might not only come again, but with much less favorable conditions of choice.

The Classic Compromise

The task of the statesman, as the cliché puts it, is to "reconcile the desirability of the possible with the possibility of the desirable." No other formulation of foreign policy has so aphoristically, yet inclusively, epitomized the operating mission of the responsible decision-maker.

Much of our preceding discussion has been leading up to this point. In any policy situation, the state has a range of ends, all desirable in terms of its interests, that can be arranged in order of preferability. Some are attainable with ease, some only by great effort, and others are beyond the range of attainability. On the other hand, the state also has a spectrum of action open to it; it has the capacity to produce a number of different outcomes. Some of these may be highly desirable, others neutral, and still others inherently undesirable. The two curves of desirability and possibility cross at the point of decision. The mission of the policy-maker is to ensure that the action takes place as far as possible along the curve of desirability.

Foreign policy normally consists of enterprises involving partial commitments of capability for the accomplishment of partial purposes. As a rule a state does not count on obtaining either all it wants or all it can get in any situation; rather it attempts *to get all it can of what it wants*. The policy decision is thus always a compromise.

Initiatives and Responses

The "strategic decision" in all states is marked by a relative emphasis on prudence and restraint. Strategy is a cautious enterprise; the consequences of failure in statecraft may be so destructive that rational statesmen refuse to give themselves the benefit of any analytical doubt in setting a course of action.

Thus it follows that, for the vast majority of states, policy is more responsible than it is initiatory. In an environment so productive of dangers and threats, policy-makers attempt first to rationalize the conditions of existence within the system before they seek to bring about changes in their own behalf. Only after a state has dealt adequately with stimuli arising from outside itself does it feel free to launch its own enterprises. Responses to challenges are a first charge on a state's resources. Initiatives are undertaken only with increments of capability thought surplus to its foreseeable needs.

Of course, the key notion in this relationship is—as so often in foreign policy—that of "adequacy." In one sense no state can respond completely to all challenges produced by the external environment. Absolute security is, as we have noted, unattainable. But even within the limits imposed by the inevitable burden of risk a state carries, difficult decisions of adequacy and the allocation of resources and effort plague policy-making.

Some states, either because of especially fortunate situations or, more commonly, relatively optimistic interpretations of the nature and extent of challenges and the necessary responses, find themselves endowed with relatively extensive capability to undertake initiatives. In other words, states with greater prowess in scientific achievement, technological innovations, and military power have greater freedom to assert themselves against lesser states. If powerful states have an interest in environmental change, they are able to blend desirability and possibility at a comparatively high level. This is a common characteristic of the strategy adopted by Communist states. Others, however, interpret their requirements as demanding that a large proportion of their capability be committed to a range of responses, with only a modest surplus left for the initiation of policies. Democratic states in the contemporary era are often accused of such caution in analysis that their policies are purely responsive. From such differences in the interpretation that each state makes of the effective environment and its capacity for initiative, as well as from its internalized image of its world role, flow fundamental differences in policy. We shall examine these variations and their implications in the next section.

TYPES OF FOREIGN POLICIES

Even after noting that each state views its own international problem as unique and develops patterns of response and initiation peculiar to its situation, we can still conclude that it is possible and useful to classify the foreign policies of states. Our system of classification is not elaborate, since it includes only two categories. The conclusions that stem from them, however, are applicable in a significant way and cover a broad range of instances.

The Two Categories of Purpose

Throughout this chapter we have stressed the basic role played in foreign policy by social values and the image of national and state purpose. Now we examine the content of purpose so as to distinguish the different ways states structure their missions.

As a people, speaking through its leaders, applies its value structure to the generalized world environment, it cannot escape passing judgment on the relationship between its society and all others. Such a verdict can be affirmative; the society may be basically satisfied with its place in the world, and such readjustments as it wishes to make are minor and do not call for major change in the international structure. On the other hand, the conclusion may be negative; the society may decide that the place it is occupying in the world is unacceptable. Either decision determines all subsequent discussion of foreign policy.

If the society is willing to accept indefinitely its place in the general shape of the world, its over-all international purpose will become a conserving (not necessarily *conservative*) one. If, however, it decides to reject the role which it is playing at the moment, it may choose to bring about change in the international order in its own interest. Every state in the world, at some time and in varying ways, has made such a choice and then based a foreign policy on it.

This selection of a generalized category of purpose is a pure value judgment. There are no objective criteria by which an observer can anticipate what evaluation of the environment a people will make. The elements that produce the eventual conclusion are embedded in their social dynamics and assume unpredictable and often eccentric forms.

Some years ago, students felt that this duality of purpose could be meaningfully reflected by a classification of states into "have" and "have-not" categories. Unfortunately, this division was not sufficiently explicit about what the "have" nations possessed that produced satisfaction or what the "have-nots" lacked that made them dissatisfied. In some cases a level of material well-being apparently served as the crucial criterion, in others, considerations of status and prestige, and in still others, obvious dissatisfaction with a historic role or nostalgia for former eminence, and so on. The best we can say is that a nation is satisfied with its world role if its critical values are receiving adequate fulfillment. Dissatisfaction follows a conclusion that certain critical categories of value needs are not being met. Each state is the final judge of the determinants and of how high a level of satisfaction is adequate.

It is from this idea of purpose that the controlling concept of national interests develops. The "general and continuing" end for which a state acts is derived from that state's interpretation of its role in the international order. Data from the external environment pass through the notion of purpose, in terms of which the information is given relevance and meaning. It is, finally, from the notion of purpose that the criteria of success and failure in foreign policy are derived.

The Policy of the Status Quo

From a concept of purpose that stresses satisfaction and conservation arises the policy orientation that we call "status quo." States that assume this international role develop policies with a number of common distinguishing traits.

Before examining the content of a policy of the status quo, we must define the sense in which we are using this common but often misunderstood concept. The status quo a state seeks to preserve is its own status vis-à-vis the rest of the international system. Acceptance of a status quo posture does not necessarily imply enthusiasm for the details of the existing state of affairs, but rather a judgment that the over-all pattern of value satisfaction extracted by the state from the international system is the most favorable it can hope for by any reasonable expenditure of effort. Thus, a status quo policy by no means condemns the state to inflexible defense of all the details of an established order; indeed, an enlightened status quo position—particularly when held by a major power —leaves ample room for extensive situational change and exertion of initiatives by the state concerned. What is beyond major modification is the state's relation to the system as a whole.

Status quo policies, therefore, are defensive in strategic orientation, however often they may call for tactical offensives. The controlling notion of national interest is couched in such terms as "defense," "preservation," and "neutralization," rather than "offense," "change," and "advantage." Status quo policies seek the stabilization of relationships rather than their modification. They normally press for wide adoption of all manner of institutional and procedural restraints on the outer limits of state action.

A state following a status quo policy accepts conflict as a condition of existence, but seldom initiates it. When caught in an overt struggle, it consciously attempts to avoid escalation in the terms of the conflict, works for resolution of the dispute at as low a level of tension as possible, and is normally willing to view an inconclusive outcome as a victory—since it is left in possession of whatever prizes it had at the beginning of the disagreement. It is axiomatic that status quo states never initiate major wars.

The policy of the status quo, whether followed by a large or a small state, is directed toward evolution of the international system into a stabilized set of relationships that incorporate the relatively advantageous situation the state enjoys at the moment. As a result, status quo policies tend to be marked by restraint in conception, caution in execution, and acceptance of only a comparatively small burden of risk. Operationally, their strength lies in their capacity to anticipate situational change and to develop rapid and efficacious responses to it. When status quo policies are prevalent in the international system, the general atmosphere is of relative quiet and relaxation; change is slow, evolutionary, and limited in extent.

The Policy of Revisionism

The second type of foreign policy—which flows from rejection of the current status and role of the state—is known as "revisionism." It is in almost every conceptual aspect the antonym of the policy of the status quo.

Revisionism aims at the favorable modification of the state's over-all international position in the system. It does not necessarily operate on the assumption that all international relationships are fluid and subject to change, but only those that it feels are crucial. It will accept no solution to those points which epitomize its dissatisfaction except one that gives it the measure of fulfillment it demands.

A policy of revisionism is strategically offensive. National interest demands major environmental change in the state's favor, and policy is directed toward the discovery or creation, and complete exploitation, of opportunities for effective action. Relationships are not amenable to stabilization until the state achieves what it seeks. Revisionist states, therefore, are normally cool to proposals for the organization of international politics that might in any way inhibit their carefully guarded freedom of action.

Revisionist states not only accept conflict, they actively seek it as long as it offers a hope for the rational attainment of an objective. They will normally accept a higher level of tension in a dispute, are less averse to escalation (at least up to a point), and are much more resistant to accepting a stalemate or a draw than are status quo states. In a struggle between an exemplar of each type, it is normally the revisionist state that begins the conflict and sets its terms; in any such controversy short of all-out war, it is usually the revisionist state that also decides how long the dispute will continue. Major wars have usually been begun by states that were revisionist in orientation, at least at the time the critical decision was made.

A revisionist policy is characterized by relative daring in conception, optimistic calculation of factors of cost, and willingness to carry a relatively large burden of risk. Its operational advantage lies in its capacity to bring about situational change or capitalize quickly upon it. An historic period dominated by revisionist policies, therefore, is marked by a high level of tension in politics and a rate of change that is both rapid and extensive.

REFERENCES

* Dahl, Robert A., *Who Governs?* New Haven: Yale University Press, 1961.
* Eulau, Heinz, *Behavioral Persuasion in Politics*. New York: Random House, Inc., 1962.
* Lasswell, Harold D., *Politics, Who Gets What, When, How*. New York: Meridian Books, 1961.

Lipset, Seymour M., *Political Man*. Garden City, N.Y.: Doubleday & Company, Inc., 1960.

* Machiavelli, Niccolò, *The Prince and the Discourses*. New York: Modern Library, Inc., 1953.
* Morgenthau, Hans J., *Dilemmas of Politics*. Chicago: University of Chicago Press, 1958.
* ———, *In Defense of National Interest*. New York: Alfred A. Knopf, Inc., 1951.

Northrop, F. S. C., *The Taming of Nations: A Study in the Cultural Bases of International Policy*. New York: The Macmillan Company, 1953.

* Osgood, Robert E., *Ideals and Self-Interest in America's Foreign Relations*. Chicago: University of Chicago Press, 1953.

Rosenau, James N., ed., *Domestic Sources of Foreign Policy*. New York: The Free Press, 1967.

* Indicates paperback edition.

Russell, Bertrand R., *Human Society in Ethics and Politics.* New York: Simon and Schuster, Inc., 1955.

Waltz, Kenneth N., *Foreign Policy and Democratic Politics.* Boston: Little, Brown and Company, 1967.

TWO

Government
and Policy-Making

W_e have already established that states act purposefully in international politics, and that an essential part of the process of foreign policy is making and implementing decisions. Our next inquiry, therefore, is into the ways states organize themselves for their international contacts, and the considerations that influence their decisions.

STATE ORGANIZATION FOR INTERNATIONAL ACTION

Government and Foreign Affairs

In the delicately balanced and perilous world of today, foreign affairs are one of the principal concerns of all states. For a small state the problem may involve no more than the basic issue of survival; the larger states usually add a variety of positive objectives that each hopes to attain in its own behalf. Each state's task in the international arena is peculiar to itself, but they all consider foreign policy a matter of high priority and major import.

As might be expected, therefore, all governments organize themselves for foreign affairs with considerable care. However inefficiently or casually domestic policy may be framed and executed, no state can afford to function internationally for very long at any except the maximum level of effectiveness. Foreign policy establishments in any state reflect the best of which the society is capable.

Organization for foreign policy is roughly identical in all governments. Atop the organizational pyramid stands the head of government, testifying by his active role to the basic significance of international affairs. He is directly assisted by whatever close advisory and administrative apparatus the government boasts, whether a "cabinet" of the British type, a "Revolutionary Council" of the military regime, a "Presidium" as in the Soviet Union, or a less institutionalized Cabinet-Executive Office arrangement, as is the case in the United States. The principal foreign affairs specialist in the government is the foreign minister (in the United States, the Secretary of State), who heads the administrative department concerned with foreign policy and is the principal official adviser to the head of government. In all states other departments participate directly in foreign policy decision; financial and military experts almost always do, and economic ministers (on questions of trade or development) have become virtually as critical. Legislative bodies play roles dependent on their constitutional place, but foreign policy is primarily an executive prerogative, only occasionally inhibited by legislative interference.

A real part in decision-making is played by the corps of representatives a nation maintains abroad. Diplomatic personnel are ubiquitous today, and economic, cultural, and military representatives are growing in number. The information they relay to their home governments obviously affects policy; in addition, they conduct many negotiations themselves.

The Head of Government

The head of government, be he President, Prime Minister, or Dictator, is the key figure in all foreign policy decisions. By virtue of the special responsibility international practice confers upon him (only he may officially speak for the state in international relationships), and as a result of his internal status as political leader of his people, he merges in his person more of the nation's foreign policy authority than can be found anywhere else. No institutional arrangements can eliminate or blur his primary responsibility.

The head of government may structure his mission in any of a great variety of ways. He naturally seeks advice and information to guide his decisions, but he may rely on the opinions of his subordinates or trust only his own judgments and intuition. He may function entirely within the official apparatus, or may rely more on informal and unofficial sources of recommendations—for example, the Communist Party in the U.S.S.R., the "kitchen cabinet" in the United States, "the Establishment" in Great Britain, or the "revolutionary command" in a military dictatorship. He may confine his personal attention only to issues of massive and general import, leaving their detailed implementation to subordinates, or intervene into the decisional process in matters of great detail and short-run impact.

The peculiar function of the head of government lies in the province of political leadership. Whatever the controlling internal dynamics may be, the head of government must somehow translate the prevailing value pattern and operative consensus of mass public opinion into foreign policy terms. Whether he be a dictator or a popularly chosen leader, it is his task as the visible symbol of national unity to formulate national purposes and give them expression in the form of concrete objectives. Under modern conditions, heads of government expend an ever-increasing proportion of their effort in maintaining this link between a changing international environment and the political community which they lead. Their policy decisions therefore tend to become increasingly general, symbolic, and direction setting, and less concerned with immediate operational choices.

Foreign Minister and Foreign Office

Foreign ministers in most states have a peculiarly taxing role. They must be specialists and technicians, concerned with the innumerable complexities of day-by-day decisions. They must also have an appreciation of the larger internal and external political problems with which their respective chiefs are faced. Simultaneously they must be administrators (as each is the head of the Foreign Office and foreign service of his state), policy-makers (insofar as permitted by their superiors), and advisers.

To this multiple responsibility has in many cases been added another task: high-level negotiation. New improvements in transportation and communication, and the need for quick decision, have given the foreign ministers of all leading powers and of many smaller ones a roving commission to travel widely and conduct all important negotiations among themselves, either bilaterally, before the United Nations, or in some form of "conference." Obviously, foreign ministers faced with complex and protracted discussions of a problem cannot always obtain workable solutions, and organizational strain and dilution of effort are predictable consequences of their profession. Whatever the disadvantages, however, foreign ministers' meetings (and their logical outgrowth, "summit" meetings among heads of government) have become a normal feature of international political life.

The foreign office of each state constitutes the primary grouping of expertise on international matters within the government. Generally speaking, its domestic personnel are relatively few, although—at least in free governments—some significant increase has taken place in recent years. It is normally organized into subsections that reflect the nature of its task. There is usually a breakdown by geographic areas corresponding to the nation's involvement in various parts of the world, and also what the U.S. Department of State terms "functional bureaus," each of which focuses on a special function in a global context.

A foreign office thus has a dual mission: to communicate with its own personnel abroad and with foreign diplomatic missions in its own country. In performing this dual role, foreign office personnel make a vast number of policy decisions at all but the highest level of importance. The foreign office also acts as a source of policy recommendations that flow upward to the higher decisional levels: the foreign minister, the cabinet, the head of government and his staff. In this respect, foreign policy bureaucrats often, by defining alternatives and selecting data, materially influence the ultimate decisions.

In most states, foreign office personnel form a part of the inner bureaucratic elite within the government. The nature of their responsibilities tends to confer an aura of preferment, and, in addition, create some residual envy and resentment in officials of other departments. As foreign policy responsibilities have become diffused throughout many executive agencies (as has been the case in most powerful states), intragovernmental rivalries have impeded the optimum mobilization of national effort. This has been particularly true in the United States.

The Diplomatic Service

Every state maintains a network of diplomatic missions abroad, one in each state with which it conducts relations; it also acts as host for similar missions sent by other states. Thus communications flow in a dual channel: a message may go directly from the foreign ministry to the resident ambassador of a second state, or it may go to the nation's ambassador abroad for delivery to the other foreign minister.

Each mission abroad is led by a "chief of mission," usually titled "ambassador." His function is multiple: he represents his state before the host government, he acts as a channel of communication, he reports information to his own government, he performs a public relations task for his state before the people of his host country, he maintains contact with his own nationals who are subject to the jurisdiction of his host country, and he may sometimes conduct negotiations. The present century has seen a great magnification of the public relations and representational roles of ambassadors, and a corresponding diminution of the function of negotiation. Though in some respects regrettable, substantial elimination of the ambassador as an important decision-maker was inevitable as soon as instantaneous communication and rapid transportation made it possible for responsible officials to conduct negotiations themselves.

Embassies vary in size and structure according to the importance of the states to each other and the prestige each wishes to cultivate. Regardless of size or detailed organization, however, some degree of functional specialization among embassy personnel is the rule. For purposes of reporting and representation, different officers concentrate on political, economic, cultural, and labor matters; specialized (non-foreign office) representatives for military, scientific, commercial, agricultural, and various other affairs are frequently found, at least in the embassies of larger and more prosperous states.

Most governments rotate diplomatic personnel between assignments abroad and tours of duty in the foreign office. There is much to be gained by this practice. Policy-makers at home gain an appreciation of the problems faced by diplomats abroad, while the missions themselves gain insight into the larger dimensions of national policy and into the difficulties of decision-making which confront their own governments.

Complicating the task of diplomats abroad in recent years has been the proliferation of what the United States calls "operating missions": task forces charged with executing within a country programs already negotiated diplomatically. The exact status of the operating mission vis-à-vis the resident diplomatic staff has proved troublesome for American officials, and has caused considerable tension. Other states that have adopted this device of implementing policy have encountered the same sort of problem. Since the lines of control and authority of the operating mission and the diplomatic mission do not coincide, resolution of jurisdictional conflicts often rotates upward to higher administrative personnel, sometimes even onto the shoulders of the foreign minister or similar government official.

Other Departments

The centrality of foreign affairs to most governments is clearly demonstrated by the wide involvement of other departments in the matter.

Every government brings a broad spectrum of insights and capabilities to the process of making and executing foreign policy.

Two departments are virtually universal participants: the agency charged with raising and allocating public funds (the Treasury Department in the United States, the Exchequer in Britain, the Finance Ministry in many states) and the military establishment. Each brings its special orientation to matters of international affairs.

Foreign policy for major states is very expensive. Questions of national survival, security, and interest are a top-priority charge on the state's resources. Any major foreign policy decision (and most minor ones) involves some charge on public finance and requires the active or tacit approval of the appropriate department. Matters of taxation, furthermore, touch sensitive nerves in the body politic, and general political considerations cannot help but affect any decision to commit public funds to international purposes. In an era in which most governments are taxing their citizens to the practical maximum and any increase will touch off resistance, great caution is required before budgetary increases for foreign policy purposes can be undertaken.

By far the largest share of expenditure for foreign policy purposes—at least for the more important states—goes for the military establishment. Most governments today are committed to the maintenance of as large a military force as is practicable. Motivations of security are responsible in the majority of cases, but for others the dominant factor is clearly a search for prestige. We must also keep in mind that the military machine in many of the new and unstable states is an instrument of government and political leadership.

These considerations all have the same effect: military leadership and the armed forces are actively involved in foreign policy-making in almost all states. They bring a special point of view—notably a distrust of "politics" in bargaining and a strong preference for direct methods—to all deliberations in which they take part. Usually they find themselves actually or potentially at odds with the foreign office.

Increasingly important in almost all states today is the economic ministry or the ministry of planning. Its primary concern with foreign policy in developed states lies in the area of international trade; for less developed ones, it is more involved with the problems intrinsic to industrial development. At times its recommendations may be absolutely controlling, as is the case with many young states in Asia and Africa. Because the economic health of a nation has a direct effect on the amount of resources it may commit to international politics, no government can indefinitely ignore the economic consequences of its policy. This fact alone would make economic specialists important in foreign policy-making.

Other agencies usually play a role more periodic and irregular. Perhaps special mention should be made of whatever organization the government maintains for propaganda. Modern mass communications are a powerful tool of domestic leadership and an effective instrument of policy, thus elevating propaganda experts to great relevance and often critical importance. Other departments with foreign policy responsibility, including intelligence agencies, tend to be called into the decisional process as their special orientation dictates and as the particular problem demands.

THE POLICY PROCESS

The entire foreign policy organization of a state exists for the purpose of making and executing decisions to advance the state's interests. Because the basic ingredients of the decision-making process are substantially identical in all states, we turn now to the policy process within any government.

The Process of Decision

Analytically, we may conceive of foreign policy decisions as flowing from the appreciation of a fluid and only imperfectly perceived situation by the corps of official decision-makers. In this effort they use criteria of interest and purpose stemming from their social milieu and professional background, modified by their peculiar institutional setting. Although national interest as a concept has deep social roots, its expression in any decisional situation is undertaken by the responsible decision-makers.

Thus the steady input of information to the decisional hierarchy undergoes constant analysis and evaluation as the officials attempt to determine which events so affect the nation as to require decision and possibly action. These stimuli come from the "external setting." For most states the majority of data are simply noted and disregarded as peripheral to the national interest; only a few major states have such widespread concerns as to make their involvement almost total. Only those matters judged to have policy relevance are actually put to analysis and enter the process of decision.

The bulk of state activity in international affairs, therefore, may be thought of as "reaction" or "interaction": responses to stimuli external to the state. A portion of any foreign policy consists of "action" in the pure sense: efforts undertaken in response to internal stimuli so as to modify the environment in a desired direction. The norms of strategic decision ordinarily make this a matter of lower priority than the crucial business of response and adaptation to external stimuli, many of which are actually or potentially hostile. A state's first responsibility is to ensure its continued existence and effective range of choice; only after it has done all it can to guarantee its participation in the system can it attempt to bend events to its purpose.

If foreign policy thus consists of the application of a set of internalized criteria of judgment to a dynamic external situation, we may conceptualize the process as consisting of the following steps: (1) establishment of the original criteria; (2) determination of the relevant variables in the situation; (3) measurement of the variables by the criteria; (4) selection of an objective; (5) elaboration of a strategy to reach the objective; (6) the decision to act; (7) the action itself; and (8) evaluation of the results of the action in terms of the original criteria.

We must keep in mind that this formulation is an abstraction applicable only to a single problem, and that in practice the procedure is never so clear-cut. States conduct many decisional operations simultaneously. Each analysis has its own peculiarities, and each affects all the others and is affected by them. Very few decisions go to completion without being modified by changing circumstances, and many enterprises are dropped without reaching fulfillment because time and new concerns have rendered them obsolete. In spite of these practical warnings, however, the schematic presentation is valuable because it distinguishes the various intellectual operations involved in a foreign policy decision.

The Analysis of Situations

Having decided that a situation merits decision, officials undertake a situational analysis in some depth, with a two-fold purpose. Initially they seek to discover the manner and extent of their involvement in the situation under scrutiny in order to arrive at the most advantageous objective for their government to seek. (In Chapter One we noted that "objectives" derive from concrete situations, in contrast to "goals," which are postulated a priori.) The second purpose of their analytical effort is to discover the different courses of action the situation makes possible, independent of their relative desirability.

Situational analysis ordinarily requires consideration of three distinct sets of factors: (1) the general pattern of forces operative in the area of decision that lie beyond the control of any single state; (2) the particular policies being followed by other states—at least the important ones—in the given context; and (3) one's own capabilities for action in light of the first two factors. In theory, this analysis is as objective and cold-blooded as professional skill can make it. However, so many intangible factors must be weighed and evaluated that no government can be more than approximately accurate in this effort.

Only after situational analysis can an objective be selected. This point is of central importance in the decisional process. It is not until after the objective has been selected that the situation permits reanalysis with an eye to selection of the optimum course of action for bringing about the hoped for state of affairs.

It should be emphasized once more that the situational context of a decision is analyzed at least three times. The first analysis stresses long-term factors so as to develop a working concept of interest. The second focuses on middle-range aspects in order to suggest an objective. The third concentrates on short-run and immediate variables; this emphasis is productive of alternative strategies and policy declarations in the narrow sense.

The Choice Among Alternatives

The key concept in the analysis of policy is "choice"; any decision-maker so conducts himself as to preserve, at any stage in the process, his maximum range of choice. In practice this results in formulating his opportunities (or imperatives) as a set of alternatives of action.

Strategically, the principle of alternatives is often formulated in negative terms: "Never put yourself in a situation in which you have only one possible course of action." As long as a state retains a choice of tactics, its opponent must go to the trouble of devising responses to each of the various lines it can follow. A lack of alternatives, however, condemns a state to a predictable response and to facing a predetermined counterstrategy. Formulating decisions as a choice among alternatives is a way of examining all opportunities, and of conserving whatever strategic advantages may flow from forcing uncertainty and risk on the decision-makers of other states.

Thus the approach to a decision is usually cast—with varying degrees of formalization, depending on the elements of time and change in the situation—as a canvass of all the alternatives open to the state in the particular context, together with estimates of the probable outcome of each alternative. This spectrum of choice forms the ultimate agenda of the "decisional unit," whether a single policy-maker or a group. The alternative selected is that which promises the greatest gain or, as often happens, the least loss in terms of the current criteria of choice.

We must understand that the range of alternatives seldom includes many bad choices and only one "right" one. Most often, the real range of choice is fairly narrow and the policy and interest differentials among the various alternatives are relatively small. Selection of one is often difficult, especially when pressures of time or administrative necessity telescope the decisional process or eliminate certain steps altogether. No state can dispense entirely with alternatives, however obscure their differences may be in a particular situation. Policy cannot be made for long on an ad hoc basis, nor can any government afford to give up the flexibility the process contributes to decision-making.

Basing a decision on a choice among alternatives, especially if the courses of action are not mutually exclusive, makes it much easier for a state to adapt itself to the consequences of an error or unforeseen circumstance in its original decision. If the selected course of action fails to evoke the hoped for response, it will be possible to shift to another line of policy without going through the entire process again.

In rapidly moving situations, it is not uncommon for a state to launch a course of action with no clear idea of its ultimate outcome. However, the general line of attack is the result of a choice among alternatives, and contains within itself further alternatives. One (perhaps several) of these will be adopted, depending on the nature of the response to the state's initial step. Thus policy is kept abreast of situational change with—if implementation is forceful—a consequent gain in effectiveness. We must admit that such extreme flexibility is usually beyond the capability of most states. Only relatively powerful states can afford to enter active maneuvering with several alternative approaches available, each equally within its competence to pursue.

The usual method of testing the validity of a choice is to take its initial steps tentatively and leave an escape route open if the judgment proves to have been faulty. In such a case, a state can hold its losses to a minimum while preserving the freedom of action to strike off later on a different tack. Only after the correctness of its assumptions and the accuracy of its situational analysis have been reasonably confirmed does a state permit itself to become fully committed to its initial choice of action.

Evaluating and Revising Decisions

Throughout this discussion of the policy process, it has been evident that state action is contingent for its effectiveness upon the extent to which it is responsive to the actual situation. Since decisions are always made upon incomplete and inaccurate information, prudence would demand constant evaluation of the results of decisions and immediate revision of policies that are not producing the desired effect.

Here modern communications media are of great utility to the policy-maker. Where in an earlier age he would have to wait weeks or months to learn the response to one of his moves, today he can get this information within a much shorter period—sometimes instantly. In this sense the process of evaluation and revision is much simpler.

But in another way, modern conditions complicate the task of making decisions. Events today move even more rapidly than decisions, which are, after all, made by human beings subject to fatigue and bad temper. Furthermore, the very complexity of foreign policy leads major states to implement their decisions by relatively fixed commitments and long-term "programs"—both extremely difficult to change even in circumstances of stress. A third factor vitiating evaluation is the press of foreign policy business. When new problems crowd in on the decision-maker, he is much more likely to deal with them than to turn to the tedious and often agonizing reappraisal of earlier decisions to see if they worked out as expected.

It is therefore not uncommon today for a particular policy to be utterly invalidated by an unexpected train of events which would have been anticipated by adequate evaluation and revision. Major powers with extensive and complicated networks of commitments are particularly prone to this danger. Although constant evaluation is the most necessary for them, it is also usually the most difficult. Smaller states, with less margin for error and with a narrower range of concerns, have proved much more adept at adjusting their policies to even modest situational evolution.

FACTORS INFLUENCING DECISIONS

Foreign policy is not made by electronic computers; it is formulated by men who lack mathematical precision but who do possess judgment. We have seen that a policy decision incorporates a choice. What factors influence the selection of one course of action rather than another?

The Appreciation of the Problem

Decision-making must begin with an understanding of what the decision itself is about. No policy can be chosen without an appreciation of the problem the decision is to affect. This truism is often overlooked in much of the discussion of policy-making in the United States.

To begin with, probably no two officials in any government see the same set of facts in identical "problem" terms. Each brings his own personality, professional and organizational bias, and intuitive skill to bear on his task, and each may have his own sources of information. A large part of the "Tower of Babel" effect in policy-making—especially in western democracies—flows from this variance in the over-all appreciation of the policy environment among those charged with responding to it. One significant task of leadership, whether political or professional, is to impose controlling criteria of problem identification upon all subordinate decision-makers.

Confusion sometimes stems from the semantic trap laid by the word "problem." Strategy is a cautious business at best, and the natural tendency (at least in western languages) to conceptualize "problem" (as incorporating an obstacle to be overcome and pressures to be resisted) only reinforces this danger. If "problem" is understood to be the factor in a situation that demands solution, and if it is borne in mind that, in logic, a "problem" is as likely to constitute an opportunity as an obstacle, the possible deadening effect of the idea can be minimized. It is as problematic to determine ways of capitalizing on an unexpected advantage as it is to develop a strategy to lessen the effect of misfortune.

A crucial element in any problem analysis is the early selection of an objective to the attainment of which the nation's effort will be committed. This is the essence of "strategy," defined as a plan for the employment of resources for the attainment of a predetermined end. On the broadest foreign policy scale, such a plan may accurately be termed a "national strategy." Since all operational decisions are made in terms of postulated goals, the identification and evaluation of strategic objectives constitute a major step in the process of problem identification. This task is more complex than it might seem at first sight.

Even if the decision-maker has a firm grasp on national goals and an adequate comprehension of the situation, he ordinarily encounters difficulty in formulating objectives. One set of possible objectives will be attractive because of its intrinsic *desirability*, while another group has *feasibility* in its favor; rarely will a single objective rank high on both scales. The task of the decision-maker thus beset by opposing constructions of the problem is to strike the best possible balance between the desirability and feasibility of the objectives he perceives, and to act on the basis of this compromise.

The Cost/Risk Calculation

A second major factor that affects foreign policy decision is the cost/risk calculation. No state can count on getting anything free in international politics. Furthermore, even with the maximum intellectual and physical effort, any policy carries with it some risk of failure. The twin cautions of cost and risk tend to delimit sharply the real range of choice of the policy-maker.

In considering a possible line of action, the decision-maker dare not give himself the benefit of any doubt. In establishing a possible cost factor, he must assume the worst possible consequences of his move. Only after he has made his decision is he free to take implementing action. Of course, the "worst possible consequences" are actually those that are foreseeable in the light of the policy-maker's supply of information. Were "possible" to be taken literally, every decision would be a peace-or-war choice, for war is a *possibility* in any international confrontation. Cost factors are actually estimated in terms of the span of probabilities open at any time. A decision to act really means that the decision-maker feels that the objective sought is worth the highest price that anyone will actually charge him and his state.

Usually simultaneous with the calculation of cost, but analytically a second step in the analysis, is determination of the risk involved in the projected course of action. "Risk" here refers to the relative odds in favor of success, and is necessary in decision-making simply because of unforeseen contingencies that perpetually endanger the peaceful interaction of states. The evaluation of risk is a recognition of the element of guesswork in all foreign policy.

For each alternative that demands a decision, the state establishes an "acceptable burden" of risk—the amount of failure that its policy will tolerate. The acceptability of such a "calculated" risk is determined by two sets of interlocking factors: how important is the objective being sought (a value judgment), and how serious will be the consequences of failure (an analytical conclusion). For important objectives, a state will bear great risk of failure; lesser objectives are sought after with a corresponding decrease in the burden of risk.

The factors of cost and risk as determined by the decision-makers establish parameters within which decisions must fall. No rational policy choice would dictate action in behalf of an objective that might cost too much if the risk of having to pay that price is beyond the level of acceptance. Thus, policy-makers find themselves hemmed in by analytical inhibitions and practical counsels of prudence.

The Domestic Aspect: Consensus

Another parameter within which the decision-maker must operate is internal (domestic) in its effect. Regardless of form of government or political philosophy, any foreign policy apparatus is bound by popular consensus and limited to whatever area of permissibility mass attitudes may allow. This is not to encourage the unsophisticated view that "all foreign policies are democratically inspired." The consensus that restricts decision-makers may be entirely synthetic and the result of a planned campaign of deceptive mass propaganda. But regardless of its origin or degree of sophistication, consensus plays a key role in staking off the area of free decision the policy-maker enjoys at any given time.

As long as war remains the ultimate sanction of state policy and wars are fought by entire populations, consensus will govern decision-making. No government can safely be divorced from the active support of its populace. Mass identification with foreign policy issues, although an enormous source of strength to all governments, is also in this sense a debilitating factor that often deprives officials of the capacity to follow their best professional judgment.

In practice, consensus operates with varying degrees of constraint. With a wide area of permissibility and on matters of lesser import, decision-makers often operate without specific reference to mass reaction. The more narrowly and specifically consensus focuses, however, the more officials feel its impact.

There is an interesting relationship between the dimensions of breadth and intensity of consensus. A broad grant of discretion to government ordinarily implies a relatively low level of mass identification. When a government increases the intensity of its popular support on a particular issue, it pays the price of the narrowing of its permissible alternatives, at least as interpreted by the consensus. Thus the paradox: the closer to war a situation drifts, the more public attitudes become inflamed, and the less control statesmen exercise over events. In gaining popular support against the worst, governments often sacrifice their ability to capitalize affirmatively upon more favorable circumstances.

Consensus is most obvious when it is most specific. Periodically— especially in moments of crisis—mass attitudes will seize upon a particular issue or problem of policy and insist on a (usually oversimplified) position. Since mass response to problems rarely takes into account either enough relevant data or practical range of choice, such manifestations are almost always sources of annoyance to decision-makers. Policy personnel in democratic and dictatorial states alike dread such developments and make considerable effort to keep popular attitudes excited but safely below the boiling point. When consensus does break out of control, policy-makers may ignore and defy popular demands only at their own risk, and even then for a brief time span.

The Incompleteness of Information

We owe to the mathematical *theory of games* the insight that decisions can be made under any of three sets of conditions: conditions of certainty, conditions of uncertainty, and conditions of risk. In conditions of certainty each action has one predictable outcome; in conditions of uncertainty each action may have more than one outcome but their relative probabilities are unknown; in conditions of risk each action may have more than one outcome but their relative probabilities are known. Decisions made under conditions of certainty are so rare in foreign policy as to be analytically insignificant. Decisions made under known conditions of uncertainty do not occur in a government of rational men. Almost all foreign policy decisions taken by states, therefore, are made under conditions of risk.

"Risk" in this sense has almost the same meaning as in the cost/risk calculation, and for the same reason: any foreign policy decision is made in a context of incomplete information, because the built-in time lag between event and decision makes it futile for a policy-maker to wait until he has the complete facts. He must act on the information available to him and arrange his decisions so as to reduce the risk to a practical minimum.

The inadequacy of information available to the policy-maker manifests itself in either of two ways: he may not have enough data, or he may have too much. In the first instance he lacks the one or several crucial informational inputs that will enable him to construct a meaningful and valid decision. If data are unavailable or if he cannot wait for more complete information, he fills the gaps with estimates, extrapolations, or assumptions, and goes ahead anyway. In the second situation, he has the information he needs, but it lies buried under mountains of extraneous and only mildly relevant data. Because of time pressures or because he lacks immediately applicable criteria of relevance, the decision-maker finds himself little better off than he would have been without the elaborate accumulation of unsifted information.

Under the heading "intelligence," governments today constantly exert themselves to improve both the quantity and usefulness of the information upon which they must base their decisions. As more areas of human life and action become relevant to foreign policy, more kinds of information are gathered up and funneled into the decision-making apparatus of each government. Once swept into the analytical net, the information is digested, evaluated, correlated, and distributed to all decision-makers whose responsibilities make these data useful and necessary to them. Those officials who consume the end-product of this information gathering and disseminating network are known in the United States as the "intelligence community."

The purpose of this greater emphasis on information is to reduce the risk factor in decisions; that is, to minimize the extent to which the outcomes of any action are unknown and to amplify what is known of the relative probability of their occurrence. This may be classified conceptually as a "search for certainty" in policy-making, but of course the realistic goal is much more modest. Any effective substitution of knowledge or informed insight for pure guesswork in foreign policy decisions is a net gain, and every state is convinced that enough improvement is possible to justify a major effort.

The Pressure of Time

Still another factor that materially affects foreign policy decisions is the simple phenomenon of time. Modern technology has speeded up the pace of international politics. With improvements in transporation and communication, events occur more rapidly than in past eras, and their outcomes reach the decision-maker in a much shorter time. This combination of forces cruelly burdens the policy-makers' task. Responsible officials lack the time needed to analyze situations, compare alternatives, and consummate choices; they can deal with most issues only in a summary (therefore usually routine and unimaginative) fashion. The best they can ordinarily do is conserve their analytical skills for the really important questions, but even in this modest and creditable effort they face difficulties. So pressed for time are they that a crucial issue—if in any way difficult to identify—often slips by as "just another problem."

In an attempt to cope with a larger and more rapidly moving flow of business, many governments have expanded their policy-making organizations. This has proved to be a self-defeating expedient, because the turgidity of bureaucracy has more than offset the gain in manpower commitment. Lateral communication within the bureaucratic structure and the need for "clearances and concurrences" often slows down decision-making unbearably, and deprives it of focus and force.

An unfortunate consequence of the pace at which most foreign policy decision-makers drive themselves (or are driven) is the disappearance of reflective thought in a climate of tension. With no time to "waste in just thinking," officials lose a quality of perceptiveness and flexibility ordinarily considered an advantage in a policy-maker. Men under pressure tend to make decisions that will clear their desks for the next problem. Being prudent, they prefer to make minimum commitments and extremely cautious responses, to follow precedent closely, and to interpret their controlling directives as narrowly as possible. A harried official always prefers a "no" answer to a "yes," for the former not only spares him the responsibility for a decision that might later prove unwise, but also obviates the necessity of opening up entirely new areas of analysis and decision for which he feels he lacks the time.

National Style

Decision-makers in any nation are materially affected by what is called "national style": the prevailing tradition and self-image of a society that predisposes its officials to perform their duties and make their decisions in a way considered unique and peculiarly appropriate. "Style" as a concept is much more useful, as well as being much easier to defend, than the once-popular idea of "national character." Although it is unreasonable to expect an entire people to conform to a given character, the bulk of a society will in their individual personalities reflect a certain stereotype.

National style is important in shaping decisions because of its effect in setting the analytical pattern of the decision-maker himself. He is usually unconscious of the extent to which he partakes of a larger code of appropriate and socially sanctioned behavior as he grapples with his special problems, but only a hopelessly alienated (and therefore largely ineffective) public servant could dissociate himself completely from his society. A common style of analysis and decision forms one of the real elements of cohesiveness in all reasonably well-integrated government structures.

The relevance of notions of style to decisions may be suggested by some examples. In Great Britain, for instance, the idea of "muddling through"—a conspicuous reluctance to relate immediate choices overtly to long-range purposes—gives British policy a remarkable resilience and adaptability that has long been the envy of other nations. Russia's obsession with secrecy is a stylistic trait that long antedates the Bolshevik Revolution. China's proclivity for suspicion is revealed in a policy style of centrism—maintenance of distance from others. The non-Western search for role and identity displays a policy style of much shape but little form. The French concern with "honor" and "glory" is far more than the mere symbolic and ritualistic matter it is for most other states; to France it is part of the national self-image and taken very seriously. The style of the United States has long dictated casting international issues in moral terms and viewing foreign policy as a series of crises broken by random intervals of relaxation.

These tricks of national style cannot help but modify the decisional dynamic each demonstrates. Considerations of style help explain both deep animosities and close associations between pairs of states, as well as many otherwise perplexing patterns of interaction. We cannot expect the United States to act with a Russian concern for secrecy, nor can the Soviet Union conceive policy along any crisis-relaxation continuum. We would not expect that the maintenance of close and satisfactory relations between two such different styles would be any easy matter, completely independent of any differences in ideology and forms of government that might exist.

Commitments and Precedents

Last in our list of the factors influencing decision, but frequently of controlling importance to the policy-maker, is the structure of already existing commitments and precedents within which the decision-maker must act. No policy decision is ever made *in vacuo* at a given moment in time; each is affected to a great degree by many earlier decisions and directed by the national interest. The state as a whole, the policy-making apparatus, and the individual decision-maker are all, in different ways, bound by the remote or immediate past.

One important type of commitment that affects decisions is that made to a state's own mass opinion. We have noted its effect in our discussion of consensus. A second includes all the understandings, arrangements, alliances, and other fixed relationships a state has developed with its fellows. A decision violating any of these, or even changing one in any significant degree, would cause a perceptible response and open many new problems. Ordinarily, therefore, any such initiative is avoided except in clearly unavoidable cases. A third type of commitment is perhaps less obvious: long-standing hostilities and disagreements with other states also function as fixed factors and materially affect decisions.

This latter category merits a final word. Since major policy undertakings today require extensive "programming" and long-term implementation, a deep-seated conflict among states (such as the Arab-Israeli imbroglio) rapidly assumes an unspoken institutional character. Any radical improvement in relations would, in strict decisional terms, present almost as critical a problem as would a major crisis. Having become one of the "givens" of a state's international position, that government's decision-makers naturally assume the indefinite prolongation of the controversy to be preferable to almost any modification in its conditions.

REFERENCES

* Almond, Gabriel, *American People and Foreign Policy.* New York: Frederick A. Praeger, Inc., 1960.

* Armstrong, John A., *Ideology, Politics and Government in the Soviet Union: An Introduction* (rev. ed.). New York: Frederick A. Praeger, Inc., 1967.

* Indicates paperback edition.

* Beloff, Max, *Foreign Policy and the Democratic Process*. Baltimore: Johns Hopkins Press, 1955.

* Cohen, Bernard C., *Foreign Policy in American Government*. Boston: Little, Brown and Company, 1965.

Crabb, Cecil V., Jr., *American Foreign Policy in the Nuclear Age* (2nd ed.). New York: Random House, Inc., 1966.

Gross, Feliks, *Foreign Policy Analysis*. New York: Philosophical Library, 1954.

Hilsman, Roger, *To Move A Nation: The Politics of Foreign Policy in the Administration of John F. Kennedy*. Garden City, N.Y.: Doubleday & Company, Inc., 1967.

* Hoffmann, Stanley, *Gulliver's Troubles or The Setting of American Foreign Policy*. New York: McGraw-Hill Book Company, 1968.

* Jackson, Henry M., ed., *The Secretary of State and the Ambassador*. New York: Frederick A. Praeger, Inc., 1964.

* Kennan, George F., *American Diplomacy 1900–1950*. Chicago: University of Chicago Press, 1951.

Lerche, Charles O., Jr., *Foreign Policy of the American People* (3rd ed.). Englewood Cliffs, N.J.: Prentice-Hall, Inc., 1967.

* Macridis, Roy C., ed., *Foreign Policy in World Politics* (3rd ed.). Englewood Cliffs, N.J.: Prentice-Hall, Inc., 1967.

* Millis, Walter, *et al.*, *Foreign Policy and the Free Society*. New York: Oceana Publications, 1958.

* Robinson, James A., *Congress and Foreign Policy-Making* (rev. ed.). Homewood, Ill.: Richard D. Irwin, Inc., and The Dorsey Press, 1967.

* Rosenau, James N., *Public Opinion and Foreign Policy*. New York: Random House, Inc., 1961.

* Rubinstein, Alvin Z., ed., *The Foreign Policy of the Soviet Union* (2nd ed.). New York: Random House, Inc., 1966.

* Sapin, Burton M., *The Making of U.S. Foreign Policy*. Washington, D.C.: The Brookings Institution, 1966 (paperback edition by Frederick A. Praeger, Inc.).

* Snyder, Richard, H. W. Bruck, and Burton M. Sapin, *Foreign Policy and Decision Making: An Approach to the Study of International Politics*. New York: The Free Press, 1962.

* Spanier, John W., *American Foreign Policy Since World War II* (2nd ed.). New York: Frederick A. Praeger, Inc., 1965.

* Ulam, Adam, *Expansion and Coexistence: The History of Soviet Foreign Policy 1917–1967*. New York: Frederick A. Praeger, Inc., 1968.

* Indicates paperback edition.

THREE

Capability in Action

An old saw that says a great deal about the nature of foreign policy and the dynamics of interstate relations alleges that "a state does what it can and suffers what it must." A state's range of action is limited both by definition and in fact. The objectives it selects, and the tactics it adopts in order to achieve them, can never be any more than functions of its over-all capacity for action within the situation in which it is placed. The tension inherent in the contrast of absolute ends and sharply circumscribed means, as we noted earlier, makes policy-making a constant process of compromise and adjustment.

The nature and extent of the state's capacity to achieve its ends is closely allied to state purpose. We have said that a state in any situation attempts to get as much as it can of what it wants. At this point we are therefore interested in how a state estimates how much it can get in a given context, how these estimates find their way into policy decisions, and what factors and elements in a state's position contribute positively or negatively to its ability to achieve at least minimum satisfaction. We shall discuss such matters in this chapter under the over-all heading of "state capability."

THE CONCEPT OF "CAPABILITY"

Definition

The broadest and most useful definition describes a state's capability as its capacity to affect changes in the international environment in its own interest. This does not include all the actions a state may be in a position to take, but only those deemed advantageous to itself. The capacity to change the environment in a way inimical or irrelevant to state purposes is regarded as exterior to capability. The concept draws its validity from certain operating assumptions about the nature of foreign policy, and is therefore meaningless except with reference to already postulated purposes.

Change in environmental conditions is obviously the core of the concept's rationale. By means of its capability a state "does what it can"; it "suffers what it must" under circumstances beyond its capability to affect. Change is to be understood in the broadest sense as situational relationships that are different than they would have been without application of the state's capability, and therefore includes neutralization of forces as well as affirmative realignment of factors by the state concerned. A state makes its intentions effective in the real world by means of its capability.

Capability is thus a summary manner of referring to the "means" aspect of the ends-means continuum in foreign policy. The policy-maker cannot afford vagueness. However generally the notion may be conceived and discussed in the abstract, capability judgments in foreign policy are useful only when made in highly concrete, specific, and immediate terms.

The Function of Capability

Capability redefines itself to some extent when it is actively committed to the service of state objectives. In the international political system, a state can achieve its purposes only by gaining the assent of its fellows. Lacking as it does an effective institutional mechanism, international politics depends for the ratification of state decision upon an informal and unstable mechanism of consensus. The entire structure of state interaction stems from this basic operating requirement.

The assent of other states may be stated or tacit, voluntary, uninvolved, or grudging. It may be extended after a relatively simple process of explanation and persuasion, or only after a struggle of will and power. Regardless of its source, nature, extent, or durability, this consensus alone makes possible the accomplishment of a national objective. A nation's foreign policy is directed and its capability is committed to the winning of this consent.

We may thus consider the operational function of state capability to be the engineering of an adequate international consensus. Almost any aspect of the policy process can be viewed in these terms. An "open course of action" is actually a series of moves a state feels it can make without running into an effective international veto. The achievement of an objective is really the creation of a favorable state of affairs which other states are willing to accept. Policy-making is really a judgment about how much effort the state must make to gain sufficient assent or acquiescence from other states involved in the situation. Conceiving capability as the measure of a state's ability to command and win agreement with its purposes gives focus and point to the concept, and highlights the way in which it is actually used in policy-making.

Influence and Coercion in Capability

A state's ability to persuade other states to agree to its designs is demonstrated in two different ways. A policy-maker may be able to obtain the consent of another government in an atmosphere of agreement. Consent may be given freely for any of a variety of reasons: the other state may approve of the projected action, it may be neutral or uninvolved in the question, or its disagreement may be so small as to be negligible. More commonly, the desired approval may be forthcoming after some measure of positive inducement: the promise of direct benefit, a modification of policy in another area, or some other *quid pro quo*. In any of these instances, absence of open conflict and mutual adjustment of positions is the significant dimension. The aspect of capability involved here is that of *influence:* the state is able to gain adequate consensus by various persuasive and/or harmonizing devices without calling into question issues of force or power.

When consent must be won for policy purposes in a context of conflict and disagreement between states, another dimension of capability becomes operative—*coercion.* This is the province of the "power struggle," as each state attempts to bend the other to its will. The forms of coercion are almost infinite, ranging from the mildest of argument through a long threat-pressure continuum to physical force, the ultimate coercive method. At whatever level coercion is employed, its purpose is always the same. In the words of the classic definition of war, it is "to break the enemy's will to resist" so as to secure his agreement.

Influence and coercion are equally genuine and efficacious manifestations of state capability. Since conflict is a more exciting and newsworthy climate of human relationships than is harmony, the coercive aspect usually receives greater attention, and is often mistaken for the entirety of the phenomenon. Yet, operationally, statesmen spend a vast majority of their time and effort manipulating such influence as they may possess and resorting to coercion only as a last resort. It costs less to win consensus by influence. Fewer undesirable aftereffects are produced, and the results tend to be more lasting. The statesman with only coercive increments of capability available to him is indeed unfortunate. His choice of policies is sharply limited by the relatively high cost that any coercive procedure will entail.

Capability and "Power"

The danger of magnifying unduly the operational role of coercion has led to the substantial discrediting of the once widely held concept of "power." Although it is possible to define and use the term "power" much as we are using "capability" in this chapter, power has come to symbolize the capacity of a state to coerce others or to avoid coercion by them. Such an emphasis on coercion leads to a concentration on the most obvious form of coercive capacity—military force. A construct of international politics grounded on "power" runs the risk of overemphasizing a victor and a vanquished in every international confrontation of will and strength. In the vocabulary of the mathematical *theory of games,* international politics is thus conceived as a "zero-sum" game: one player can win only to the extent that other players lose.

This is simply not the way international politics usually proceeds. Although the values states seek may be mutually exclusive and their prosecution possible only in an atmosphere of conflict, even this does not make all relationships coercive. The values may instead overlap or coincide, making conflict and disagreement irrelevant to the establishment of necessary equilibrium. A simplistic "power theory" of international politics ignores far too many aspects of the actual relations of states to be a reliable guide.

The concept of "power" contains another built-in conceptual trap. Capability is always the ability to do something, to act purposefully in an actual situation. Power should mean this also; in popular political discourse, however, power often becomes a status to which states aspire and which a chosen few achieve. Unsophisticated observers speak of a "powerful" state in the abstract, regardless of how much that state can actually do in immediate action situations. Capability preserves the necessary nexus with policy and action that a careless use of "power" often overlooks. It is for that reason that we use the former term in this book to refer to the over-all action competence of states.

CAPABILITY JUDGMENTS IN FOREIGN POLICY

Having outlined some of the ingredients in the concept itself, we turn next to a brief analysis of how capability is used in policy-making.

What Is a Capability Judgment?

A capability judgment made in a policy context is no more than an analysis of the opportunities and limitations implicit in the operational environment of the state concerned. Its end result is the formulation of a range of possible action by the state—insofar as the analyzing statesmen can identify it. The key idea in any capability judgment is *possibility;* capability provides the state with the resources of action, but in no other way predisposes the state to act in any particular way among those alternatives possible. The choice among alternatives is a value choice; capability judgments do no more than spell out the viable alternatives.

Thus a capability judgment is a special form of situational analysis. The policy context dictates the specific elements of capability that enter into the analysis, while the capability judgment establishes the parameters within which the operational decision will eventually be made. It is obvious that no sane statesman will attempt a policy that requires an effort beyond his state's capability.

Judging the State's Own Capability

The policy-maker must be fully informed about the several things he can do in the situation before he adopts a course of action. He must know what part of his nation's total resources is available to him in the particular situation; he may be (and usually is) restricted by the fact that much of the state's capability is already invested in other commitments, and also by policy decisions that limit him to certain forms of action (for example, military power may not be available, but he may use all the propaganda and economic measures he wishes). He must also have attempted to foretell the consequences of applying any of the available forms of capability.

This process, carried out to whatever necessary and appropriate level of detail, leads to an appreciation of his span of meaningful choices. On the basis of this judgment he proceeds to apply the criterion of desirability to the several courses of action he has formulated, and to select one of them as policy.

Modern governments are acutely sensitive to the concept of capability, and make such a massive effort to keep up-to-date on the choices they have open at any time that a policy-maker rarely finds it necessary to go through the entire analytical operation sketched above. Usually he has at his fingertips generalized formulations of state capability applicable to detailed situations. The essentials of the process remain the same, regardless of how extensively it may become institutionalized.

Capability Judgments of Other States

Capability judgments are really exercises in the determination of relationships. No capability judgment is of real use except in comparison with the capability of another state. Governments spend at least as much time and effort in attempting to judge the capability of other states as they do their own.

It is critical to a strategist to have an appreciation of the range of action open to other states, particularly those with which he is directly involved at the moment. If he can sense the parameters of action accepted by his opposite number in the other government, he will have a great advantage in developing his own policy. As a result, the major focus of political or "strategic" intelligence work in contemporary international politics is devoted to the development of elaborate formulations of the capabilities of all other states.

The method of reaching a capability judgment about another state is not radically different in nature from that used on one's own, but is of course a more difficult task. Information on which the judgment is based is much more fragmentary and difficult to obtain, since no state is eager to have any other gain complete insight into its own capabilities. Even more perplexing is the problem posed by differences in analytical points of view. Capability analysis, in spite of its purely possibilist focus, still requires interpretation and evaluation of data, and no two states interpret facts in quite the same way. For capability judgments to be of maximum use in devising strategy and tactics, a state must somehow modify its own possibilist formulations of the situations of other states with empathetic consideration of how the other policy-maker views his own situation.

FACTORS IN CAPABILITY ANALYSIS

Capability analysis, we have concluded, is a crucial step in policy-making. We have also sketched out the essentials of the approach to reaching capability judgments. It is now appropriate for us to review the factors that enter into these analyses.

Analytical Point of View

Perhaps the most important element in capability analysis is the point of view adopted by the analyst. Since a capability judgment is an estimate of the opportunities and limitations intrinsic to the decisional milieu, there is inevitably a gap between the environment as the analyst apperceives it and as it exists in reality. The policy-maker, subject to all the perceptual and behavioral limitations of any human being, must act on the milieu as he sees it, in full knowledge that many factors of the situation are unknown to him and will serve to modify and possibly upset whatever capability judgments he may make. We have already noted the impact of this element of unpredictability on policy-making as leading to caution and tentativeness in commitment and to a strong preference for a sizable margin of error in any decision.

Any "outside" capability analyst—anyone who makes estimates without bearing responsibility for official action—necessarily has a different point of view from that of an official. He may know many things that the official does not, and may be free from the institutional and social biases that complicate the decision-making process. His freedom from the burden of facing consequences of his decision may well induce a greater measure of optimism and a willingness to bear greater risk than is normally characteristic of an insider. The "grandstand quarterback" of foreign policy, be he student, journalist, electoral politician, or concerned citizen, can never more than approximate the special analytical point of view of the responsible decision-maker wrestling with questions of capability.

The Policy Context

The next factor in capability analysis that merits attention has been alluded to several times previously. Capability is a useful concept and capability judgments can be made meaningfully only in terms of a set of policies under analysis and evaluation. It is nonsense to speak of "capability" in the abstract as long as we grant that states move and act in international politics to some purpose. The policy assumptions underlying a capability analysis may frequently be left implicit or phrased as contingencies; this in no way frees the analysis from its policy roots. Even the most ephemeral of policy assumptions may serve as the base for capability analysis.

Capability judgments made without reference to a policy context lend themselves to semimystical deterministic manipulation. The various deterministically-oriented "theories" or "laws" of international politics tend to find their empiric root in one of the physical "foundations" of national strength. Geographers, demographers, military scholars, experts on raw materials, industrial and agricultural economists, and other specialists have all at some time developed a single-factor theory of capability and politics that purported to forecast the future of international relationships. None of these formulations has been able to explain more than a fraction of the totality of interstate maneuvering, and none has escaped the necessity of allowing for the supremacy of the policy considerations of statesmen and governments.

The Situational Base

If capability makes sense only in terms of a policy context, it is also true that the concept is useful only within a specific situation. This is partly because the "open courses of action" and "opportunities and limitations" in terms of which capability is phrased exist only within a concrete context. The measure of the state's ability to influence or coerce agreement is also a function of the particular situation in which it is operating.

Specifically, a state never has more than a fraction of its total theoretical or actual capability available for its immediate purpose. An over-all "favorable" capability position—a relatively large sphere of freedom of action within its general policy—may not translate into an equivalently high range of capability in a particular situation. A small and ordinarily weak state may, in an appropriate situation, have greater capability not only to influence a larger one but also to coerce it.

Certain forms of capability, whether influential or coercive, are appropriate to the peculiarities of any situation, while others are irrelevant. The actual capability a state enjoys in a situation is determined by which of its available increments of action are effective in meeting the exigencies of the context in view of the policy the state is pursuing at the moment. In this way the actual outcome of most international confrontations—especially those cast in an atmosphere of disagreement and attempted coercion—tends to be less a reflection of any generalized "power" relationship than a function of time, place, and the policies being carried out by the respective states.

Relativity of Capability

Capability is, as we have observed, a concept of relativity in two different ways: in the first instance, a judgment is made of the state's capacity to act in behalf of an already selected objective; second, any capability judgment is actually the state's capacity to act in comparison with the capabilities of other states to act.

Capability measured with reference to the state's ability to achieve an objective produces only one rational answer to the question, "How much capability does a state need?": "Enough." The criterion of any contingency planning is "adequacy"—sufficient capability to fulfill the anticipated needs of policy. There is no advantage in compiling action capacity beyond what a state sees itself as likely to need, with a generous overallowance for analytical error and unpredictable quirks of fate. Development of capability which has no policy relevance is merely an international political example of "conspicuous consumption."

Furthermore, with capability rooted in policy and situational contexts, its manipulation clearly requires comparison of relative ranges of choice and action open to whatever states are involved in the problem. Regardless of what a state may be able to do in a situation, its net capability is zero if other states can cancel or neutralize each of its moves. On the other hand, even a narrow range of action may be enough to give the state absolute capability if other states are relatively less well-off. The significant dimension in capability analysis is less that of absolute levels of environmental change than whatever margin of operational superiority one state may enjoy over another. This is particularly pertinent in questions of military confrontations today. Several states have the "capability" to destroy each other with thermonuclear weapons. Since neither is able to focus its absolute military strength to gain a strategic advantage, for operational and policy purposes the massive military machines of contemporary great powers are without relevance to the functional capability of their possessors.

Capability: A Dynamism

Capability is a highly dynamic concept. A capability judgment involves correlation of a broad variety of factors within a state with an international situation, all elements of which are moving at different speeds. Any final conclusion about relative capabilities, no matter how up-to-date the information on which it is based, is obsolete by the time of its formulation. To make such an analysis applicable to an existing situation, it is necessary for the statesman to project into the future whatever trends and variables he feels are controlling, both in his own state and with regard to all others involved.

In pure theory, any single capability analysis should serve as the basis for only one action decision. Any later consideration of the same situation would require a new calculation of the relative status of all the states concerned. Literal adherence to this principle would render decision-making almost impossible; most governments merely adjust a generalized capability formulation with such additional data as they may have available, and then proceed to a new decision. Even this partial re-calculation suggests the transitory character of the ingredients of a capability comparison, and the constant necessity of keeping it up to date.

ELEMENTS AND FACTORS OF CAPABILITY

Even after stressing that capability is a relative rather than an absolute phenomenon, and that any absolute "objective" formulation of a nation's capability, irrespective of a situational and policy context, suffers from unreality and a lack of usefulness, we must admit that it is necessary and desirable to make at least a rough catalogue of the elements and factors in a state's position that contribute to its capacity to act effectively. The list and discussion that follows may be thought of as a kind of checklist that indicates the disparate sources from which a state may, in a particular situation, draw resources with which to support its policy. By no means should it lead to absolute operational conclusions about the "strength" or "power" of any state.

The Major Categories

The "elements and factors" of capability are usually broken into two broad categories for convenience of discussion, although the classification is a rough one. Any overprecise conclusions based on the differences between categories will be at best questionable, and possibly in error. With this warning in mind, we may generalize that the capability of a state comes partially from tangible sources and partially from intangible ones.

Tangible factors are listed in various ways; here we include five categories: (1) geographic position; (2) population and manpower; (3) resource endowment; (4) industrial and agricultural productive capacity; and (5) military power. Each of these is obviously capable of further subdivision; their use in an actual capability analysis requires that they be broken down into greater detail.

The intangible factors we use here are four in number: (1) political, economic, and social structure; (2) educational and technical level; (3) national morale; and (4) international strategic position. As was the case with the tangible factors, these four as named are extremely broad and necessarily vague, and they must be given specific content and applicability if they are to be meaningfully used.

A quick comparison of the two categories leads to the conclusion that the so-called tangibles each have a generous measure of intangibility about them, while the intangibles all have certain aspects of tangibility. The major dimension used in analysis of the tangible factors is that of *quantity*—as modified by such notions as availability, convertibility, and substitutability. The significant dimension in the intangibles is *quality*—estimated not only in terms of "excellence," but also by such criteria as appropriateness and relevance. The analyst *measures* the tangible factors but *evaluates* the intangibles; the quality factor built into the intangibles has a great influence upon the effectiveness with which the tangibles are employed.

Thus a capability analysis in logic begins with the most obvious physical factors, such as geography, that are not only the most easily measured, but also have the slowest rates of change. It proceeds through the less manifestly concrete and thus more dynamic factors, and ultimately comes to rest at the opposite pole of intangibility, where there is little empiric data on which to rely but a rapid rate of change and evolution with which to cope.

The Tangibles

1. GEOGRAPHY. Geographic factors enter into state capability in a number of ways. Among the more immediately remarkable are such characteristics as the size of a state (which is either an advantage, a handicap, or a neutral factor, depending on the policy being pursued), its shape, topography, location, and climate. More subtle geographic influences include the nature of the state's frontiers, its neighbors, its insular, peninsular, littoral, or landlocked condition, its internal penetrability, and the distribution of its population over the landscape. None of these factors affect any state in the same way, yet any capability analysis, either over-all or specific, must take such geographic factors, which are relatively fixed conditions of state existence, into account.

Various theories of geographic determinism have plagued students for many years. An elaborate theory of civilization can be grounded on climatological data; an insular position is claimed to "destine" a nation (like Britain or Japan) for maritime greatness. The most inclusive deterministic interpretation of geography is found in the several theories of "geopolitics," an approach built on perhaps the most fundamental geographic fact of all—the arrangement of land and water on the face of the globe. One nineteenth century school of thought found mastery of the seas the key to world power because of the critical role of seaborne commerce and military power. This doctrine was replaced by the "heartland" theory identified with the British Sir Halford Mackinder and the Nazi German Karl Haushofer in the 1920's and 1930's. In the latter doctrine, land power was held to be supreme, and the "heartland" of the "world island"—roughly coterminous with the territory of the U.S.S.R.—was declared the one unassailable power base for world conquest.

Both the sea power and the "heartland" theories demonstrate the danger of drawing conclusions of inevitability from geographic facts, since each was in turn outdated and invalidated by changing technology. Sea power was overtaken by land power with the advent of the internal combustion engine; the "heartland" lost its immunity with the appearance of intercontinental ballistic missiles and other sophisticated delivery systems that overcome historical geographic barriers. Geography is neutral in its basic effect on state policy; it may be a handicap or an advantage depending on the purposes to which policy is committed.

2. POPULATION AND MANPOWER. A second tangible factor of immediate relevance is population and manpower. The basic datum is the gross number of human beings the state incorporates. On the assumption that other things are equal, greater population means greater capability to perform more tasks at a higher level of effectiveness. But other things are seldom equal; population data must be qualified by such factors as age distribution, sex distribution, and spatial dispersion. For military purposes, as an example, a population clustering heavily in the upper age groups or with an imbalance of females may make less of a contribution than might be estimated from its size alone.

Population is perhaps a less meaningful notion for purposes of capability analysis than is "manpower," that portion of the population available for broadly defined foreign policy purposes. All individuals who are politically useless, as well as those needed simply to keep the society functional (such as food producers), must be subtracted from the gross total. The result is the manpower quotient that, with appropriate direction, leadership, and administration, can be used to contribute to the miltitary, productive, and political capability of the state.

Capability estimates involving manpower, especially when any but the briefest time spans are concerned, must take into account trends of evolution and development within the population. A comparison of birth and death rates, for example, will suggest such insights as the net growth rate, and trends in age levels and life expectancy. It is possible, over a fairly long period, for government action to bring about perceptible change in population trends by the encouragement of early marriage and large families. France is today the outstanding example of a state that has done this successfully.

3. NATURAL RESOURCES. The third more or less quantifiable element of capability is natural resources, which include the state's natural endowment and those additional reserves it can control. Natural resources are both agricultural (mainly food and fiber) and mineral. The latter category has been crucial since the Industrial Revolution, as industrial processes have contributed so many new forms of capability to states. In this sense, mineral resources include energy sources (coal, petroleum, wood), the metals of ferrous metallurgy (iron ore and the various metals involved in steelmaking), nonferrous metals, and nonmetallic minerals.

Resource endowments clearly are limiting factors on capability; no state can function at a level beyond that permitted by its resources. But the rigid raw material theory of international politics, popular several decades ago, has few adherents today. Development of synthetics and other new industrial processes, elaboration of stockpiling techniques, and the unexpectedly high capacity of embattled populations to endure chronic shortages have all served to liberate states from the more rigid absolutes of the theory. Today an analyst may draw only the most general capability conclusions (with only peripheral relevance to immediate policy situations) from resource data.

4. INDUSTRIAL AND AGRICULTURAL PRODUCTIVITY. In one sense, industrial and agricultural productivity as a capability factor is a function of the two preceding factors of manpower and resources: production is the application of human effort to the transformation of resources from raw materials into finished products. Thus the level of industrial and agricultural production is determined in part by the initial resource endowment, and in part by the amount and quality of manpower committed to the task.

Production levels are obviously of more immediate relevance to capability than are resource potentials; whatever is produced is available for utilization. Sheer amounts of production, however, or even a less specific concept such as "productivity," are of only limited relevance to immediate capability judgments. Production takes many forms, and only a portion of the total output has any but the most general political applicability. The crucial capability factor involved in production is best suggested by asking: "How much are we producing of what we need at the moment?" Once more we see the critical part played by the policy context of capability.

Particularly apposite in dealing with productivity are such modifying considerations as availability, convertibility of facilities, and "lead time." Since capability judgments normally involve some attempt to estimate future requirements and capacities, these "quality" interpretations of productivity provide estimates of what the state might be doing at some point in the future. Estimates of the ability of the state to increase its politically significant production must take into account the willingness of the population to undergo relative hardship, since a major share of increased productive capability involves subtraction from the civilian-consumption sector of the economy. The development of new productive capacity is never more than a minor factor.

5. MILITARY POWER.   At once the most obvious, and at the same time the most relativistic, of the tangible factors of capability is military power-in-being. Capability judgments must pay deep attention to military factors, and are frequently based on them. It is by military means that states take overt action at the highest level of intensity, and final solutions are arrived at in international politics. The military element in capability is obviously central to all estimates.

Such being the case, it is no wonder that a great deal more effort has been lavished on the development of doctrines and techniques for estimation of military factors than has been spent on any other elements of capability. Analysis and evaluation of the several variables that enter into a state's military capability has been raised to a fine art in almost all states.

As with all the other tangible factors, the initial consideration is one of size: How large is the military establishment in terms of manpower? A second criterion is that of equipment and arms with regard to modernity and sophistication, as well as to the capacity to produce more. Third, inquiry is made into deployment, involving both the relative allocation of men and material among the various arms and services, and the pattern of their placement within the state's territory and (sometimes) its overseas bases. Finally, the full military capability of a state is comprehensible only in terms of whatever strategic and tactical doctrines are controlling at the time of the analysis; these principles will govern the way in which the armed forces are actually used in support of state purposes.

As we shall see in later chapters, in no area is the danger of absolute capability judgment greater and easier to fall into. There is a consoling but deceptive objectivity and clarity about raw manpower and equipment figures that often leads analysts into unsound, absolute conclusions. This difficulty has been compounded by the development of modern weapons and military techniques. What really counts in military capability is the military margin of superiority that may exist between two states, not the absolute level of military power either may have mobilized. Switzerland, it is sometimes said, is a pygmy to France but a giant to Liechtenstein.

1. POLITICAL, ECONOMIC, AND SOCIAL STRUCTURE. We have pointed out that the tangible elements of capability tend to be measured, whereas the intangibles are evaluated. In his approach to the intangibles, the analyst is not seeking a quantitative finding so much as he is interested in establishing the extent to which the phenomena he is studying contribute to or detract from the state's effectiveness in a specific situation.

This becomes obvious when we examine the first in our list of intangibles—the political, economic, and social structure of a state. The efficient capability analyst should be free from any stereotyped prejudices concerning the intrinsic superiority of one political, economic, or social system. Instead, he must apply the yardstick of efficiency: considering the mission which the state under analysis has set for itself, do these three structures represent the best possible way of mobilizing the nation's effort? Does the political system, for example, provide for both efficient administration and a workable rapport with mass consensus, or is there sufficient disaffection to constitute a drag on governmental effectiveness? Does the economic system reduce waste, lost motion, uneconomic production, and inefficiency to the practical minimum, or are many opportunities for a rationalized productive system lost? Is the society integrated and coordinated and thus capable of unified effort, or is it split apart so that internal tensions dilute the nation's international effort? These and analogous questions ultimately produce an over-all verdict on the general subject of how the nation organizes itself for international action, and their answers constitute a significant if imprecise factor in its over-all capability.

2. EDUCATIONAL AND TECHNOLOGICAL LEVEL. In a technological and scientific age, another societal characteristic that bears directly upon capability is the educational and technological level of the nation. Industrial productivity, military effectiveness, and simple social cohesiveness are all major functions of the extent to which education and technical facility are dispersed within the society. Level of education is one of the major qualitative modifiers of any quantitative finding regarding manpower.

Fundamental to the matter of educational and technological level is the simple question of literacy. No state can muster a significant national effort if reading and writing, the basic communication skills, are mysteries to the bulk or even a significant minority of its people. For reasons of both effective consensus building and efficient administration, a literate population is a necessity if a state is to play a meaningful international role; the massive efforts made by such nations as China and India to bring minimal literacy to their people underscores its importance.

A second, almost as crucial, basic element in capability is what we might call tool skill, which means orientation toward and facility in the employment of the tools and techniques of modern industrial civilization. This involves emotional adjustment and acculturation as much as the actual learning of skills and procedures. Unless a people are familiar with the subtle ramifications of an industrial system, they will waste a good deal of effort in making the machinery work. Extensive training and inculcation of the necessary discipline are prerequisites to effective tool skill.

The factors of literacy and tool skill are characteristics of the mass of a population. A third factor, and in many ways as crucial an element in a nation's educational and technological level, is the quality of the higher stratum of educated specialists. Does the nation have enough specialists of the right sort? Is their training and level of performance adequate to the demands the nation will make of them? Is the over-all standard of scholarly, scientific, and technological effort advancing, declining, or merely static? These and related questions may, even in short-run situations (such as a "crash" program of weapons development), be the real determinant of the state's working range of capability.

3. NATIONAL MORALE. Among the difficult factors to measure, yet one of the few constant determinants of capability, is the elusive notion of national morale. We use this term here to describe the mass state of mind in a nation, with particular reference to the extent to which the society feels itself committed to the government's policy.

A state has high morale when the government feels itself supported by an active, well-informed, articulate, and involved consensus. Such a condition requires that politically self-conscious people constitute the bulk of the society, that these individuals be convinced that the foreign policy enterprises in which the government is involved are derived from the prevailing mass values of the society, and that the consensus include a favorable vote of confidence in the capacity of the policy-makers to meet and overcome challenges implicit in the policy.

Thus national morale has a direct effect on the vigor and human dynamics with which officials mobilize and employ the tangible factors in capability. Widespread apathy toward foreign policy establishes restrictive parameters on decision, and active disagreement within the body politic virtually paralyzes the government. In this sense, morale involves not only the affirmative characteristics of zest, dedication, and confidence, but also such negative elements as discipline and the capacity to endure stress, disappointment and temporary failure.

If a government concludes that the state of national morale is sufficiently questionable as to raise doubts about the endurability of the
consensus on which decision-makers must rely, improvement of morale
becomes a primary charge on the government. What strategies the government may employ depend upon its judgment of the nature of the
deficiencies and peculiar dynamics of the society and its controlling
values. It may choose to frighten its people or seek to encourage them;
it may become more generous with information and explanation, or control tightly the flow of communication to the public. It may increase the
pace of stimulation of the public psyche, or it may deliberately minimize
tension. Whatever the devices adopted, however, its policy must remain
largely in suspension until its morale goals are achieved.

4. INTERNATIONAL STRATEGIC POSITION. The final element of capability
—the state's international strategic position—brings us almost full circle,
since it is the general strategic role played by a state in world politics
that raises issues of capability in the first place. We have stressed that
capability is comprehensible only in a specific policy context. Now we
conclude that the state's own policy and strategy contain factors that
contribute to its working capability.

This is most apparent in terms of the state's need for the support of
other states in the service of its own policy. Its effective capability vis-à-
vis its actual or potential associates is reduced exactly to the extent to
which it feels it needs allies; it must so conduct itself as to establish or
maintain the desired cooperative relationship. Were it following a different policy, it would not require this particular alliance pattern and
would have a greater freedom of choice and action in these areas.

A second manifestation is derived from the state's interpretation of its
position in the world. If the state feels itself under great and constant
danger, it will obviously devote a much greater share of its available
capability to defense of its home territory, leaving a restricted margin
available for affirmative action on the world stage. Any revision in a
state's estimate of the threats it faces automatically affects its capability
in other areas. A judgment that the threat has grown less frees the state
for more extensive action elsewhere; if the threat is deemed to have
become greater, adequate responsive action normally calls for contraction
of effort at other points.

In a peculiar and paradoxical way, the very objectives a state selects
for itself, and the way it interprets the situation in which it must operate,
have a major influence on its capability to achieve those objectives and
to function in the situation. A state's international strategic position is to
a large measure determined by itself; a state is to a great extent the
architect of its own capability.

No more graphic proof could be advanced of the relativistic and policy-grounded nature of the concept of capability. The universe of the policy-maker and the capability analyst is largely of their own making. The judgments and decisions they make are expressions of their interpretations of the reality of their world. It should not be surprising that their conclusions about the ability of their state to achieve its purposes are so directly derived from their formulations of the nature of the problems they face.

REFERENCES

* Aron, Raymond, *The Great Debate: Theories of Nuclear Strategy.* Garden City, N.Y.: Doubleday & Company, Inc., 1965.
* Berle, Adolf A., Jr., *Twentieth Century Capitalist Revolution.* New York: Harcourt, Brace & World, Inc., 1960.
* Black, Cyril E., and Thomas P. Thornton, *Communism and Revolution: The Strategic Uses of Political Violence.* Princeton, N.J.: Princeton University Press, 1964.
* Campbell, Robert W., *Soviet Economic Power* (2nd ed.). Boston: Houghton Mifflin Company, 1966.
* Cole, J. P., *Geography of World Affairs* (rev. ed.). Baltimore: Penguin Books, Inc., 1963.
* De Jouvenel, Bertrand, *Power: Its Nature and History of Its Growth.* Boston: Beacon Press, 1962.
Friedman, Milton, and Robert V. Roosa, *The Balance of Payments: Free versus Fixed Exchange Rates.* Washington, D.C.: American Enterprise Institute for Public Policy Research, 1967.
* Halperin, Morton, *Limited War in the Nuclear Age.* New York: John Wiley & Sons, Inc., 1963.
* Huntington, Samuel P., *Common Defense: Strategic Programs in National Politics.* New York: Columbia University Press, 1961.
Knorr, Klaus, *On the Uses of Military Power in the Nuclear Age.* Princeton, N.J.: Princeton University Press, 1966.
Lasswell, Harold D., *et al.*, *A Study of Power.* New York: The Free Press, 1950.
Mouzon, Olin T., *International Resources and National Policy.* New York: Harper & Row, Publishers, 1959.
* Nove, Alec, *Soviet Economy* (rev. ed.). New York: Frederick A. Praeger, Inc., 1965.

* Indicates paperback edition.

Osgood, Robert E., and Robert W. Tucker, *Force, Order and Justice.* Baltimore: Johns Hopkins Press, 1967.

* Rostow, Walt W., *Stages of Economic Growth.* New York: Cambridge University Press, 1960.

* Russell, Bertrand R., *Power: A New Social Analysis.* New York: Barnes & Noble University Books, 1962.

* Indicates paperback edition.

FOUR

The Implementing
of Decisions

After the policy-maker has stipulated the objective he will seek and determined his capabilities for action within the particular situation, he next turns to the selection of the appropriate means of implementing his decisions. We have already suggested that he has a considerable range of choice in selecting detailed procedures, and that he attempts to develop a course of action which will carry him to the goal he has adopted. In this chapter we shall examine and characterize categories of state techniques, the four general channels through which the statesman may act in world politics. We shall not attempt to elaborate a complete catalogue of state procedures in policy implementation, since these are infinite in number and largely dependent upon random and unique factors in the operative situation.

First, we ought to make one basic point that will be implicit in all our subsequent discussion. Although this chapter concentrates on the various ways states may act, action of any sort is not a necessary consequence of a policy decision; the net result of the elaborate analytical process outlined in Chapter Two may be a resolve not to act at all. While it is true that inaction is a form of action and proceeds (or should proceed) from the same intellectual process as does action itself, the strategy of inaction obviously raises fewer questions of implementation. For our purposes, we should always keep in mind in our consideration of state techniques that a state decision to act represents a deliberate choice of action over inaction in the particular context.

If a state decides to act, the nature of the state system opens four possible channels for the application of its strength. These four are in the literal sense classic in that they are intrinsic to international politics and represent the totality of the *ways* states may act. The increased complexities of contemporary life have opened countless doors for state action on behalf of policy, but in the last analysis all techniques may be fitted into one of the four standard categories.

The first of the four different sets of techniques is political in nature, and its most conspicuous manifestation is the device of diplomacy. The second is economic, probably the most varied and complex of the four in its richness of artifice and stratagem. Third in the list are psychological techniques, of which propaganda and its operational derivatives are examples. Finally there are military techniques, ranging from nonviolent use of armed force to open warfare.

In pure theory, a state may place its entire reliance in a particular situation upon any single one of these generalized techniques. More commonly, however, states develop an approach based on a "mix" of techniques, blended in such proportions as will, in the estimation of the policy-maker, produce the greatest effect. It is axiomatic that a statesman may develop combinations of techniques in perfect analytical and operational freedom; the only "correct" technique is that one that best achieves the purpose of the state.

A state attempts to preserve flexibility with the implementation of policy. Since its capability to act is a function of the exigencies of the situation, it is most important that any operational commitment permit intensification, reduction, modification, or even abandonment if circumstances should dictate. The need for such flexibility has been redoubled as modern technology has led to the drastic reduction of available action time.

POLITICAL TECHNIQUES: DIPLOMACY

In one sense all foreign policy techniques are, or ought to be, political. No matter what a state may do in the execution of its purposes, its orientation and goal are always political in that it seeks the maximization of its value system. Yet in practice the word "political" is applied more narrowly to those methods that involve direct government-to-government relations. The contacts that governments have with each other and the manner in which this intercourse is carried on are generally subsumed under the name of diplomacy.

The Nature of Diplomacy

Diplomacy, considered as a technique of state action, is essentially a process whereby communications from one government go directly into the decision-making apparatus of another. It is the one direct technique of state action, in that it exerts its diplomatic power upon the crucial personnel of the other government or governments. If the operational purpose of policy is to secure the agreement of other states to national designs, it is only by diplomatic means that such assent can be formally registered and communicated. In this sense, diplomacy is the central technique of foreign policy.

Diplomacy is both a full-fledged technique in its own right and the instrument by which other techniques are often transmitted. A state can act diplomatically in a purely political context, using only the methods and resources of the diplomatic instrument, or it may implement economic, psychological, or even military action by diplomatic maneuvering. Although the operating requirements of pure diplomacy and what we might call "mixed" diplomacy differ to some extent, their fundamental rationale remains essentially the same.

The actual procedures of diplomacy are many, ranging from such highly formal devices as notes, *aides-memoires*, and *communiqués* to more informal and almost casual conversations. At bottom, diplomacy is a method of negotiating between sovereignties, and although the elaborate ritual and protocol that surround the practice may sometimes seem pretentious and time-consuming, their roots lie in the nature of the task. By diplomatic means a state transmits its position on an issue to another state and receives the other state's response. Whatever changes may take place in the respective positions are registered diplomatically, and the eventual elaboration of whatever relationship develops also lies in the hands of diplomats.

The Functions of Diplomacy

We can distinguish several distinct functions of diplomacy. Which of these the working diplomat may be called upon to perform depends on the nature of the policy his government is following.

First, diplomacy is to a major extent a technique of *coercion*. Coercive moves made by other means are communicated diplomatically, and the narrower framework of pure diplomacy contains significant resources of pressure. In many cases, rupture of diplomatic relations has a coercive element, as does exclusion of the target state from international conferences or organizations. Coercion may also be applied in negotiation by an ultimatum, by establishment of a rigid time limit for the conclusion of an arrangement, or by the registration of a formal or informal protest or complaint. In the past few decades, "pragmatic" dictators have added an element of psychological coercion to diplomacy by eliminating the courtesy and good manners traditional to the art, and conducting relationships in an atmosphere of vilification and intensive emotion. This procedure has had its undeniable advantages.

Second, diplomacy is a technique of *persuasion*. The advancement of arguments and the proffering of a *quid pro quo*, both persuasive devices, are within the exclusive province of diplomatic technique. In terms of our discussion of the forms of capability, diplomacy is the most frequently used and best suited of all state techniques for application of the influence component of state capability. While the actual line between coercion and persuasion is often vague, and the two approaches frequently blend into one another, there is a real difference in both motivation and atmosphere, and most diplomatic initiatives are at least initially cast in a persuasive form.

Third, diplomacy is uniquely a procedure of *adjustment*. It is admirably suited to the task of enabling two states to modify their positions on an issue in order to reach a stable relationship. Its directness of communication, its potentially noncoercive nature, and its subtlety and flexibility all contribute to its usefulness. States may prosecute their differences and intensify their conflicts by a great variety of methods, but they may reduce tensions between themselves only by diplomatic means. However, the adjustment function of diplomacy is effective only if both parties are amenable to negotiation; nothing in the diplomatic instrument can overcome a state's unwillingness to change a policy.

Finally, diplomacy is a technique for reaching *agreement;* indeed, it has been said that diplomacy is the art of negotiating written agreements. Formal written agreements are the most binding strictures on international commitment offered by world politics, and can be brought into existence only by diplomatic procedures. We must note that agreement may involve coercion, persuasion, or adjustment, and that no agreement is possible unless both parties wish it. On the other hand, even a strong interest in formalizing and understanding would be pointless if instruments and procedures for reaching one were not available. Here diplomacy comes usefully into its own.

Success and Failure in Diplomacy

What are the characteristics of good diplomacy? More directly, what are the marks of the policy of a state that is making good use of diplomatic technique? Conversely, what is wrong with the normal practice of diplomacy in the contemporary world that has given the diplomat such an apparently small role in the conduct of international politics?

There is little disagreement about the requirements for success in diplomacy. The essentials of the diplomatic art have been well-known for centuries, and the actual practice of its masters furnish us with clear guidelines. We may here reduce the vast literature into four basic operative requirements.

1. *The diplomat must have a clear understanding of the situation in which he is operating.* He must be sensitive to the forces at work in his problem area, and must also be quite clear about his own purposes and the ultimate implications of his policy with respect to long-range goals. Last, he must have a clear understanding of the points of view, interests, and goals of other states, because without such empathy he will be virtually powerless.

2. *The diplomat must be fully aware of his real action capability.* He must appreciate how much coercive capacity his government will support him with, and how much influence he may enjoy at that particular moment. He dare not attempt initiatives that lie beyond his capability, nor should he content himself with less than full exploitation of the resources appropriate to his objectives.

3. *The diplomat's approach must be flexible.* He must be prepared for unforeseen developments or for withstanding the consequences of analytical error by having some alternate policies and approaches in reserve, by having an unpublicized "fallback" position available, and by being consistently eclectic in methodology. He distinguishes as much as possible between abstract "principle" and concrete interest, and remains firmly committed to the latter while being quite flexible on the former.

4. *The diplomat is eager to compromise within limits of nonessentiality.* A clear priority system is essential to a diplomat because only in this way can he determine what issues are subject to bargaining and which are not. Priorities also suggest quantitative criteria to guide him in determining how extensively he may compromise without giving away matters of importance in return for lesser concessions. In theory, a good diplomat should always be willing to give up a position of lower priority to secure one of higher rank; although subject to drastic modification in practice, this rule does have great importance in diplomatic maneuvering. The

criterion of a good diplomatic bargain is less how much is given up than how much is won, for only the prize can determine whether the price was too high.

Diplomacy in the contemporary era has not proved able to cope adequately with the dilemmas of politics. Its inadequacy has been so obvious that some critics have been moved to speculate on "the end of traditional diplomacy." In practice, since the end of World War II, the four roles we have formulated have been honored more often in the breach than in the observance. Situations are analyzed far too often in ideological and nationalistic terms, and too seldom realistically. It is currently unfashionable to admit that one's opponent has any point of view, let alone one meriting consideration. Capability factors are grossly misinterpreted, especially in the military realm. Flexibility, thanks to ideology and nationalism, is usually a lost cause, and compromise is normally rejected as striking a bargain with sin.

In these circumstances, diplomacy cannot flourish, and current practice has involved either ill-concealed and blatant attempts at coercion, or nonpurposive propaganda. Real negotiation, persuasion, and adjustment of positions culminating in agreement have been accidental phenomena instead of the normal procedures of states in the system. Deep popular involvement in foreign policy by means of absolutist and emotional sloganizing, common in both large and small states, has seriously impeded the force of diplomacy by depriving it of the necessary "elbow room" in which to maneuver.

Some recent hopeful signs, however, augur a revival of diplomatic activity in the true sense. The height of the cold war era had been marked by constant advocacy of absolute solution to problems. More than two decades of struggle have had their effect; absolutist positions are advanced somewhat less seriously, and responsible and increasingly prudent governments are willing at least to entertain the possibility of partial solutions. With this frame of mind becoming more common, the opportunity for diplomacy to work its harmonizing and adjusting effect becomes somewhat brighter. The future will undoubtedly see relatively greater reliance on diplomacy and possibly a much more favorable record of its success.

ECONOMIC TECHNIQUES: THE CARROT AND THE STICK

Economic techniques of state action are as old as the state system itself, but their full flower dates only from the Industrial Revolution. The increasing complexity of modern economic and industrial life has made the states of the world to a large degree mutually interdependent; this reciprocal involvement serves to open a broad range of action possibilities to states. Various sorts of international economic action aimed at the achievement of political goals have become a part of foreign policy for all states.

The Rationale of Economic Methods

Probably the most obvious characteristic of economic techniques is their bewildering diversity. Almost any aspect of economic life can, with sufficient ingenuity on the part of policy-makers, be turned into a tool of state action. However, certain generalizations are possible concerning the rationale of economic methods in foreign policy.

First, economic techniques are indirect in their application, in contrast to the directness intrinsic to diplomacy. Their immediate target is not the decsion-making apparatus of the other state, but rather the totality of that state's society. The consent sought for is supposed to flow from internal pressures of that society upon its government rather than from any direct action by the initiating state. It can be thus said that economic techniques are designed to force the hand of the other government and to urge or coerce it to accede to the wishes of the first state.

Second, as the title of this section indicates, economic methods are two-sided, in that they may be either coercive or persuasive in intent. A coercive economic move is one that, in general or specific terms, threatens the target state with deprivation or impoverishment unless it submits. A persuasive move holds out the bait of economic reward or advantage in return for satisfactory modification of a target state's behavior. A single economic maneuver may frequently partake of both intents, threatening economic damage if no agreement is forthcoming but simultaneously promising rewards for acquiescence. Such ambivalence in effect is usually thought of as ideal.

Third, economic techniques are almost entirely creatures of the particular situation, the effectiveness of any such device being completely dependent upon the nature of economic relations between the states involved. A state with no economic leverage on another would simply be ignored or ridiculed if it threatened economic reprisal to an unacceptable policy. Therefore, maximum use of economic instruments is reserved to those few states with widespread economic influence or to those controlling crucial economic goods or services. An otherwise weak state controlling huge oil reserves, for example, has a considerable range of capability made possible by its atypical and accidental economic situation.

Fourth, economic techniques are productive of generous amounts of resentment, resistance, and retaliation by the target state. Coercive economic moves obviously create hostility, since no people can stolidly accept either the threat or actuality of economic deprivation. Even persuasive and advantageous economic policies engender almost as much enmity among recipient peoples, on the ground that it is humiliating and status-destroying to submit to bribery and blackmail for policy reasons. Much of the agitation in the nonwestern world for "foreign aid without strings" flows from this orientation.

Fifth, as a result, purely economic techniques have a much more limited range of effectiveness than was suspected until fairly recently. Strategists have learned to take account of resistance to economic pressures and to discount accordingly the return expected from their use. As a rule, economic techniques today are rarely used alone. A persuasive economic policy is usually linked with extensive propaganda and diplomatic initiatives, while coercive programs are accompanied by a strong diplomatic line and frequently by military pressures of various sorts.

Persuasive Economic Techniques

Under the conditions of contemporary world politics, certain persuasive economic techniques have proved useful and appropriate.

Probably the best-known is "foreign aid": the direct grant or favorable loan of either cash, credits, or goods to other countries. These may be "economic" in nature, and consist of foodstuffs, capital goods, or consumer products. The first decade of the cold war placed a high premium on "military" aid, including all types of military material and what the United States called "defense support" in the form of economic aid committed to military purposes.

A second technique, of great importance since the nonwestern revolution has become a reality, is development assistance, through which advanced industrial states assist unindustrialized states in developing productive plants and fostering a higher standard of living for their people. Originally undertaken in a cold war context, development assistance has proved to be so expensive, so long-lasting, and so unproductive of cold war advantage that its leading practitioners are seeking a less intensive and therefore more rational climate for its application. Its full political effect can obviously be determined only over a very long time span.

Third, much effort has gone into the use of trade policy as a technique of state action. Bilateral or multilateral trade agreements are a familiar feature of international politics today; most of them have clear political overtones, and some—particularly those between a large and powerful state and a smaller one—formalize the exchange of economic advantage for political rewards. In recent years, another aspect of trade policy has appeared: the creation of trading blocs and the extension of an invitation to join such a group as a form of persuasion to political cooperation. So powerful has this lure been that some traditionally neutral European states have been tempted to abandon political non-alignment in order to secure the economic rewards of membership.

Closely linked with trade agreements are the many kinds of moves possible in the area of currency stabilization and control. This technique was quite common in the early postwar period, when currencies throughout the world were unstable and in need of assistance from those few nations with adequate reserves. Current widespread stability has served to minimize its effect, although one peculiar anomaly exists: the United States, once the financial pillar of the entire free world, has for several years been suffering a balance of payment deficit and a consequent outflow of gold. Today, the United States is subject to some extent to the policy influence of the currency stabilization drive utilized by its erstwhile clients in Europe.

Coercive Economic Techniques

Coercive economic techniques are limited in number and variety only by the imagination of the implementing state within the particular political and economic situation. Here we do no more than attempt a rough classification.

The first type we may call restrictions on economic relations, which include the whole apparatus of currency control, export licenses and quotas, tariffs (selective and otherwise), foreign exchange blocking and control, and freezing of credits. The intent of all of these is to ensure that economic relations continue in a way favorable to the dominant state. An implicit aspect of these restrictions is the suggestion that an improvement in political relations would have immediate economic consequences.

More overtly coercive is the outright interruption of economic relations, primarily international trade. If the target state is sufficiently dependent upon trade with the dominant state, interruption will cause serious hardship and impel the victim toward reestablishment of normal patterns at a political price. Interruption of relations may be effective when the powerful state is a critical supplier of certain categories of goods, or when it is a major market for the product of a single-commodity agricultural economy. Such a boycott is perhaps the most infuriating of all economic practices; since it usually leads to strong pressures for retaliation, it is seldom employed, and then only under especially favorable circumstances.

A special type of coercion stems from the cancellation or suspension of a program of economic aid. Recipient states become accustomed to a steady flow of assistance once such a program is established; their dependence upon continuation of aid makes them peculiarly vulnerable to the pressures that develop if the regular supply is interrupted. Again, this technique is most valuable when the coerced state is completely at the mercy of the state extending aid. If the former can actually do without the assistance, or if it should develop another source of aid, then net results of the effort may well be zero or even a minus factor.

There remains a collection of coercive economic steps that do not readily lend themselves to classification. These are markedly dependent for their effect on almost accidental situational elements, and their impact tends to be random and almost unpredictable. They include such trading practices as dumping, such politico-economic moves as pre-emptive purchase of raw materials (sometimes for the purpose of depriving another country of these supplies), and such manipulative tricks as unilateral currency devaluation or barter trade agreements.

Conclusions on Economic Techniques

The most significant conclusion about economic techniques is that they are of only limited and special usefulness by themselves, because of both the unpredictability of their results and their relations-worsening effect. "Economic man" is no more real in international life than in domestic affairs.

A second conclusion, however, is that, under appropriate circumstances, economic techniques may have an effect at once devastating and controlling. Coercion in economic terms may cause hostility, but it may also move its victim to rapid and extensive policy revision. At the persuasive end of the spectrum, an imaginatively conceived and skillfully presented program has often earned major political dividends in a noncontroversial climate. Discrimination in the use of economic techniques, adequate understanding of the operative factors in a situation, and a refusal to adhere only to a particular technique all contribute to the over-all usefulness of these techniques.

Third, economic techniques are of less value in short-term situations than over a longer period. To attempt to extract short-run political gain from application of a single economic device is frequently to court disappointment; seldom is a target state so tightly caught as to be obliged to respond politically in a single dimension to an economic initiative.

Over longer time spans, however, the correct economic policies may well develop a pool of consent (or at least reduce barriers of disagreement) that will ultimately prove of major value. This caution has been violated consistently by both major powers during the cold war era, with predictable frustrating results.

PSYCHOLOGICAL TECHNIQUES: PROPAGANDA AND CULTURE

Psychological techniques, aimed at the mass psyches of relatively large bodies of people, are also an indirect technique of state action. Thanks to improvement in the art and science of mass communication, propaganda and culture have become major elements in state capability and constitute in themselves a significant area of political action.

The Nature of Propaganda

Propaganda has been defined in many ways, but all definitions agree that, operationally, it consists of messages in a context of action; that is, the purpose of communication is to inspire the audience to act in a particular way. From the propagandist's point of view, however, this generalized concept breaks down into two subcategories. Some propaganda is basically a problem in audience conditioning, designed to increase both its size and its sympathetic receptivity, while the remainder is directly action centered with the goal of persuading the audience to act in certain specified ways. Both forms have an important place in policy implementation.

Propaganda as a Foreign Policy Tool

We should distinguish among the four distinct "audiences" to which the foreign policy propagandist speaks. The first is the propagandist's own people, whose morale and dedication require that they be kept adequately informed, inspired, and indoctrinated. The second is the populace of those states associated with or friendly and cooperative to the propagandizing state. These also need to have policy explained in such a way as to impress them with the necessity of remaining true to their allegiance. The third is the audience formed by those who are neutral toward the propagandist's policy. Newly important today, they may be won to the state, or at least be prevented from active opposition, by a well-conceived program of information. Finally, there is an audience composed of the people of states hostile or in opposition to the propagandist. Propaganda in this context seeks to reduce their support of their own official policy and perhaps to loosen their bonds of loyalty.

We have phrased "audiences" in terms of "people" because propaganda is largely a mass phenomenon. Decision-making personnel are normally too committed and too sophisticated to be particularly amenable to propaganda from abroad. Most mass communicators believe that they obtain the greatest results for a given effort by aiming at the broadest possible audience, and the record of their accomplishments in international politics confirms this judgment.

The great bulk of the propaganda messages put out by states are aimed at audience conditioning and sympathy building, a focus which is today called "image projection": the state seeks to be viewed in a favorable light by its several audiences. Direct calls to action are relatively few, partly because of the remote likelihood of their being heeded except in special circumstances, and partly because of the ease with which they can be neutralized by domestic counterpropaganda.

Therefore, most foreign policy propaganda is auxiliary to diplomatic efforts, and propaganda is seldom the single dimension in which a state acts. Effective propaganda may increase the policy impact of diplomatic, economic, or even military moves, but it can rarely accomplish a specific end by itself. It is crucial, therefore, that propaganda be rooted directly in the state's ongoing policy, and that major efforts to maintain consistency of word with action be axiomatic.

A factor seriously inhibiting propaganda today is the fact that virtually everybody is using it. With each audience bombarded by messages and appeals from every point of the compass, and with almost every policy point of view receiving eloquent and repeated expression, the listener has difficulty in formulating a clear impression by which to guide himself. He is likely to select from the welter of propaganda those messages and appeals with which he is already familiar, and simply ignore the remainder. Thus the policy impact of propaganda is seriously reduced, since it has relatively little influence on established patterns of behavior and response. This helps explain the great emphasis on audience building displayed by so many propagandizing states.

The Role of Subversion

Although subversion—the attempts of a state to overthrow or weaken another by means of internal agitation and conspiracy—is a direct action technique in its own right, it is included in this discussion of psychological techniques for a special reason. Crucial to a state's establishment and implementation of a subversive activity is the psychological problem of destroying the loyalty that binds a citizen to his government. His loyalty must be replaced in turn by a willingness to follow the commands of an alien and hostile state.

Subversion is an old technique, but it has been raised to its highest peak in the contemporary era. This has been due in part to the increasing militancy of modern ideologies—particularly communism, fascism, and anticolonialism—and in part to the improvements in communication that have made it possible for a government to control a subversive movement (or many subversive movements) from a great distance. However, more important than either of these in explaining the rise of subversion as a technique is the fact that the present age is one of great social disaffection, change, and revolution. When any society develops substantial internal divisions and deep animosities, the potential for subversion is present. Aggressive and shrewd agitators can often capitalize on such internal cleavages by enlisting key leaders and groups to prosecute their own purposes under the sponsorship of a foreign government.

In theory, subversion is a technique of revolution, the ultimate purpose of which is complete overthrow of the government and its replacement by the revolutionary group. As a technique of foreign policy, however, it is valuable even at a much more restrained level. Organized subversion can deepen divisions within a society to the extent that the government's integrity is compromised, its vitality weakened, and its attention diverted from vital questions of foreign policy. If, as was said about some European countries immediately following World War II, a government must validate each policy decision twice—once in the government structure and once in a street riot—it obviously cannot act with the dispatch and firmness demanded by important foreign policy questions.

The current importance of subversion and its "counterinsurgent" handmaiden, guerrilla warfare, should not obscure the fact that it is a technique of opportunity, usable only in those special circumstances when social and political revolution is at least incipient. Societies in which disaffection is minimal may be annoyed but never inhibited by subversion. Only states with frankly revolutionary policy can exploit popular discontent successfully, since only they have adequate appeal to emotionally involved rebellious individuals and groups. Thus it is almost axiomatic that states pursuing a stabilizing and mollifying status quo policy must combat subversion, but are not in a position to make much use of it themselves.

Cultural Techniques in Foreign Policy

A special development in the field of psychological action is the "cultural offensive." Using the standardized techniques of public relations, states have taken in recent years to active international promotion of the more prominent manifestations of their indigenous culture patterns. Aided markedly by advances in mass communication, nearly every government today seeks to "put its best foot forward" culturally through a vigorous advertising campaign aimed at a global audience.

The operational demands of propaganda partially explain the cultural attack on mass consciousness. A favorable cultural image of a nation and its government might well lead an audience to listen approvingly to policy positions expounded by that same government. But there is a more far-reaching rationale to cultural techniques. Culture patterns—whether economic, social, esthetic, or political—are manifestations of the basic value system of a society. Winning favorable international response to certain cultural symbols is a major step toward winning acceptance of the fundamental values on which they are based. Since foreign policy is at bottom an exercise in value maximization, it can be argued that in one sense cultural techniques are a form of direct state action on behalf of national objectives.

Some cultural programs have become so powerful that some governments, concerned that their people might be seduced by attractive but specious cultural manifestations from abroad, have voiced such disparaging terms as "cultural imperialism" in recent years. It has seemed as if many newer nonwestern states have reserved their greatest anti-colonialist tirades for certain symbolic examples of western culture, such as articles of clothing and items of diet. They seem to feel that a deliberate cultivation of their own cultural traits will free them from an unhealthy dependence on western ways.

We should also note that many aspects of culture have a vitality of their own, and display their influence without dependence on overt government action. Jazz music, Coca-Cola, and television are only three symbolic representations of American culture that have spread widely abroad with obvious—if not always favorable—results. This effect of uncontrolled culture spread is more important to relatively free societies than it is to authoritarian societies, which make a much greater effort to shape a consistent and integrated international cultural image. Also, the process of cultural diffusion is particularly marked in less developed countries.

MILITARY TECHNIQUES:
WAR AND ITS APPROXIMATIONS

We come now to the fourth and final set of techniques of state action —military capability and the role of force. We should establish our logical base by pointing out something of a paradox. In logic and in the practice of statecraft, there is no substantive difference between military techniques and any others. War is thus "normal" in interstate relations, since the criterion of appropriateness governing use of military power is exactly the same as that used in any other policy decision. Yet statesmen have always recognized that the use of military techniques is predictably more costly and more dangerous than other ways of acting, and have normally considered military techniques a last resort, to be used only if lesser measures prove inadequate for attaining a necessary objective. The great technological revolution in warfare has sharpened the impact of this dilemma. Today, one of the more hotly debated theoretical issues, as well as one of the most pressing practical problems of policy-making, is that of the utility of military power—offensive, defensive, and deterrent—in foreign policy.

War in Foreign Policy Calculations

The phrase "military techniques" really refers to some sort of application of military power, the ultimate being actual conduct of war. Reconciling policy considerations to the threat, initiation, conduct, or avoidance of war has long been one of the major concerns of the statesman.

It is important that we keep in mind that employment of military power is a means to a policy end, not an end in itself; "victory" is a technique and not a goal. The object of the exercise of military power is exactly the same as that of any other type of state action: achievement of enough international consent to permit attainment of the preselected objective. The extent to which military power is used in active pursuit of policy goals is determined initially by the value placed on the objective and by the amount of resistance the state expects to meet. The objective of combat—the manipulation and application of military force —is to "break the enemy's will to resist"—not necessarily, be it noted, his *capacity* to resist.

Resort to military techniques is derived from the same type of cost/ risk calculation that precedes any policy decision. Although there is a significant difference in an ultimate decision for war, it is less in quality than in quantity. Costs in war are obviously much higher, since they must be measured to a great extent in human life. The risk factor demands greater odds in favor of success because the price of failure in war is much higher than in any other policy enterprise. Thus cost factors demand that war be reserved for purposes great enough to justify the inevitable expenditure.

In principle, therefore, use as policy tools of military techniques which may culminate in war demands that the magnitude of the force and violence be in reasonably accurate relationship to the worth of the objective, and appropriate to the extent and nature of the resistance to be met. It is this concept of the role of violence—phrased by Montesquieu as doing no more damage to the enemy than is absolutely necessary to the attainment of one's purposes—upon which the state system is founded, and it is in this way that war figures in the policy judgments of states.

Technology, Nationalism, and War

Two of the great historical forces of modern times have seriously complicated the role of war in statecraft. The first is technology, which has made possible new horizons in weaponry and expanded incalculably the ability of states to inflict damage on each other. The second is modern nationalism, which has involved entire populations in warfare and largely dissipated the ability of governments to control the magnitude of their military effort. Technology and nationalism have made war a struggle between peoples rather than between states. The objectives of war have become the total submission or utter destruction of the enemy, rather than the lesser purpose of winning his assent to a particular policy.

The world has entered the era of "total war," a situation divorced from single policy objectives which is instead a simple if desperate matter of survival. Under contemporary combat conditions, a total war cannot be considered a rational application of capability to foreign policy, although this may be true of conflicts on levels below the "total nuclear war" stage. Total war represents a catastrophic breakdown in the international political process, while limited wars, internal wars, proxy wars, and the use of threat and bluff may all signal that the system is operating with some prospect of resolution short of annihilation.

The Appropriateness of War

The statesman of today, knowing that the use of military techniques will trigger extreme nationalist emotions in his people and open himself and his state to the possibility of attack by the most horrible of new weapons, is cruelly inhibited in his policy choices. While in theory he is as free as ever to resort to techniques leading to war, the logic of the cost/risk continuum is inexorable and frustrating to him.

With war certain to cost far more than it ever has before, the number of objectives for which such an expenditure is justifiable has shrunk alarmingly; prolongation of a list of such goals past the initial entry of national survival has become extremely difficult. By the same token, if any war in which the statesman becomes engaged is potentially a war of survival, risk factors assume a new relevance. The odds he must have in his favor before risking combat have climbed almost to the absolute, for his enemy is just as likely to assume that the struggle is total, and therefore commit his ultimate capacities in his own defense. Total war can knowingly be unleashed only by a state that has a "first-strike" capacity to destroy or cripple the enemy, and an approximation of in-vulnerability to whatever retaliatory capacity the enemy may possess, either before or after the initial onslaught. Attainment of such dominance in the contemporary world is effectively beyond the capacity of any state.

Thus war, total or otherwise, has not become impossible, since either an irrational distortion of reality or a serious analytical error could lead a government to take the risk. What has happened is that war, particularly total war, has become inappropriate to foreign policy conceived and im-plemented in a climate of calculation, prudence, and rationality. This situation, so disruptive of many operating assumptions of international politics, has engaged the attention of scholars and statesmen ever since the dawn of the nuclear age. A considerable body of speculation and doctrine has been concerned with the implications of modern warfare for the future of foreign policy and international politics. We shall be examining these contentions in some detail in Chapter Nine, but may anticipate the conclusion we reach there, at least in general terms: a persuasive case for the continued relevance of military considerations to world politics has been built up, but the ubiquitous factors of cost and risk have served to deter states, particularly nuclear powers, from ventur-ing too far into the dangerous waters of open warfare. The American frustration in Vietnam has illustrated this situation.

Military Techniques Short of War

The role of military techniques in policy implementation has by no means been confined to actual warfare. As a matter of fact, military fac-tors have long been an ingredient in the normal conduct of foreign policy by all states.

Relative military rank of states has been one of the fundamental structural elements in the state system. The relations of any two states in time of "peace" have long been materially affected and often dominated by their respective military postures, due in part to the direct impact of military differentials that always involved a subtle or blatant threat to the weaker states. As long as a state retained the right and capability to back its demands by military force, a weaker state was obliged to include this consideration in its situational context and to guide itself by a quantitative and qualitative evaluation of the likelihood of this threat becoming a reality. Even more importantly, military differentials had a crucial status-conferring effect. Something very much like a class system gave form to the international scene as great military powers, medium military powers, and weak military powers developed standardized relations to one another, with differing rank, role, and status in world affairs. It is impossible to overestimate the historic impact of this factor.

But both the element of threat and the element of status (perhaps most usefully conceived as the institutionalized reflection of the threat) depended for their energizing effect upon the credibility of the military means. The threat of military power could influence a weaker state only if that government believed that the more powerful state was willing to risk the commitment of force and was also in a position to use that force meaningfully. The status reward of military capability—by no means entirely inoperative today—also flowed indirectly from the credibility of military superiority. As soon as smaller states came to realize this paradox —that the more military capability major states acquired in the nuclear age, the less real opportunity they had to use it, and the less interested they were in committing themselves to its use—credibility began to erode. Threats lost their compelling character, and status began to be dissipated as well.

This reevaluation of the real role of military techniques in foreign policy has gone so far that some analysts contend that the world has tied its hands in a military sense, and has entered the era of the "tyranny of the weak." It is argued that if the purpose of high capability is to broaden the area of freedom of choice enjoyed by a state, then the greatest measure of such freedom is enjoyed by states almost entirely devoid of military power, while those governments with the largest establishments discover that their real freedom is drastically circumscribed by the very existence of their military machines. In practice, therefore, the weaker the state in a military sense, the more actively it can prosecute its policy.

If this dour conclusion on the place of military techniques reflects a fundamental change in the nature of international relationships rather than a temporary distortion of regular patterns, the international political system will inevitably undergo far-reaching modification. The military channel of action is historically not only the *ultima ratio* of states, but is essential to the operation of orderly relationships within the traditional system. If, however, either technological or conceptual progress results in a recapture of the controlling place of military factors, the system will find it possible to stabilize itself again.

REFERENCES

Abelson, H. I., *Persuasion: How Opinions and Attitudes Are Changed*. New York: Springer Publishing Co., 1959.

* Baldwin, David A., *Economic Development and American Foreign Policy*. New York: Frederick A. Praeger, Inc., 1966.

Barghoorn, Frederick C., *Soviet Cultural Offensive*. Princeton, N.J.: Princeton University Press, 1960.

Biderman, Albert D., and Herbert Zimmer, eds., *The Manipulation of Human Behavior*. New York: John Wiley & Sons, Inc., 1961.

Clausewitz, Karl von, *War, Politics and Power*. Chicago: Henry Regnery Co., 1962.

Clews, John C., *Communist Propaganda Techniques*. New York: Frederick A. Praeger, Inc., 1964.

Dyer, Murray, *Weapons on the Wall: Rethinking Psychological Warfare*. Baltimore: Johns Hopkins University Press, 1959.

* Feis, Herbert, *Foreign Aid and Foreign Policy*. New York: Delta Dell, 1966.

George, Alexander L., *Propaganda Analysis: A Study of Influences Made from Nazi Propaganda in World War II*. Evanston, Ill.: Row Peterson and Co., 1959.

* Graebner, Norman S., *Cold War Diplomacy: American Foreign Policy, 1945-1960*. Princeton, N.J.: D. Van Nostrand Co., Inc., 1962.

Griffith, Samuel B., *Mao Tse-tung on Guerrilla Warfare*. New York: Frederick A. Praeger, Inc., 1961.

Holt, Robert F., and Robert W. Van De Velde, *Strategic Psychological Operations and American Foreign Policy*. Chicago: University of Chicago Press, 1960.

* Iklé, Fred C., *How Nations Negotiate*. New York: Frederick A. Praeger, Inc., 1961.

* Liddell Hart, Basil H., *Strategy* (2nd rev. ed.). New York: Frederick A. Praeger, Inc., 1967.

* Indicates paperback edition.

* Mason, Edward S., *Foreign Aid and Foreign Policy.* New York: Harper & Row, Publishers, 1964.

* Montgomery, John D., *Foreign Aid in International Politics.* Englewood Cliffs, N.J.: Prentice-Hall, Inc., 1967.

Muller, Kurt, *The Foreign Aid Programs of the Soviet Bloc and Communist China.* New York: Walker and Co., 1967.

* Paret, Peter, and John W. Shy, *Guerrillas in the 1960's.* New York: Frederick A. Praeger, Inc., 1962.

* Whitaker, Urban G., Jr., *Propaganda and International Relations* (rev. ed.). San Francisco: Howard Chandler Publishing Co., 1962.

* Indicates paperback edition.

part **II**

THE POLITICAL SYSTEM: STATES AND THEIR RELATIONS

FIVE

Ideas and Patterns
of International Politics

The second part of this book is devoted to the international political system: those more or less regularized patterns of relationships formed by the contacts of states with each other. Our focus will continue to be political, in that we are most concerned with those relationships of states that stem from their respective attempts at value maximization. International politics results from the reactions and interactions of the foreign policies of states. These initiative, responsive, ameliorative, combative, and compensatory forms of state behavior demonstrate sufficient regularity to form what we call here the "international system."

THE SYSTEM OF STATES

The international system is a special type of "social system," an arrangement created when a number of operating units—individuals or groups—so regularize and pattern their relationships with one another that system-centered behavior becomes to a large extent predictable. The states of the world are the operating units in this case, and something like three centuries of experience has brought such a degree of regularity to the structure and dynamics of their relations that the general shape of international behavior is very orderly. It is with this concept that we begin our discussion.

The Characteristics of the System

Although it can be included within the general definition of a social system, the international political system has a number of characteristics that mark it as distinctive and unique. It is this measure of difference that lends international politics its distinguishing characteristics.

First, international politics goes on within a *system*, and not within a *society* or a *community*. Although writers are frequently moved to discuss the "community of nations," or the "society of states," such terms must be taken as literary hyperbole rather than accurate reflections of reality. An indispensable element in either a society or a community is acceptance of a common set of goals for social action and a common value consensus. The international system has neither common values nor any mutual goal other than survival within the system. No state feels responsibility to anyone or anything outside itself. Society or community feeling is impossible without a common loyalty.

The international system therefore lacks the essential aspects of a more highly organized and articulated community: a controlling moral consensus, a socially sanctioned code of behavior that prohibits certain lines of action as destructive of good order and demands others as socially necessary, and an institutional structure to implement the moral consensus and enforce the behavior code. Instead, the system gains its form and energy from a much more rudimentary set of controls, particularly a calculating kind of prudence that we have already characterized as "strategic," and a thrust to maintain and preserve the system in its essentials as preferable to any other basis of organization, either more or less restrictive.

The operating assumptions of the international system may be classified as a semiorganized anarchy. The anarchic presumptions of the free will of the individual state, the right of the state to choose any goal it wishes and take any appropriate implementing action, and the resolution of conflicts of interest in terms of the relative strength of the disputing parties are absolutely controlling. The principle of sovereignty, if taken literally, permits none but an anarchic base for political action among states. It is true that state policy in world affairs is always rooted in the possible necessity of the state's being thrown entirely upon its own resources, with every other state's hand turned against it, and it is common for the rhetoric of statecraft to evoke images of the individual state bravely making its way against the active or passive opposition of the remainder of the system. Yet the logic of anarchy is surprisingly unreliable as a base for predicting the outcome of state relations in the real world. Statesmen have made considerable progress in softening and diverting the more onerous consequences of the relatively underorganized international system.

This is due in part to the strong tendency of policy-makers to prefer an expediential to an absolute formulation of both goals and tactics. We already know how willing statesmen are to settle for half a loaf in foreign policy, especially as the consequences of failure in an all-out effort become more awesome. But the regularities of international politics are also due in large part to the impact of habit and inertia; statesmen no less than ordinary individuals are prisoners of their own past action patterns. The influence of custom and standardized practice has been almost uniformly on the side of stabilization and regularization in the relationships of sovereignties. Today, although the anarchy of international politics is conceptually as obvious as ever, the international system is more elaborately and tightly organized than is generally appreciated.

The Nation-State in the System

The individual nation-state, viewing itself as a functional unit within the international system, is a solitary, self-contained, and self-justifying entity. It draws its motivations for action from within itself, feels itself obligated to no other state, is prepared to devote its own resources to satisfaction of its needs, and is ready to enjoy the rewards or suffer the consequences of its own actions. It judges all situations and the actions of all other states by the single criterion of its controlling version of interest, and acquires enemies or friends and acts cooperatively or controversially in response to its internal evaluation of the ebb and flow of political action.

This emphasis on the internalized mission and function of the state in the system reflects the dominant note in the reality of international politics. The state is theoretically a free agent, and attempts to achieve as close an approximation of this freedom as possible. Nonidentification of the political unit with the larger community and the greater operational freedom from restraint enjoyed by the state marks the difference of international politics from other forms of social action.

It has been argued, by Machiavelli and his later disciples, that the state's control over its own international role is so complete that it is the architect of its own moral code. In these terms the only "good" the state serves—the supreme value of foreign policy—is the accomplishment of its own ends. Although it is in one sense circular reasoning and not especially useful as a criterion for determining ultimate moral questions, the notion of "reason of state" is of great value in formulating and executing foreign policy. Whatever the state decides to do in international politics is transformed by the very fact of decision into a moral goal. Qualms of conscience need never trouble the working policy-maker, for if he concludes that something is demanded by the national interest, it automatically becomes moral and good. Success in achieving an objective, regardless of other factors, is in itself a "good" thing, while failure is intrinsically immoral and therefore reprehensible.

Thus the motive force of the international system does not flow from any centralized source but from the nation-states themselves. The "climate" of world politics—the general atmosphere within which relations are conducted and which is subject to change over time—is neither a cosmic force nor an accident of history, but stems from the prevailing patterns of assumptions and action accepted by the dominant states of the system. Any basic change in the system will find its initial expression in modifications in the way states conceive of their international roles.

The Interstate Relationship

These operational postulates govern the approach of states to one another. We have already mentioned that states, lacking any consensual base, must develop their respective postures on a purely ad hoc basis. Initial stages of any new interstate relationship are always tentative and probing, as each seeks to discover the nature and extent of the involvement of its own interest with the interests of all the others. Only after each state has determined the essential ingredients of the evolving relationship does it feel free to elaborate and exploit a strategy.

The relations of any two states within any situation can be located somewhere along a continuum ranging from total agreement to total hostility, the determining factor being the extent to which the respective interests coincide or conflict. In one sense, therefore, the outcome of any particular collision between states can be termed inevitable. Each has a predetermined notion of interest, and the forces liberated by the interaction of these notions determine the shape of the relationship with almost mathematical precision.

Two further points should be made in this connection. First, inevitability develops after the respective notions of interest are determined; each state has complete freedom until then to formulate its interest as it may please. Thus, because the states set their own goals the relationship is under complete control at one stage, although almost entirely beyond manipulation after the critical point of goal-setting. Second, the degree at which interests clash does not dictate the level of hostility or tension at which the disagreement is prosecuted. The magnitude of an area of disagreement merely outlines the arena of conflict; whether the conflict is fought at a high level, a low level, or allowed to lie virtually dormant depends upon further policy decisions by the governments involved.

We have already discovered that this primacy of interest in the calculations of statesmen has made strategy and policy a cautious business. With no certain foreknowledge of how other states will react to a given stimulus, a government, to be safe, must assume the worst—any other nation is capable of becoming its enemy at any time and for causes, in the last analysis, beyond its own control. The potentiality of total opposition in any interstate relationship materially affects the substance and formulation of policy.

The Pole of Order and the Pole of Disorder

The state system is perpetually torn between the attractions of what we might symbolically call the pole of order and the pole of disorder. Conceptually and logically, the system postulates disorder so complete and controlling as to reduce world politics to a law-of-the-jungle war of all against all. Operationally, although violent outbreaks of disorder and open physical conflict may be "normal," they are also relatively infrequent. States spend a much larger proportion of their effort in prosecuting their ends in a context of order and restraint than they do in any type of open conflict.

The order-disorder dichotomy tends to stabilize the norm of international political interaction somewhere between the poles because of dynamic equilibrium. At times, pressures leading toward disorder may become relatively more powerful than countervailing tendencies, and the system may head toward breakdown. Disorder has taken over twice within the twentieth century, during World Wars I and II. Normally, however, the closer toward open disorder the system drifts, the more powerful becomes the urge toward reestablishment of order, and equilibrium is likely to be restored. In the same way, there is such a thing as too much order in the system, in the sense that many states feel that an overstabilized set of relationships might deprive them of the freedom of decision and action they feel is intrinsic to sovereign status. An excess of stability may well trigger disorderly forces within the system into deliberate attempts to gain elbow room.

EQUALITY AND INEQUALITY IN INTERNATIONAL POLITICS

One of the paradoxical aspects of international politics is the constant tension between the claims of states to substantial equality and the practical fact of their actual inequality. Both equality and inequality are manifested concretely in the conduct of the relations of states; both affect the way peoples and governments view the world and the tasks they attempt to accomplish in their foreign policies. Since states do exist simultaneously on the planes of conceptual equality and operational inequality, the student must understand the implications of either factor and the significant relations between them if he is to gain a grasp of the realities of international politics.

The Law and the Myth of Sovereignty

Equality of states as a characteristic of international politics has its roots in one of the basic concepts of the entire discipline of political science—sovereignty. From both the legal and mythical consequences of sovereignty flow many fundamentals of international politics.

Sovereignty is legally a key characteristic of a state: to be accepted as a state, a political society must have within itself a supreme lawgiving authority with the power to issue commands from which there is no rightful appeal. The concept was born during the formative era of the modern state, and today does no more than state a truism. No one would quarrel with the necessity of having a central source of political and legal authority within a state.

Difficulty arose when this internalized idea of considerable utility was applied to interstate relations. What in law and in logic could be the appropriate relationship between two sovereign states, each incorporating an alleged supreme authority which recognized no superior? No relationship except complete legal and status equality was conceivable. It is on this basis that international law, the body of jurisprudence that regulates the relationships of sovereignties, is built.

Accordingly, sovereignty in international relations and law has come to stipulate the absolute and perfect legal equality of all states. None may rightfully dictate to another; each is declared the equal of all others in status, dignity, and honor. All of the protocol and procedure of formal international intercourse pays respect to this symbolism of sovereign equality; even the Charter of the United Nations states that "the Organization is based on the principle of the sovereign equality of all its Members."

Legal sovereignty was given an added dimension with the birth of modern nationalism. As popular self-consciousness evolved into intensive nationalist identification, the doctrine of sovereignty, with its insistence that all states were equal and independent, became of great value in molding nations. From this has developed the contemporary myth of sovereignty.

Nationalism demands that the nation-state be at least symbolically free from responsibility to external authority. The "national will" is sacred and not to be tampered with, while the symbols of national identity—the flag, the uniform, the historical monuments—acquire overtones of mystical sanctity. Any impairment of sovereignty is to be resisted as a major patriotic duty.

Thus the myth of sovereignty and the concept of nationalism, both grounded in a formalized concept of state equality, unite to reinforce the anarchistic tendencies of the state system. The insistence that the state cannot be controlled by any larger community has contributed to the instability of world politics. Operationally, the incapacity of the conceptual state to accept coercion (for to do so would deny the equality and independence of states) has made it necessary for all international arrangements to be ratified by the (free or forced) consent of the participating states. So long as states consent formally, the integrity of sovereign equality is at least preserved on a *pro forma* basis.

The Political Inequality of States

Sovereignty as law and concept is a reality of contemporary political life, so it does little good to argue (as devoted protagonists of international organization and world government frequently do) that the doctrine of sovereignty is "invalid." The persistence of states in acting as if sovereignty were a reality gives the doctrine great political significance. But another equally stark fact must be faced: the conceptual equality of states exists alongside an absolute inequality in political competence. States are completely equal in their right and capacity to develop ego-images, select goals, and adopt action strategies, but they are inequal in their competence to fulfill their purposes. Either in absolute terms or with reference to a particular situational setting, no two states are ever equal in capability and must adapt their behavior to the verdicts of comparative strength.

This political inequality, long recognized as dominant within the state system, is most clearly seen in the surprisingly formalized horizontal stratification of states into great powers, medium powers, and small powers. Great powers are those few states whose capabilities are sufficiently large to permit them to establish and implement a totality of interest; in other words, a great power asserts the political right to interfere in and be consulted with regard to the resolution of any issue anywhere in the world at any time. A medium power is treated with a modest degree of formal deference by great powers, but is expected to confine its concerns to matters geographically or politically closer to home. A small power is permitted to exist but cannot ordinarily maintain an interest in opposition to either larger type; the conditions of its political activity are imposed upon it by the decisions of more powerful states.

In political terms, there are an infinity of gradations and discriminations of rank, power, and status. One of the most trying tasks of statesmen is to conduct relationships so as to preserve the useful fictions of legal equality while making certain that the political solutions accurately reflect the controlling inequality. We already know that the favored device for accomplishment of this purpose is the technique of consent.

The Trend Toward Greater Inequality

The gap between the mystique of state equality and the reality of political inequality is not decreasing, but instead is growing greater. The augmented store of capability conferred by modern technology on industrial states, contrasted with the birth of so many new, less developed, and unstable states, has vastly extended the spectrum of inequality. The powerful, both absolutely and relatively, are far more powerful, while the weak are relatively much weaker than ever before. In such a general context, to speak of the "sovereign equality" of the members of the United Nations is to compound fatuity.

To some extent, however, the growing disparity between equality and inequality has been mitigated by certain other factors. Politically relevant forms of capability have changed drastically under postwar conditions; for example, military differentials are no longer so absolute an element of inequality. Such universally relevant supranational entities as the United Nations have also provided a way in which aggregates of strength can be constructed by small states. By the creation of a sufficiently impressive bloc, they can go far to offset the political dominance of larger states.

But these measures can only soften the inexorable advance of inequality. There is ample evidence today that popular leaders and professional policy-makers are beginning to question the rationale of a political system that posits equality among states, and yet attempts to function with such disparity among its members. Whether the familiar political system can survive such a widespread contradiction is one of the major issues of the comtemporary era.

POWER POLITICS

The controlling dynamic of the state system has long been known as "power politics." This term, brought into English as a translation of the German *Machtpolitik*, has both a pejorative and a descriptive connotation. It may be used to characterize the relationships of states as being governed almost entirely by force or threat, without any consideration of right and justice; this meaning is perhaps closest to the sense of the original German word. Since our purpose here, however, is less to condemn power politics than to understand a process, we shall confine the term to a purely descriptive use. Power politics in the discussion that follows simply characterizes the way in which the international political process actually works.

The Assumptions of Power Politics

Our discussion of the state system and the respective roles of equality and inequality in the relations of states pointed out the underpinnings of the doctrines of power politics. Granted the doctrinal and operating fundamentals of the nation-state, a political system including all states can develop in only one way. Power politics rests on a set of assumptions that are consciously accepted and deliberately implemented by all governments.

1. *There are no absolutes of right or justice in the relations of states.* Each state is the judge of the correctness of its own actions, and international politics goes on in a climate of moral relativism.
2. *The only collective value shared by all participants is the desirability of preservation of the system.* Except for the common concern not to destroy the system and its members, states are conceived as being entirely on their own.
3. *Self-help is the rule of action.* Lacking common values, the system cannot boast institutions and mechanisms of collective action. Individual states must therefore enforce their own rights and can count on support from no external source.
4. *Each state has only as many rights as it can enforce itself.* The state,

thrust on its own resources, is obliged to content itself with such rewards as its strength and the wit of its leaders can extract from the system.

5. *The relations of states are determined not by the application of any general principles, but by the expediential interaction of their respective capabilities.* This is the crux of "power politics": considerations of "power" (capability) govern the outcome of state contacts.

6. *Operationally, therefore, factors of power determine questions of right.* In this sense, might (broadly interpreted) actually makes right.

We can see the extent to which these organizing and operating assumptions flow logically from the postulates about the nature of the sovereign nation-state. If the test of any institution is appropriateness to its social situation and efficacy in solving its problems, these assumptions—seldom verbalized by statesmen as baldly as we have stated them, but always sedulously adhered to in the practice of statecraft—establish an admirably effective institutional structure for the conduct of international politics.

Of course, the validity of these assumptions depends ultimately upon the extent to which the phenomenon of power or capability can be meaningfully quantified. Such a relativistic and purportedly value-free system of regulating a set of relationships demands the existence of a completely objective and universally accepted arbitral apparatus. Power has played this role for centuries. The generally blurred appearance of the international political system today is partially due to the diminished skill of statesmen in clarifying and quantifying the several categories of power. As a result, many of these assumptions are under serious fire.

Power Status in International Politics

The process of power politics became formalized as a basis for state interaction only as status configurations reflecting the power and strength (actual, potential, or formal) of states were crystallized into institutional form. The social system of international politics has traditionally been sharply stratified, because the three "classes" of states—great powers, medium powers, and small powers—have structured the entire political process. Essential to a working class system is a full appreciation by each class of its relative place in the system and a recognition of the peculiar roles of all other classes. In this regard the international political system qualifies as a fully-developed class society.

To continue our analogy, the relatively small group of great powers have, throughout history, insisted on their right to regulate all matters within the system in their individual and group interest. For many years the study of international politics actually involved no more than analysis of relations among a cluster of between four and eight major states. So great was their influence and so complete their collective monopoly over the relevant instruments of coercion that these few states repeatedly demonstrated their capacity to police all international relationships.

Membership in the elite inner circle of states was not the result of any mathematical calculation of power components, but rather a function of international practice and consensus. Certain "qualified" states were taken into the group by joint agreement, frequently registered in a major international conference culminating in a reordering peace treaty, such as the Peace of Westphalia (1648), the Treaty of Utrecht (1713), the work of the Congress of Vienna (1815), and the several peace treaties known as the Peace of Paris at the end of World War I (1919). Each of these epoch making (and epoch ending) instruments brought erstwhile outsiders into the group of great powers, and also temporarily or permanently expelled certain states.

We have already indicated the chief reward of great power status: the implicit right (rooted in action capability) of the state to extend its interest as far as it wishes and to act in support of this interest. Great powers have always asserted that no question is inherently out of their province, and insist on being consulted on the ultimate disposition of any problem in which they may care to involve themselves. The fact that they may override longer-lived and deeper-rooted interests of lesser states is regarded as irrelevant, although some doctrinal efforts have been made toward formulating principles of an alleged "responsibility of power" that would authorize formal, universally accepted great power intervention anywhere.

The consensual base of great power status is clearly shown by the periodic appearance of states that are given membership in the circle for various political reasons, but which in fact lack a large reservoir of action capability. Spain, for example, was kept in the great power class long after its effective role had been extinguished in the seventeenth century. Italy was given courtesy membership after its unification in 1870. France and (Nationalist) China were included at United States insistence in the immediate aftermath of World War II. Such states may enjoy great prestige among lesser powers, but their actual influence on the deliberations of the inner circle is usually minimal.

The international system gives formal recognition to the controlling place of great power status through the mechanism of the "concert of power": formal assemblies of leading states which attempt to arrange a set of relationships to their mutual satisfaction. In the past this has been most apparent at major peace conferences, such as the Congress of Vienna, and at periodic gatherings for the resolution of particular problems, such as the Congress of Verona (1822) and the Congress of Berlin (1878). Since 1945, the "concert of power" has had a dual aspect; the conference of opportunity continues in the form of the so-called "Conference of Foreign Ministers" of the great powers, while permanent concern activity is made possible in the Security Council of the United Nations.

Less need be said of the two lower status groups. The values of great power status tend to be automatically accepted by all states, so each smaller state seeks to act as much as possible like a great power. Each seeks as broad an international role as it can effectuate; each is active in augmenting its limited store of status and deference. Both classes (medium or small powers) contain an infinity of gradations, and something like an international pecking order is the norm. So dominant is the role of great powers, however, that these distinctions flow less from analyses and judgments made by lesser powers themselves than from (sometimes almost casual) discriminatory evaluations made by the elite states.

Patterns of Power Politics

Within the general characteristics of the power political system we can distinguish four clear patterns of relationships that have recurred frequently and are operative today. Two of these patterns involve only the great powers, two also involve the smaller powers, and each relates to the general area of great power–small power relationships.

The first pattern develops when the great powers are in substantial agreement about the existing shape of their own relationships within the entire spectrum of issues. Such a situation occurs only when the entire group—or all but a fraction of the membership—is, in terms of the prevailing situation, committed to a generalized status quo orientation. Great power agreement results in the combined force of the concert being exerted upon the arena of world politics, and the almost inevitable control of international politics by the leading states. A notable historical example of this pattern is provided by the course of affairs in Europe between 1815 and, roughly, 1848.

The second pattern is the converse of the first in that the great powers, instead of agreeing on the preferable state of relationships, split into hostile and competing camps. This situation normally develops when revisionist points of view take control of a sizable slice of the total power represented by the group of major states; the dominant dimension of struggle is between status quo and revisionist policies. When major states fall out, the over-all control of the elite group on world affairs inevitably diminishes, since the break in their common front and the dynamism that characterizes a great power struggle offer opportunities for small states and coalitions to act effectively. The neatest example of such a pattern is also the most recent: the cold war era that split the great powers between 1947 and the early sixties.

The third pattern arises when the smaller states of the world (including both medium and small powers) develop a common interest, point of view, and over-all strategy to govern their responses to major states. This is a relatively recent development in world affairs, made possible only by the appearance of the United Nations as a universal actor that derives its motive force from its many small members. Under appropriate conditions—notably the military balance of terror that inhibits great power use of armed force—this pattern has surprisingly great scope. Contemporary world politics, especially the rise in importance of the General Assembly of the United Nations and the increasing militancy of the small state anticolonialist bloc, is a clear demonstration of the pattern.

The fourth pattern, consisting of small state disorganization, lack of communication, and incipient or actual mutual hostility, is historically far more common. In this pattern each small state is subject to isolation and pressure from predatory medium or great powers, irrespective of the state of unanimity of the elite group itself. This tendency of the more numerous but less well-organized medium and small powers to break into uncoordinated fragments has simplified the controlling and dominating mission of the great powers.

One final point about these patterns should be made. Either the first or the second may be controlling the relations of the great powers, while either the third or the fourth may be controlling the status of the remainder of the states. Whichever pair (one *or* two, three *or* four) is simultaneously functional determines the general shape of international power relations at any particular moment in history.

THE REGULARITIES OF INTERNATIONAL POLITICS

The anarchy of the international system, at least in concept, contains the constant potential of explosion. Managing the affairs of states in a lawless environment requires the development and application of a variety of relatively unstructured but very pervasive principles of action. These regularities of international politics function to control the external manifestations of power in the international order, and to regulate by limiting the effect of power differentials among states. Acceptance by the controlling consensus of states of one or another of these patterns is reflected in their policies. Self-preservation in a context of change is the controlling motivation for the willingness of states to submit to a regularized structuring of their over-all responses.

Patterns of Equilibrium of Power

If we assume that the normal tendency of state relationships is to seek equilibrium, we may classify the equilibrium patterns of politics and power as a three-fold system. Our first type is characterized by widespread dispersal of action capability among the states of the system; this pattern has long been known as the "multiple balance of power," and received its most explicit institutionalization in the classic European system of the seventeenth through nineteenth centuries. The second pattern is marked by concentration of power on a bipolar basis around two great powers. This is the predominant pattern of the post-1945 world and is usually identified as a "simple balance of power." Finally, there is the pattern of integrated power radiating from a single central point, like the spokes of a wheel. Although never realized since the decay of the Roman Empire, the League of Nations and the United Nations represent attempts at its achievement in the modern world.

The multiple balance system, based on a concentration of power in individual states, is uncentralized. The simple balance is in one sense a midpoint in that the number of poles of concentration is reduced to two. The integrated system theoretically does away with dispersed power and replaces it with an integrated power structure.

Multiple Balance of Power

The multiple balance was the controlling pattern of interstate relations throughout the seventeenth, eighteenth, nineteenth, and early twentieth centuries. The international system during this period was consistently pluralistic in that a multiplicity of great powers—at least five at any time—dominated the course of world politics.

In a multiple balance system the great powers act so as to complement each other and—sometimes intentionally but more often instinctively—maximize the prospects of their survival as individual states and the durability of the system. This system demands an implicit agreement to respect each other's existence and sphere of interests, and to confine disagreements to issues considered marginal. Coalition formation is normal, as is the tendency for these action groupings to balance each other. Any reduction or (to a lesser extent) increase in the number of great powers is considered undesirable, since either modification runs the risk of upsetting whatever stability the system may boast. No great power in a multiple system, therefore, should seriously plan to eliminate another.

World War I signalled the final breakdown of the multiple balance system. Several profound historic trends, imperfectly understood at the time, had undermined the operative conditions essential to the perpetuation of the tidy world of an earlier period.

1. The emergence of Germany and Italy dramatically increased the number of great powers, while the two new major states energetically pressed for the expansion of the system to include their own interests.
2. The end of imperialist expansion terminated the digressive effect of colonial conquest and again focused great power interests on each other.
3. Britain lost the freedom of action it had once enjoyed as the self-conscious "holder of the balance," and found itself drifting into opposition to Germany and a blurred but binding affiliation with the Franco-Russian alliance.
4. The ramshackle empire of Austria-Hungary could no longer function meaningfully as a great power.

After 1907, the inner political world of the great powers had become almost bipolar as two rigid blocs confronted each other in a situation permitting no real maneuver. "Balance" had become an irrelevant concept.

Simple Balance of Power

Bipolarization of power between the United States and the U.S.S.R., due in part to historical accident in the World War II era but also the result of deliberate policy choices by both sides, has characterized world politics since 1945. In this simple balance (simple in its structure, but difficult and dangerous to operate), alignments shift around the poles of the two major powers, and all states draw their international orientation from the general configurations of strength. Movement and change in a tight bipolar system is minimized, since the rationale of great power policy is to reduce the pluralism of international politics to a concentration on the single issue of the bipolar struggle. The simple balance, therefore, is reminiscent of a seesaw in contrast to the multiple balance of a chandelier.

Integration of Power

Integration of power is best represented in political terms by the classic concept of collective security, exemplified today by the United

Nations. Collective security is simply a system to make real the idea of "one for all and all for one."

The obligations of collective security are spelled out in Articles 39 through 51 of the Charter of the United Nations. The "teeth" of these provisions are found in Article 42:

> (The Security Council) may take such action by air, sea, or land forces as may be necessary to maintain or restore international peace and security. Such action may include demonstrations, blockades and other operations by air, sea, or land forces of Members of the United Nations.

The "other operations" obviously include military action under United Nations direction, first implemented in Korea and later in the Suez Canal Zone and in the Congo.

Collective security and integration of power have never been real successes in the contemporary world. Pending the transfer of state sovereignty to a single world government of some sort, collective security may function only upon the basis of a massive consensus among the world's leading powers. So long as the political world remains divided into hostile camps, collective security demands the impossible, for the system was never designed to restrain part of the community on behalf of the remainder. Its rationale demands that any potential aggressor be an outcast, with every man's hand turned against him the moment he threatens to violate the peaceful climate of relationships. Thus collective security is a viable pattern only when the vast preponderance of action capability is in the hands of states with a deep interest in the preservation of at least the essentials of the status quo. A significant revisionist faction among the major states renders the idea irrelevant. It is in no sense pessimistic to insist that the contemporary world is favorably disposed to the policies of revisionism, and therefore true integration of power is not a real prospect in the foreseeable future.

Methods of the Balance of Power

There are seven different techniques employed by states to maintain or rectify a balance of power: intervention, compensation, buffer zones, divide and rule, spheres of influence, armaments, and alliances.

1. INTERVENTION. This is the interference by one state in the internal affairs of another, and may assume either defensive or offensive forms. Defensive intervention aims at the preservation of a particular regime or system; offensive intervention is directed at altering such a system.

Defensive intervention is based on the assumption that a state, particularly a great power, cannot permit the balance of power to be materially changed to its disadvantage by another state's change of government or policy. Examples of defensive intervention are numerous in contemporary international politics: Allied intervention in Russia (1918) to maintain the pre-Bolshevik regime; Soviet intervention in Hungary (1956) to protect the Kádár government; American intervention in Lebanon (1958) in support of the Shamoun administration.

Offensive intervention is expansive and is primarily manifested by penetration. Its purpose is to bring about a change of policy or government in another state, or, if necessary, eliminate its independence completely. The manner in which both Italy and Germany became united in the second half of the nineteenth century represents offensive intervention employed by Prussia and Piedmont respectively. The establishment of communist governments in Eastern Europe following World War II illustrates Russian offensive intervention, while the old American custom of "dollar diplomacy" is still another example of this form of intervention in Latin America.

2. COMPENSATION. This involves giving a state the equivalent of the territory of which it is deprived or the equal of what is given to other states. This usually applies only to victorious states and their allies; defeated states customarily lose territory without compensation. Peace treaties normally result in territorial changes which reflect the principle of compensation. This was the spirit of the territorial settlements embodied in the peace treaties that followed World War I and World War II.

The basic assumption underlying compensation is that one state resents seeing another state increase its power without obtaining a compensating aggrandizement of its own, a principle that characterized the approach of the great powers toward the partitioning of Africa and the Far East during the second half of the nineteenth century. It was an insistence on compensation that made Mussolini join actively the side of the Axis after the fall of France; he refused to permit Hitler to settle Europe's future without deriving benefits for Italy. The assignment of mandated areas to France and Great Britain following World War I and the authorization of the United Nations trust territories following World War II are more recent examples.

3. A BUFFER ZONE. This is a small power situated between two or more great powers. It may also be a relatively weak state located between the spheres of interest of great powers. The assumption underlying this technique is that it is in the interests of each of the great powers to prevent the other from controlling the buffer zone. Each competing power seeks to preserve the integrity of the small state in the middle as preferable to its falling prey to the other.

Switzerland and Belgium have long been considered buffer zones between Germany and France. During the latter part of the nineteenth century, Afghanistan was a buffer zone between the British Empire and Russia, and the Spanish colonies in Africa played the same role between the colonial empires of France and Britain. At present, we can classify Austria as a buffer zone between the Eastern and Western spheres of influence in Europe, and Nepal a buffer zone between India and Communist China.

4. "DIVIDE AND RULE." This means that a great power follows the policy of dividing its opponents and competitors into hostile camps, or at least heightens their disunity. The principal assumption underlying this principle is that disunity and partition will keep the competitor weak.

The principle of divide and rule has been the traditional policy of France toward Germany. The present policy of the Soviet Union in regard to Europe represents another example of the divide and rule formula.

5. THE SPHERE OF INFLUENCE. This is a device by which competing great powers delineate their areas of hegemony. Each of the great powers concerned undertakes to respect the others' power rights in its own zone, assuming that in this manner disputes between great powers can be minimized. North Africa was considered a French sphere of influence from the late nineteenth century until only a few years ago, while Egypt and the Sudan became British spheres of influence after 1882. The Balkans are presently regarded as belonging to the Russian sphere of influence.

6. ARMAMENTS. These are the principal means by which a great power tries to maintain and reestablish a balance of power to its favor. The underlying assumption is that a greater quality and quantity of armaments maximizes the capabilities of a state for attack and deterrence. Hence, the inevitable corollary of the armaments race is a spiraling burden of military preparedness consuming an ever greater portion of the budgets of states. We shall examine this point in detail in Chapter Ten.

7. ALLIANCES. These are the most important manifestations of the methods of balancing power. An alliance is an agreement between two or more states for the defensive or aggressive purposes of its members against a state or states outside the alliance. Leading contemporary alliances include the North Atlantic Treaty Organization, the Warsaw Pact, the Rio Pact, the Central Treaty Organization, and the South East Asia Treaty Organization.

Alliances are an essential function of the balance of power within the international system. They are grounded in the belief that through alliances a state can increase its own power, either by adding increments from other states or by withholding the power of other states from its competitors. Alliances are dynamic; their changing pattern is not stimulated by principle, but reflects the circumstances of expediency as viewed by the state concerned. Common interests are the primary considerations in the establishment of alliances between states, with the alliances themselves defining the general policies and concrete measures serving these interests. Although the typical interests which unite states in an alliance against an opponent are explicit, they are less precise regarding the policies to be pursued and the objectives to be sought.

Alliances may be regarded as essential methods in the regulatory process of international politics. They are important instruments in the adaptation of the nation-state to the international system, and help to fill the gap between the ideals of organization and the realities of quasi-anarchy in the system.

REFERENCES

* Carr, Edward H., *The New Society*. Boston: Beacon Press, 1964.

Cassirer, Ernst, *The Myth of the State*. New Haven: Yale University Press, 1946.

Claude, Inis L., Jr., *Power and International Relations*. New York: Random House, Inc., 1962.

Cox, Richard H., ed., *The State in International Relations*. San Francisco: Chandler Publishing Co., 1965.

* Dehio, Ludwig, *The Precarious Balance*. New York: Alfred A. Knopf, Inc., 1962.

* Gulick, Edward V., *Europe's Classical Balance of Power: A Case History of the Theory of European Statecraft*. New York: W. W. Norton & Company, Inc., 1967.

Herz, John, *International Politics in the Atomic Age*. New York: Columbia University Press, 1959.

Krader, Lawrence, *The Formation of the State*. Englewood Cliffs, N.J.: Prentice-Hall, Inc., 1968.

Laski, Harold J., *Authority in the Modern State*. New Haven: Yale University Press, 1919.

———, *The Foundations of Sovereignty and Other Essays*. New York: Harcourt, Brace & World, Inc., 1921.

* ———, *Introduction to Politics*. New York: Barnes & Noble, Inc., 1962.

* Lerche, Charles O., Jr., *The Cold War . . . and After*. Englewood Cliffs, N.J.: Prentice-Hall, Inc., 1965.

* Indicates paperback edition.

* MacBridge, Roger Lea, *Treaties Versus the Constitution*. Caldwell, Idaho: The Caxton Printers, 1955.

Meriam, Charles E., *History of the Theory of Sovereignty Since Rousseau*. New York: Columbia University Press, 1928.

Moon, P. T., *Imperialism and World Politics*. New York: The Macmillan Company, 1926.

Nicolson, Harold G., *Diplomacy* (3rd ed.). London: Oxford University Press, 1963.

Niebuhr, Reinhold, *The Structure of Nations and Empires*. New York: Charles Scribner's Sons, 1959.

Satow, Ernest M., *Guide to Diplomatic Practice*. London: Longmans, Green & Co., Ltd., 1957.

* Schampter, J., *Imperialism and Social Classes*. New York: Meridian Books, 1955.

Whight, Martin, *Power Politics*. London: The Royal Institute of International Affairs, 1946.

* Indicates paperback edition.

SIX

The Conditions of
International Politics Today

The international political system, incorporating the historically validated ideas and patterns that we have just examined, has in this generation come into conjunction with modern technology. The several
revolutions of the contemporary era—in transportation, communication,
energy, production, weapons, and space—have all had their direct effect
on the relation of states. The conditions of international politics today
are radically different from those of even a half century ago. Many of the
tensions of international politics in the nuclear era come from the inevitable frustrating effort to fit the contemporary environment into traditional
political categories.

Today the states of the world function within a closed political system.
In analytical terms, the frontier of international politics has disappeared.
Every explosion of political, economic, or social force within this closed
system inevitably radiates to all portions of the globe. No part of the
earth's surface can be classified as politically undesirable or strategically
unimportant. Every state is in some way relevant to every other state.

THE STATES OF THE WORLD

One manifestation of the new dimensions of international politics is
the great change in the number and nature of participants in the process.

With the members of the international political system so different, it is no wonder that the process has been greatly modified.

The Contemporary International System

The total number of national actors (states) in international politics has more than doubled since the end of World War II. When the United Nations was established in 1945, its membership included 51 states; a quarter of a century later membership had risen to 126. This increase in number is further highlighted by the current geographic distribution of membership. In 1945, the United Nations had 19 members from Central and South America, 19 from Europe and other western areas, nine from Asia, and four from Africa. The number of Central and South American states remained unchanged until Jamaica, Trinidad-Tobago, Guyana, and Barbados became independent in the early and mid-sixties, while the states of Europe and the West have increased by 13. In contrast, the number of African states has increased to 42 and those of Asia to 29. Together, the non-western states of Africa and Asia constitute nearly 60 per cent of present membership. Of the 75 new members, more than 60 have escaped from colonial status since the end of World War II.

Thus the system which was once a purely western cultural pattern has been invaded by non-western peoples and their value structures. This great shift in the background and general orientation of the bulk of participants in international politics has had a number of immediate consequences for the system.

1. Consensus on many issues is more difficult to obtain than it was when all important states shared a common moral and historical orientation. The new states arrive at world politics with a point of view different from that of the older states, and apply different criteria of judgment and evaluation. The resulting communication between West and non-West has thus been marked by great suspicion, misunderstanding, and confusion of motivations.
2. A new force—non-western nationalism, usually expressing itself in the form of anticolonialism—has come to play a major determining role in the course of political life. Many of the new states look upon their former colonial masters as natural enemies and press their case against colonialism almost as a matter of principle. The older states with a history of rule over alien peoples are almost morally and intellectually powerless against this onslaught.
3. The dawn of political consciousness in many once-somnolent peoples has shown them the startling contrast between their familiar way of life and the much higher standard long enjoyed by older states. They have

pressed their governments to win by international action what they feel to be their just share of the good things of life. This familiar "revolution of rising expectations" is a direct consequence of the broader membership in the international political system.

4. The older and better established members of the system have been obliged to broaden their own political horizons to take account of the new conditions of international life. Not only have they been required to extend their interests to include many once-neglected areas of the world, but they also have been constrained to deal with a broad range of substantive problems (e.g., economic development, human rights) that rest outside the traditional context of international politics.

The Origins of the System

The world political order as we know it today emerged from the European state system that followed the collapse of feudalism. The Renaissance and Reformation transformed the political conditions of the medieval period into a milieu that made possible the development of the modern European nation-state. The Renaissance laid the foundation for secularization of European thought, whereas the Reformation set in motion nationalization of the once-universal concept of Christendom. In addition, new means of communication and the so-called "commercial revolution" shook the foundations of feudalism. These forces led first to the modern idea of the state, and subsequently to the European nation-state system that was formally institutionalized in the Peace of Westphalia in 1648. Prior to World War II, "international politics" was largely synonymous with the politics of Europe and European-rooted culture. The basic concepts which energize international politics today—such as sovereignty, nationalism, war, and international law and organization —were systematized over three centuries ago.

Gradual development of a multiplicity of independent units that acknowledged no universal political superior, and establishment of continuous and organized relations among the western national states, marked the beginning of what has come to be called power politics. Beginning with the fifteenth and sixteenth centuries, the newly-established European states began to reach out and circle the globe. Leaders in this effort were those maritime powers located on the circumference of Europe: initially Portugal and Spain, and later France, Great Britain, and Holland. Wherever they went in the non-European world they planted their flags and established outposts for what rapidly became empires. The Industrial Revolution accelerated the rate of European colonial expansion because many of the raw materials for the new European industries were located outside Europe.

By 1900, the concepts which originated in European institutions during the fifteenth century had become a global system incorporating the political values and structures of the West. This cultural root of international politics points up a significant contemporary paradox. The new states of Asia and Africa are admittedly in revolt against a system which they feel "enslaved" them, and yet at the same time are seeking to join that system themselves and to use as their instrument of revolt a state form frankly borrowed from western models.

Diversity and Integration

As long as power in the international order was confined to a limited number of European and western states, there was no need for any supranational authority to regulate the relations of states. The balance of power, as practiced by the statesmen of Europe, served to stabilize the international political process. Since effective action of the balance of power depended on the configurations assumed by an unequal distribution of power among states, the services of Great Britain, as the self-conscious holder and wielder of the balance, were required most of the time.

The new dimensions of international politics have given rise to a drastic modification of the traditional patterns of power distribution. The fundamental conditions upon which the old system were based have evaporated, and in their stead the devolution of power since the Industrial Revolution has created an entirely new situation. Three current trends merit separate mention.

1. The number of *national actors* in international politics has increased. The number of independent states has more than doubled since World War II, from about 60 to roughly 135 today,[1] an increase almost entirely in the category of small states. By using the normal criteria of classification, the number of small powers increased from about 40 in 1945 to approximately 105 today. Middle powers increased from only 12 to less than 20—a one-third gain.

2. The number of *essential national actors* has, on the other hand, actually decreased. During World War II there were eight essential national actors (great powers)—the United States, the Soviet Union, the United Kingdom, France, Italy, Germany, China, and Japan. Today the number has been reduced to two unimistakably essential states (the United States and the U.S.S.R.), two near-essential states (the United Kingdom and France), and three aspirants to essentiality (India, Japan, and

---

[1] This figure is not to be confused with U.N. membership; it includes states not members of the United Nations.

China). If and when the process of European integration reaches fruition, this listing will probably include an entity called "Europe" as a new essential national actor. The number of great powers in the world today, however, is the smallest it has been since the beginning of the state system.

3. The differentials between categories of national actors are becoming wider, due to differences in industrial, political, and military conditions rooted in the newer aspects of technology. Barring some reversal of trends, many experts fear the indefinite prolongation of this evolution, with important consequences for the future of international politics.

These trends, operating within the more intimate international environment created by technology, have had a significant dual effect. First, they have led to concentration of the visible forms of international power within the major political blocs that dominate contemporary world affairs. These rigid groupings, expressing in their most intense form the traditional values of the state system, emphasize the diversity on which the political approach of states to one another has long been based. Second, the integration of power demanded by the newer questions facing the system has received its institutionalization in the form of a new phenomenon: the universal actor, epitomized by the United Nations and its subordinate and associated multilateral agencies. The struggle between diversity and integration, although as old as political life itself, has acquired a new and portentous dimension; the bipolar system and the United Nations system as ways of organizing power stand in direct confrontation.

NATIONALISM: OLD AND YOUNG

Nationalism is the common sentiment or feeling of solidarity which transforms a people into a nationality and expresses itself in an attitude which ascribes to the collective activity of the nation a very high (frequently the highest) place in the hierarchy of social value. Nationalism converts a state into a nation-state; the latter is thus the political structure that reflects a people considering themselves a nation. Nationalism is one of the absolutely controlling phenomena of world politics today, as it has been since American and French Revolutions.

Characteristics of Nationalism

Nationalism grows from a variety of sources. Some of the more obvious factors that impel individuals to join with others in a national group include a common language, religion, historical background, cultural tradition, and racial background. Several of these may interact in subtle ways to reinforce a cohesive tendency in a people. The nationalist ethos is best expressed in the broadly based and deeply felt philosophy of political, economic, and social life that becomes the operational creed of the nation. It is also reflected in a complex variety of symbols: external enemies, myths, heroes, history, and folklore.

Traditional European Nationalism

Rudimentary forms of nationalism can be traced to the states of antiquity. Ancient peoples commonly considered themselves divinely chosen and believed that their gods were the sworn foes of other states. Regarding themselves as greatly superior in all aspects to the rest of mankind, they viewed others as approaching excellence in proportion to their acceptance of the particular values of the state.

Development of the European state system and the expansion of western civilization gradually brought into sharp focus the effect of nationalism in international politics. The Hundred Years War (1337–1451) between France and England may be considered the beginning of modern nationalism. The initial foundations for the union of Norman and Saxon into Englishmen were laid down in England during the twelfth and thirteenth centuries, to be fully achieved by the middle of the fourteenth century. In France, an elementary form of French national consciousness first appeared during the Hundred Years War. The French, however, lacked the more elaborate political institutions of the English, and the development of full national identity was slower in France than in Britain. By the seventeenth century, England and France had become nations in almost a contemporary sense, to be followed shortly by Sweden, Holland, Spain, and Denmark.

In these European societies, nationalism was originally directed at the centralization of government through the unity of law and administration. It gradually evolved into a more liberal movement dedicated to the termination of royal absolutism, following the principle that the state belongs to the people, and thus became a condition of civilized life and functioned as a principle of political order and freedom. The European tended to turn to nationalism in order to discover a more meaningful relationship to his increasingly secularized environment. So powerful did it become that in many societies it acquired the characteristics of a secular religion, partially filling the gap left by destruction of the medieval synthesis.

The unifying influence in nationalism, which initially brought order and stability within the national state, ultimately promoted a highly diverse community of sovereign states. Whereas during the early stages of its growth nationalism promised peace, order, and justice predicated on the fulfillment of national aspirations, the paradox of nationalist logic was highlighted after the middle of the eighteenth century. Since then it has functioned more as a force of disintegration and fragmentation than of unity.

In an important way nationalism is self-contradictory. Two principles make up its substance: the expression of aspirations for personal and civil liberty by the individual, and the thrust for political dignity and freedom for the society. In practice these two principles are inescapably antagonistic. Either can serve as the basis for political action, but never both together, at least for any period of time.

The Impact of Nationalism

The development of international politics since the middle of the eighteenth century furnishes much evidence of the difficulty of effective implementation of nationalism without aggravating the conditions of international politics. A people's aspiration to create a nation-state has almost always conflicted with territorial claims of other states. Nationalists, generally not satisfied with internal achievements, tend to seek glory through expansion and empire, whether territorial, economic, or cultural. Furthermore, intense nationalistic identification tends to undermine flexibility in policy and the capacity to compromise in interstate disputes.

The series of major wars that have been waged since 1815—especially World Wars I and II—embodied overt attempts to apply the principles of nationalism. Almost every one was fought by one or more belligerents in the name of national self-determination, and the results of these wars were reflected in peace settlements allegedly predicated upon the same principles. Yet a victory of nationalism, instead of bringing peace and order to international politics, only led to an exchange of the roles of oppressor and oppressed. Far from creating a more stable system, nationalism contributed to the "Balkanization" of the international order and exaggerated an already strong proclivity to tension.

Unable to cope with its own success, nationalism has not developed into a broad enough political concept to unite political institutions, ideologies, and economic systems in the same way that science and technology have compressed the world. It is eroding both Communism and democratic liberalism, and has created a polycentric mosaic in place of these two supranational ideological blocs that emerged following World War II. These ideologies have been transformed from universal political faiths into power techniques to promote the national interests of individual states. One can safely say that creeping nationalism is currently awakening secular and parochial bonds.

Nationalism in the Non-Western World

Modern nationalism in the emerging Asian and African states shares only one aspect with the principle of early European nationalism: the nation is held to be the ultimate point of reference for political loyalties and actions. Otherwise non-western nationalism is a special, almost exotic growth.

The goal of the original phase of nationalism in Europe (sometimes called the "liberating" phase) was "one nation in one state" and nothing more. In twentieth-century western nationalism (known as "integrating" nationalism), the phenomenon of the nation in a state is usually no more than the starting point of a universal mission of value dissemination whose ultimate objectives extend in some cases to the entire world. This "nationalistic universalism," a type of political Messianism, claims the right of one nation, acting through a set of state institutions, to impose its own values and institutions upon as many nations as it wishes.

The impact of both forms of western nationalism on the non-western world has been explosive, partially because the environment was peculiarly prepared to respond to the stimulus of these ideas. Since the middle of the nineteenth century, non-western peoples coming into contact with the expanding West have been searching for some orienting concept upon which to base an adequate response. With their old societal and personal values eroded by the technological transformation everywhere in the underdeveloped world, these peoples have found in nationalism a method of giving new meaning to their lives.

The non-western world is finding it necessary to reconcile tradition with the demands of modern thought and life. Success in this effort has been minimal because of the peculiar dimensions of the problem; non-western leaders, seeking a sufficient mass revival to produce a political and cultural renaissance, fear massive social or political revolutionary change. Caught between the necessity of doing something and the reluctance to do too much, leadership in the non-western world faces the danger of fleeing from overcontradiction into moral and intellectual skepticism. Old codes no longer meet the social and political need, but new principles of intellectual life from the West are unpalatable. Sociopolitical stasis has been the consequence.

Into this vacuum has moved the ambivalent concept of nationalism, originally imported as part of colonialism but given peculiar twists by native spokesmen. Nationalism in most of the non-western world is difficult for the older and more settled western societies to comprehend, since the emerging nations are not really pursuing nationalist aspirations in any traditional sense. The operative goal of these states is the rejuvenation and ultimate vindication of their respective civilizations, to be effected by the reconciliation of old aspirations with new values.

Although they use the language of western political discourse, national arguments in Asia and Africa do not incorporate the familiar assumptions of the West; the full implications of the nation-state are not appreciated. Consequently, it has proved dangerously easy for ambitious leaders of mass movements to use nationalist slogans as devices of apology and self-defense against past failures and present difficulties.

A nation in the western sense does not exist within the boundaries of any present state in much of the non-western world. These states do not reflect spontaneous political growth, but rather the aftereffects of the division of the world by European colonial powers. In many instances no concept of nationality exists; family and tribal loyalties still form the central core of the society. Government is minimal in organization and in effect, and the visible symbols of national identity are few and unimportant. The intelligentsia are too sophisticated to respond to the call of nationalism, while the masses are so insensitive that only the crudest and most obvious stimuli have any effect.

Thus nationalism in Asia and Africa is grandiose and disorganized in its expression, with incompatible ideas conjoined in the same breath. Past grandeur is lovingly evoked at the same time that the people are exhorted to slough off their old ways and join the mainstream of modern life; withdrawal and pervasive self-expression are equally prominent. The non-western world wants simultaneously to escape from the "vulgarities" of western life, to emulate the comforts found there, and to reform the rest of the world in its own "spiritual" image. Nationalism in the new states is more of an expression of an attitude toward life and a reflection of culture shock than it is a formalized belief system and a base for governmental action.

Despite these shortcomings, non-western nationalism evokes a sense of self-respect which was unknown during the colonial period. It stimulates social solidarity and helps create a relevant community to which diverse peoples can claim common loyalty. It is of prime significance when it helps create the national unity of purpose and readiness to sacrifice which are required for development and even survival. It is not at attempt to express what is, but what is perceived as desirable.

The elites of the nationalist movements, usually products of the modernization and education which have not yet touched the mass of their countrymen, are the mediators between the old and the new. They must set the ends and employ the means of modernization, yet the values and techniques which they have adopted are often inappropriate to their traditional societies.

Therefore, the elites are strangers in their own lands, subverting the existing order and society, which they want to change in order to satisfy their own needs. Their desire for change is in part a narrow personal wish, but it is also rooted in an intense desire to bring to their country-men the "better life" which they have seen elsewhere. However, the amount of change needed to arrive at political and cultural awakening necessarily disrupts orderly transition. The endeavor to create a united nation-state through common effort usually runs into traditional patterns which strengthen factionalism and division. Such obstruction of national-ist ideals is often met by the creation by the elites of one party states which suppress opposition and deal ruthlessly with the obstructionists and factionalists.

THE TECHNOLOGICAL REVOLUTION

The technological revolution has accelerated the pace of history. Ideas covering all domains of human activity—political organization and in-stitutions, economic and social organizations, religion, fine arts, science, and strategy and tactics—radiate quickly from their sources of origin and penetrate the rest of the world. This process has been breaking down ancient customs, introducing seeds of doubt and hope, initiating con-troversies between political groups within states, and giving rise to new concepts of ends and means. Social institutions everywhere are in flux. The technological revolution has ushered in revolution in many other phases of life as well.

The increased pace of history and the conquest of time have had a curious double effect. Men everywhere are involved in international affairs to an extent undreamed of only a generation and a half ago. In this sense, the technological changes of this era have gone far in making men members of one global community of interest. However, technology and the pace of change have helped to consolidate human organization and loyalty behind the one familiar institution in an age of transition— the nation-state. Thus technology both simplifies and complicates the formulation and resolution of the problems of international politics.

The Revolution in Communication and Transportation

The new revolutionary means of communication and transportation make it possible to travel to any point in the world in a matter of hours, and to communicate with any part of the world within a few minutes. These developments have obvious consequences for both the conduct of interstate relations and the substance of the questions that concern states.

Operationally, the revolution in transportation and communication has affected all the instrumentalities of foreign policy. Diplomacy has been heavily invaded by direct intervention from the foreign office, markedly reducing the role played by resident ambassadors. Electronic and printing media have completely changed the rationale of propaganda and other methods of psychological warfare. Economic measures can now be applied much more rapidly to specific situations. By far the most obvious effect of the revolution in transportation and communication, however, is in the field of military methods. A ballistic missile, for example, is both a vehicle and an unmistakable message; delivery systems are means of transportation, while guidance systems reflect the application of modern communications science.

Substantively, the technology of transportation and communication have made the world smaller and much more constrictive; the tension between diversity and integration is heightened by the shrunken arena of world politics. On the other hand, a greater sense of unity and common destiny is sensed by men everywhere, who are in a much greater variety of ways mutually interdependent. At the same time, states as organizational units have all become more vulnerable to a greater range of pressures and actual or potential attack. As individuals, men are increasingly driven together by modern transportation and communication; as political groups, they are driven apart by fears and suspicions.

The Energy Revolution

Probably the most spectacular of the several aspects of the new technology is the successful attempt to release the energy of the atom and its nucleus. Since 1750 the roots of modern political power have been in industrial power, and industrial power is no more than a function of its energy base. Industrial establishments of modern states are built on the technology of steel, with familiar sources of energy such as coal (by far the most important), water power, petroleum, and—as a derivative—electricity.

If (or when) the theoretical potential of nuclear energy is realized in practice, many fixed assumptions about the relative power positions of states will be invalidated. At present the energy released by nuclear fission (to say nothing of the vastly greater energy potential in thermonuclear fusion) is expensive to produce and of little industrial import. But any significant lowering of the cost level would raise a host of tantalizing possibilities.

States presently debarred from effective industrialization because of poor energy source endowments could acquire the potential of large-scale industry overnight. Already industrialized states that lagged behind in the conversion might find themselves hopelessly outstripped by relative newcomers. The ranks of the great powers could suddenly be increased, and the classification of "small power" might require extensive redefinition. Like almost all aspects of the new technology, however, the energy revolution might take two directions. While at first its effect might be to exaggerate differences and potential conflicts, logic might ultimately demand its effective implementation on the broadest possible international base.

The Production Revolution

Even within the context of the coal-iron technology, a revolution in production methods is occurring and has already had major effects. The most notorious aspect of the new production is automation—performance by computer-programmed machines of incredibly complex processes of manufacture—but its political ramifications are almost endless.

For example, the states of western Europe were forced to rebuild their war-ravaged industrial plants almost from scratch after 1945. Today their new factories, incorporating the latest theories and techniques of production, are able to gain competitive advantages over the older and less rationalized establishments in the United States and Great Britain. When modern industrialization takes firm root in the non-western world, it will almost certainly forego the earlier evolutionary steps and move quickly into equally revolutionary methods of manufacture and distribution. Coupled with the new horizons opened by the energy revolution, the possibility arises that the future will see relatively small but superlatively efficient productive plants located in now underdeveloped parts of the world. What this might mean for the economic dimension of international relations seems self-evident.

The Weapons Revolution

Modern technology, using both the energy potential of nucleonics and radical innovations in transportation and communication, has consummated a frightening revolution in the weapons of warfare. Man is becoming aware of the awful consequences to the entire fabric of human life if the application of advanced technology should develop only new methods of killing people.

Weaponry has been drastically expanded in at least two major dimensions: the "projectile" that does the damage to the target and is in one sense the weapon itself, and the "delivery system" that moves the projectile from its point of launching to the target. In the Roman empire, the spearhead or the edge of the sword was the projectile, and the delivery system included the remainder of the spear or sword and the soldier himself. Today the logic remains the same, but technology— which has progressed through bows and arrows, muskets, rifled artillery, and engine-driven aircraft—has now improved to the extent that entirely new concepts are needed to encompass the requirements of warfare.

So damaging are the new weapons and so long-range and speedy are the modern delivery systems that the new weapons (epitomized by the intercontinental ballistic missile [ICBM] and anti-ballistic missile [ABM] with its hydrogen-bomb warhead) have almost priced war out of the international political market. In every nuclear state and in many non-nuclear ones as well, military scholars and strategists are seeking a rationale that will make employment of these weapons efficient instruments of national policy. Their failure to break through conceptually as clearly as the scientists have broken through technologically has made war an exceptionally hazardous gamble, and given international conflict since 1945 a frustrating and inconclusive character.

The Space Revolution

In recent years the "nuclear age" has also become the "age of space," as both the U.S.S.R. and the United States have made successful forays into the nearer reaches of outer space. The venture is so vast and its possible ramifications so awesome that the international system and the political consciousness of men have not yet discovered any viable basis of adjustment to the phenomenon. All governments realize that the penetration of space by man is fraught with consequences for the relations of states on earth, but none is yet certain of their significance or even the direction in which the space revolution will lead. There is little doubt, however, that space technology strengthens some of the assumptions of international politics and utterly invalidates others. Coming to terms with space in all its implications is a task statesmen must take on with no delay.

The Human Revolution

Technology has also had its way with man as a biological entity. Medical research and public health techniques have produced revolutionary effects on the human condition. Massive research campaigns to combat the more prevalent diseases hold out the prospect of the "conquest" of tuberculosis, cardiac disease, malaria, cancer, and other widespread causes of death. Application of even rudimentary measures of sanitation and preventive medicine has had spectacular results on epidemic diseases that breed in squalor and filth. Man has come to expect increased longevity and the possibility of relative immunity to the ordinary ills of the body.

Western morality teaches that this is a noble cause; to preserve human life is the highest calling of men of good will. However, the operational consequences of this effort are being questioned: What advantage is it to a society for its people to be spared deaths by malaria only to have them starve to death, or die in mob riots or in a war? Ecologists raise questions about the ultimate danger in upsetting the natural balance of life on the planet; demographers warn of the already frightening "population explosion" and its future political consequences.

Yet the effort to conquer disease and early or unnecessary death goes on. Men are living longer, and greater numbers of human beings inhabit our planet. The challenge of overpopulation may require a massive technological effort by the combined forces of governments everywhere. We shall return to this subject and other aspects of the technological revolution in more detail in Chapter Eleven.

Technology and the State System

Retention of the nation-state, in the classic form, is imperiled by the preponderant influence of the new technology. The devastating effect of a nuclear war would endanger the longevity of the sovereign state and usher in an era of a precarious balance of terror. Despite the potential destruction of nuclear war, nations have evidenced little willingness to modify their traditional unilateral approach to diplomacy and engage in a collective pursuit of security. The international reception accorded the 1968 Nuclear Non-Proliferation Treaty is characteristic of the apprehension and fear displayed by most states regarding the possibilities of world-wide disarmament.

The contemporary nation-state system is plagued by the fact that all major nations which industrialized during this century had a lengthy period of totalitarian dictatorship; some are still governed by a totalitarian dictator. There is a danger that the scientific-technological process has created conditions in less developed states which form a negative environment for bourgeois politics and later evolution to mass democracy. The growth of totalitarianism in the nation-state system has chauvinistic overtones which could be injurious to the furtherance of multilateralism.

THE NEW INSTITUTIONS OF
INTERNATIONAL POLITICS

Institutions usually develop as responses to compelling societal needs within any given historical period. Hence the compulsion to satisfy unprecedented needs, generated largely by the technological revolution, has given rise to new institutions in international politics whose function has been to deal with systemwide or regionally defined issues, some of which had heretofore been considered only by nation-states acting unilaterally. The experience of two world wars, the increasing vulnerability of the national actor (with the resultant inability to guarantee national security), and the recognition that economic and social instability produces political instability, which may in turn threaten general systemic instability, have combined to produce an accelerated growth in multilateralism. The institutions created by national actors which manifest the trend toward multilateralism have at least minimally assumed the role of actors themselves. The bounds of action permitted these multilateral actors, however, are determined by the collectivity of national actors comprising each institution, and these bounds are usually situationally determined—the interests of the members and the issues of the moment determine the extent to which the multilateral institutions can act in the international political system. The multilateral actors which have developed in the contemporary era may be classified as blocs, universal organizations, and limited (or regional) organizations.

The Multilateral Actors

The term *multilateral actors* designates a class of international actors whose structure, composition, and interests transcend national boundaries and whose membership is composed of national actors. There are three major types. *Bloc actors* are groups of states that share certain controlling political and/or security interests, and usually a common orientation in their foreign policy objectives. The *universal actor* comprises within its structure almost all the existing members of the international system, and has the capacity for including all members of the system. This actor takes the form of a general or specialized international organization (a general organization incorporates all aspects of international life, whereas a specialized organization is restricted and incorporates only a few). *Limited (or regional) actors* are associations of states sharing common interests that are more inclusive than the mere political and/or security interests of blocs, yet less comprehensive than the interests of the universal actor. Membership usually follows a geographic rationale. Like the universal actor, limited or regional actors may be either general or specialized in terms of the problems, issues, and interests which are considered.

Bloc Actors

Bloc actors are not completely new phenomena in international politics. By virtue of the technological revolution, ideological competition, and the emergence of a large number of economically and socially underdeveloped and politically incompetent entities as independent states, they have become more common, and on occasion more cohesive. Today, most of the essential national actors in international politics are more or less bound into two blocs by means of alliances. Each bloc is led by a dominant essential national actor (the United States and the Soviet Union respectively) and comprises a number of middle and small powers which act in conjunction with their respective leaders on many issues. These alliances are not as monolithic or cohesive as they were in the immediate postwar period, since their cohesion is directly proportional to the consensus produced by the situation and issue of the moment. In other words, alliances today are much more fluid and, according to some, in a state of decay and increasing irrelevance as middle and small powers grow reluctant to focus their foreign policy within the restricting context of alliance or bloc policy. Intrabloc conflict has become increasingly important in contemporary international politics inasmuch as national actors outside the bloc are often compelled to formulate foreign policy toward factions within each of the blocs.

The identity and integrity of each bloc depends on the ability of the dominant essential actor to preserve its capacity as the leading producer of all those things—materials, money, moral stimulus, and leadership— thought necessary to the vital interest of all other members of the bloc. This is not a simple matter of the bloc leader exercising internal hegemony over its minor associates. Each of the essential actors makes great commitments to the other members, but this protection is reciprocal; even relatively small and weak bloc members contribute in some measure to the over-all viability of the grouping.

The foreign policy tasks of the United States and the Soviet Union have become more complex as the range of their bloc interest has expanded. Each bloc has attempted to extend its span of effective action to whatever area of the world in which it might wish to operate. Interbloc conflict, familiar to the history and logic of the traditionally structured western state system, has in recent years come forcibly into contact with the emerging, newly sensitive, and operationally viable non-western world.

The new nations, most of which came on the international scene after the major blocs had been institutionalized, have reacted by resisting affiliation with either, and by developing a variety of workable definitions of "neutralism." Although admittedly imprecise and laden with emotion, this idea unquestionably reflects both the instinctive leanings of many non-western states and the practical range of possibilities open to them in the pattern of interbloc relations. This range is increased as the fluidity of the major blocs grow and as opposing factions within the major blocs become more manifest.

So consistent has been the reaction of the bulk of emerging nations to the massive confrontation of the two groupings that today it is common to speak of a neutral or "third world." While this is an overstatement (as is the popular term "Afro-Asian bloc"), since the neutral group displays neither the relatively high degree of integration nor the policy consensus that marks a genuine bloc actor, it is undeniable that, on East-West issues, the otherwise incongruous neutral states have frequently been able to form a common front in opposition to the attempt of bloc leaders to universalize their dispute.

On other sorts of issues, however, especially questions subsumed under the energizing but vague issues of "anticolonialism," the neutral bloc demonstrates clear splintering tendencies. Sub-blocs are often formed, frequently on a geographical basis (an African bloc, a South Asian bloc), and these smaller groupings function as independent units in the process of developing a viable systematic consensus on a particular issue.

The Universal Actor

The pressures toward multilateralism that have given rise to the evolution of blocs have also contributed to the creation of the most inclusive institutional form: the universal actor, with both specialized and general competence. Universal actors with general competence, defined as having the capacity to consider all aspects of the international system (political security, economic, social, and humanitarian), have included the League of Nations and the United Nations. Universal actors with specialized competence are usually restricted to consideration of selected economic or social concerns. The essence of the universal actor in international politics is that it acts in the international system in the name of all members of the system, subject to the authority granted by the membership. It is armed at any moment with whatever measure of effective systemwide consensus is available, and performs restrictive, ameliorative, or affirmative functions as the case may dictate.

THE LEAGUE OF NATIONS. The League of Nations, founded as part of the peace settlement after World War I, was the first serious attempt to create a universal actor. Although the total membership ultimately included the majority of national actors then active, significant absences in the membership virtually doomed it to ineffectiveness. The United States never became a member, and never during the League's brief history were all the other great powers members at the same time. After a hectic period of prosperity in the mid-1920's, the League fell apart under the successive shocks of the depression of 1929, the Japanese invasion of Manchuria in 1931, the rise of Hitler, Italy's aggression in Ethiopia, the Spanish civil war, and the Russo-Finnish war of 1939–40. It went out of formal existence in 1946 when its property and personnel were transferred to the United Nations.

The League of Nations may have been premature, because the machinery for responding to these crises was certainly available. Either the members of the League elected not to use the machinery, or were incompetent to do so, indicating that the system had not developed to the point where such a sophisticated tool could be utilized.

THE UNITED NATIONS. World War II stimulated the establishment of the United Nations. The real history of the UN begins with the London Declaration of January, 1941, the Atlantic Charter of 1942, and the Moscow Conference of October, 1943. Churchill, Roosevelt, and Stalin, during the Teheran Conference of 1943, strongly supported the movement. In the Dumbarton Oaks Conference between August and October, 1944, the governments of the United States, Great Britain, the Soviet Union, and China drew up the blueprint for what later became the Charter of the United Nations. At the Yalta Conference in February, 1945, the United States, Britain, and the U.S.S.R. agreed that a conference (the United Nations Conference of International Organization) designed to draft the Charter of the United Nations should meet in San Francisco on April 25, 1945. The San Francisco Conference met between April 25 and June 26, 1945, with 51 states attending. On October 24, 1945, the United Nations was officially established.

The declared purposes of the United Nations are to maintain international peace and security, to develop friendly relations among states based on respect, equal rights, and self-determination of peoples, to cooperate in solving economic, social, cultural, and humanitarian international problems, and to promote respect for fundamental freedoms and human rights.

The United Nations has a number of operational principles set forth in its Charter:

1. The sovereign equality of all its members is assumed, at least theoretically.
2. Members are to fulfill in good faith the obligations they have assumed under the Charter.
3. Members are to settle their disputes by peaceful means and refrain from the threat or use of force.
4. Members are to give every assistance to the United Nations and refrain from giving assistance to belligerent states.
5. The United Nations is not to intervene in matters essentially within the domestic jurisdiction of member states.

The United Nations is different from the League of Nations in a number of respects, the most important being that the essential national actors of the international system are all members. The United Nations has developed a more elaborate organizational structure and hence is better equipped than the League to carry out its functions.

THE SPECIALIZED AGENCIES. The development of the United Nations has stimulated the growth of nonstate actors operating in the form of specialized agencies—multilateral institutions to assist the United Nations in carrying out the economic and social stipulations of the Charter. The specialized agencies have emerged in functional response to the new technical, economic, social, and humanitarian conditions of the international system. The Economic and Social Council (a "principal organ" of the United Nations) is responsible for their coordination.

There are now 14 specialized agencies. Three were established before World War II: the International Telecommunication Union (ITU) and the Universal Postal Union (UPU) were originally founded in the latter part of the nineteenth century, whereas the International Labor Organization (ILO) developed with the League of Nations. The remaining 11 agencies, products of World War II and the United Nations, include: the International Bank for Reconstruction and Development (IBRD), the International Monetary Fund (IMF), the International Finance Corporation (IFC), the International Development Association (IDA), the Food and Agricultural Organization (FAO), the United Nations Education, Scientific, and Cultural Organization (UNESCO), the World Health Organization (WHO), the International Civil Aviation Organization (ICAO), the World Meteorological Organization (WMO), and the Intergovernmental Maritime Consultative Organization (IGMCO). Since the proposed International Trade Organization remains only a charter with insufficient adherents, the actual work of expediting international trade is done through the General Agreement on Tariffs and Trade (GATT), established in 1948.

THE ROLE OF THE UNITED NATIONS IN THE INTERNATIONAL SYSTEM. Since its inception in 1945, the United Nations has modified the international milieu in a number of significant respects.

1. The United Nations provides the international system with channels for cooperation and negotiation between national actors. The mere fact that contending states are members of the same organization often facilitates the prospects of peaceful settlement of their disputes.
2. The United Nations furnishes states with an opportunity to express their interests and policies before a global audience and a multilateral vehicle for securing those interests and policies. Thus it increases each state's appreciation of the views of other states and makes them all more aware of the importance of world opinion.
3. The United Nations provides states with an interest in preventing or avoiding conflict within the system, and a forum within which to make their influence felt. Thus the organization increases the capability of each national actor to influence other national actors. By combining its votes with those of other states, a small state has the opportunity to increase its bargaining power. A great power, by lining up small states in its support, may give the moral sanction of a majority vote to what could otherwise be purely an act of force.
4. The United Nations provides the international system with a forum for the mobilization of world opinion. Small states may use this forum to embarrass the great powers that could easily overpower them, but may not prefer to do so in the full light of international publicity.
5. The United Nations contributes to the development of a feeling of belonging to a world community. This often concretely reflects the evolving integrative trends of world affairs.
6. Finally, the United Nations equips the international system with the means to improve general economic and social conditions. This broadening of the bases of cooperation between states is inevitably a force toward greater order and stability.

Limited or Regional Actors

There are two types of limited or regional actors (regional organizations) operating in the international system—general regional actors and specialized regional actors, of which the latter deal with specific economic and technical matters. The distinction between the two categories is determined by differences in competence or purpose and scope of activities.

General regional actors are more inclusive in membership. Their range of interests tends to be broader and less defined than that of the regional actors for specific technical and economic cooperation. They are associations of national actors with a community of interest. There are only two general regional or limited associations of states which have recently been institutionalized into formal organizations: the Organization of African Unity and the Organization of American States. Such associations as the Commonwealth of Nations and the French Community do not have the structure or competence to be considered formal organizations, but may be more akin to the bloc actor.

Regional actors for specific technical and economic cooperation are more exclusive in membership. Their interests are limited to economic, social, and technical matters. Examples of this type of regional actor are the Organization of Economic Cooperation and Development (OECD), composed of 17 European states, Canada, and the United States, and the Council for Mutual Economic Assistance (CEMA), comprising the Soviet Union and the communist states of Eastern Europe.

Regional actors have appeared in response to the need for units of action larger than the nation-state but short of the full range of universalism. Their usefulness depends in great measure upon whether the problems they face can actually be solved on a regional basis. Because of their smaller and generally more cohesive membership, wherein consensus on common interests is more easily developed, regional actors have proved to be more effective action organizations than has the United Nations.

REFERENCES

Barghoorn, Frederick C., *Soviet Russian Nationalism*. New York: Oxford University Press, Inc., 1956.

Bloomfield, Lincoln, ed., *Outer Space: Prospects for Man and Society* (rev. ed.). New York: American Assembly, Columbia University; Frederick A. Praeger, Inc., 1968.

* Claude, Inis L., *The Changing United Nations*. New York: Random House, Inc., 1966.

Crabb, Cecil V., Jr., *Elephants and the Grass: A Study of Non-Alignment*. New York: Frederick A. Praeger, Inc., 1965.

* Dean, Vera Micheles, *The Nature of the Non-Western World*. New York: Mentor Books, 1957.

* Emerson, Rupert, *From Empire to Nation*. Cambridge, Mass.: Harvard University Press, 1960.

* Indicates paperback edition.

Hayes, Carlton J., *Historical Evolution of Modern Nationalism*. New York: The Macmillan Company, 1931.

* Kedourie, Ellie, *Nationalism* (rev. ed.). New York: Frederick A. Praeger, Inc., 1961.

Kohn, Hans, *American Nationalism*. New York: Crowell-Collier and Macmillan, Inc., 1961.

————, and W. Skolsky, *African Nationalism in the Twentieth Century*. Princeton, N.J.: D. Van Nostrand Co., Inc., 1965.

Mangone, Gerald, *Short History of International Organizations*. New York: McGraw-Hill Book Company, 1954.

* Northrop, F. S. C., *Meeting of East and West: An Inquiry Concerning World Understanding*. New York: The Macmillan Company, 1946.

Pye, Lucien, *Southeast Asia's Political Systems*. Englewood Cliffs, N.J.: Prentice-Hall, Inc., 1967.

* Said, Abdul A., *The African Phenomenon*. Boston: Allyn & Bacon, Inc., 1968.

* Sharabi, H. B., *Nationalism and Revolution in the Arab World*. Princeton, N.J.: D. Van Nostrand Co., Inc., 1965.

* Stoessinger, John G., *The U.N. and the Superpowers*. New York: Random House, Inc., 1966.

Toynbee, Arnold J., *World and the West*. New York: Oxford University Press, Inc., 1953.

Whitaker, Arthur D., and David C. Jordan, *Nationalism in Contemporary Latin America*. New York: The Free Press, 1966.

* Indicates paperback edition.

SEVEN

Conflict and Adjustment

The view of politics as the pursuit of the common good as understood by a given community underlies the conduct of the relationships of states. The controlling idea of the common good energizes the formulation of aims and objectives which, for all their shifting and changing qualities, mark evolving stages in the pursuit of the ideal. Every attempt to organize the international system is in this sense a response to the urge to attain the common good.

In international politics, however, states are concerned with practicalities. Absolute ends are less immediately germane than relative means, so conscious search for the common good is reduced to a secondary place in the international system. The unequal distribution of power and the mystique of sovereignty make the international order relatively unresponsive to ideas of the public well-being on any basis transcending the nation-state.

This emphasis on state centered common good has immediate consequences for the process of dynamics and change in the international system. No community of interests sufficient to control all members exists. Any change in relationships is as likely to be the result of conflict as

143

of peaceful adjustment; in fact, conflict of some form is quantitatively the more usual atmosphere of change and realignment in world politics.

THE NATURE OF CONFLICT

Competition, whether actual, seeming, or potential, is a normal relation between states, as a result of the growth of the nation-state system. International conflict has become an intermittent but inevitable feature of world politics.

The Sources of Conflict

The nation-state system is inherently competitive, since it is based on an ego-centered concept of state destiny—an aspiration to preserve and increase the power and stature of a state relative to those of all of its fellows. When a state insists upon universal recognition of its political independence and freedom of choice and action, it finds itself in a dilemma. It must grant every other state the same freedom and independence, yet cannot really trust anyone but itself. The state must seek salvation by its own efforts and maintain a guarded attitude toward every other state; absolute security is possible only if it controls more power than the remainder of the world combined. When one state makes even slight progress toward this objective, however, all other states feel less secure, and are impelled to seek some corresponding advantage to rectify the balance.

The logic of this paradox derives from the fact that a state's political decision is always an expression of the relative priority that its government assigns to certain objectives and interests. The interdependence of states exercises a pacifying influence in international politics only so far as political conflicts remain limited; the needs of interdependence are virtually powerless to disarm political antagonisms that are already consolidated.

The absolute character of interests and objectives inherent in the national policies of states reinforces the tendency toward interstate conflict. While a limited objective spelled out in concrete terms is capable of achievement, an absolute objective tends to involve the state in continuous struggle. Enhancement of prestige, aggrandizement of power, and promotion of ideology are common examples of absolute objectives which attract opposition and conflict because of their lack of rational content and clearly defined limits. On the other hand, unilateral defense of territorial integrity and of political independence, even though they are themselves concrete, have on occasion been conceived in such absolute terms as to bring on intense conflict.

Types of Conflict

There are two broad categories of international conflict, with the criterion of classification being the principal technique utilized. Nonviolent conflict involves the use of diplomacy, pacific methods of settlement, or forcible procedures short of war as means of prosecuting national purposes in a climate of disagreement. Major reliance by contending parties in violent conflict is placed upon military measures and wars.

VIOLENT CONFLICT IN INTERNATIONAL POLITICS.   War, a condition in which two or more states carry on a conflict by armed force, is the most common form of violent international conflict. War is, of course, a legal status as well as a means of executing policy, but its policy relevance is much greater.

Since the sixteenth century the devastation of war has grown as weapons increased in effectiveness and new theories of warfare were developed. Today entire populations are personally involved and identified with military operations as combatants, targets, or producers. The objectives of war are now usually formulated in terms of one nation gaining an absolute triumph over another. The once limited conduct of warfare has become universal in scale, and great powers, forces, and ideas are hopelessly caught up in it.

Wars do not usually arise out of disputes concerning the respective rights of the belligerents, but spring instead from conflicts of interest. State motives in war are entirely political, even though a legal discussion of "rights" and "justice" often furnishes the pretext for violence. Many causes of war have been isolated by scholars, but rather than enumerate them here we will simply generalize that, since war is rooted in the international system, any specific war is more a product of the general dynamic of that system than it is of the unique circumstances out of which the conflict has grown.

NONVIOLENT CONFLICT IN INTERNATIONAL POLITICS.   In essence, the difference between nonviolent and violent conflict is of degree rather than kind. Nonviolent conflict has the same rationale as war, with the single exception that the states involved conclude that cost and risk factors as related to the worth of the disputed objective demand that the struggle be prosecuted at a lower level of intensity and commitment. Otherwise both the purpose and conduct of the conflict is governed by the same principles of strategy and tactics that control the most violent warfare.

As a rule, states accept nonviolent conflict as routine but look on violent conflict as exceptional. The over-all costs of nonviolent conflict are always less than those of a war, at least within similar time spans. By the same token, the penalty for defeat in a nonviolent struggle is almost always less than that demanded by a military victor.

VIOLENT AND NONVIOLENT CONFLICT: PROBLEM OF DISTINCTION. Before the advent of twentieth-century military technology, the distinction between violent and nonviolent forms of conflict was relatively clear and unambiguous. A state of war was recognizable militarily, politically, and legally. The devastating nature of modern military technology is blurring the traditional contrast between the two types of conflict, which had formerly been marked by qualitative and quantitative distinctions of a legal and military character. In part, this reflects a response to what has been termed the "technical surprise" of modern weaponry (initially experienced in World War I), in which the means of warfare have far outdistanced rationally conceived ends. Military means, once employed, tend to force a reappraisal of ends so that the objectives of conflict will appear justifiable and proportional to the physical and emotional commitment of the belligerents.

This traditional view of the conflict ends-means relationship has been transcended through the threat of escalation into mutually destructive nuclear war. Therefore, the extremes of conflict expression have been discarded from the spectrum of usable means and more ambiguous and less overtly provocative forms have taken their place. In this sense, unconventional warfare and limited warfare represent a return to the familiar Clausewitz doctrine that war represents a continuation of diplomacy by other means. But although the post-World War II experience with conflicts of this order would seem to validate such a conclusion, it is equally clear that conflict and war have taken on special meanings unknown to their eighteenth or nineteenth century predecessors.

The difference lies in part in the more modest nature of political objectives (as distinct from goals) for which states are apparently willing to commit military forces, and the diminished relative magnitude of the forces actually employed in support of these objectives. Each of these affects and is affected by the other. Thus violent conflict is limited (both as to means and ends) in a way unknown even to the eighteenth century. Such an assertion does not imply that this condition of conflict could not be changed and escalated through miscalculation, desperation, or reckless aggression. However, the post-World War II experience of violent conflict, actual and potential, has resulted in an awareness of the inescapable dangers of nuclear conflict, with a mutual if tacit willingness to control the means and ends (objectives) of military and political policy within a framework of tolerance so that international politics can be pursued in a modified, though relatively traditional, manner.

The return to modified traditional forms of violent conflict is largely dependent upon the continuing credibility of the threat of nuclear destruction. Should this threat subside markedly, or should peoples and decision-makers become conditioned to its presence and immune to its demands, it is possible that the level of permissible conflict might be raised, thus closing the gap between limited warfare as a condition and nuclear warfare as a possibility in the spectrum of violent conflict.

Objectives of Conflict

We can distinguish analytically between two major categories of conflict objectives. The first, *balancing-objective* conflict, is endemic to a relatively fluid international situation characterized by wide dispersal of power and the operations of a multiple balance system. Under such circumstances, the purpose motivating the participants in an interstate conflict is primarily restoration of a disturbed equilibrium. The range of choice open to all parties is narrow, and their efforts tend to be concentrated upon a single object of controversy substantially independent of their relations in other policy areas. *Hegemonic-objective* conflict, on the other hand, has a goal of domination rather than balance. The disputing parties are less concerned with specific objectives than with the establishment of a clear margin of superiority over the other in a very broad range of issues. In other words, balancing-objective conflict concerns itself primarily with a particular set of relationships in the real world, while the controversy over details in hegemonic-objective conflict is no more than a pallid reflection of much deeper maladjustments in the political approach of the involved states.

Balancing-objective conflicts assume many forms, since they stem from the essential requirements of the international system for simultaneous dynamism and equilibrium. Among the broadest categories are the clash of expansionist politics, the revisionist-status quo confrontation, disputes between aroused nationalisms, conflicts growing out of history, and a variety of racial, religious, social, and cultural involvements. Hegemonic-objective conflict has only one real form, although it is almost infinite in its manifestations.

Balancing-Objective Conflict

EXPANSIONIST POLICIES.   The form of conflict that arises from a collision between two or more states following policies of expansion or revision is the most dynamic and potentially dangerous. Such states are usually driven by such strong motivations as prestige, acquisition of raw materials, new markets, cheap labor, military bases, or various internal pressures. When a revisionist policy encounters resistance, the government will usually increase its own pressure; when two such states conflict, the dispute is marked by rapid increase in the power each commits to its objective and rapid development of crises. Furthermore, because of the internal and international pressure, revisionist states find it difficult to reverse policies short of their ultimate objective.

Imperialism and the colonial methods in which it is expressed are a common historical example of conflict of expanding policies. The traditional methods of expansion underwent steady decline beginning with the first half of the twentieth century; half a century later the great colonial empires were dissolving. But new types of expansionism are developing in the forms of economic dependencies and satellite states. Economic dependencies are nominally independent states whose major economic activities are heavily under the control or influence of a great power, while satellite states are nominally independent states whose political life and foreign policies are in varying degrees under the control or direct influence of a more powerful state. Conflicts growing from these relationships are prone to be both intense and prolonged.

REVISIONISM VERSUS STATUS QUO. A frequently recurring form of conflict arises from a situation in which a policy of expansion collides with the interests of a passive, status quo state. The distinction between this type of conflict and the first is important. In expansionism, the motives of the contending states, both seeking expansion in their span of control, are basically identical. In the type we discuss here, the objectives of the contending states are complementary. The revisionist state seeks to take away from the passive state a particular object of advantage. The latter, seeking nothing, tries to retain what it already has.

The revisionist state always takes the initiative in this form of conflict. It seeks through any appropriate means to detach the passive state from its control. The status quo state confines its strategic actions to defensive measures, countering each affirmative step of the revisionist state. On occasion, however, it may assume a tactical initiative.

CONFLICT OF NATIONALISM. Many of the areas of tension in contemporary international politics are characterized by a battle of embittered or exaggerated nationalist attitudes. An aroused nationalistic group becomes heedless of the regularities of international politics and uninformed about the subtler details of the policy of either its own government or the government of its enemy. When mass emotions are aroused in a particular state, great pressures are brought upon the government to take forceful measures against the offender. The other state is impelled to react in a similar manner, and a web of conflict is woven from which both states find it difficult to extricate themselves.

Another example of nationalist conflict is furnished by colonial revolutions and their aftermath. No subject people can become free of alien control without first developing a keen sense of nationalistic particularism and making the achievement of independence a primary objective. When independence is gained, the hatreds that evolved through the struggle for self-determination continue and form a significant part of the policy of the new state toward the former colonial masters.

Still another source out of which nationalist conflict grows is the clash of expanding great power nationalisms. When a people with a "universalist" outlook live in a state having great power resources, a powerful dynamic element is injected into international politics. When two such states exist simultaneously, a serious and long-lasting conflict develops. This was the case of French and British nationalism in the Napoleonic era; the rival nationalisms today are the Russian and the American.

CONFLICT OF HISTORICAL EXPERIENCE. The foreign policies of many states are characterized by nationalist animosities nourished by a long history. Despite the origins of these hatreds often being veiled in obscurity, they have become to the concerned people a familiar and expected part of the way their government formulates its foreign policies. While these animosities lie dormant for long periods, they often flare up at critical moments. Familiar examples of such historical animosities are the Russo-German, the Franco-German, and the Greco-Turkish nationalist hatreds. Some of these, of course, slowly recede in the face of changed circumstances.

CONFLICT OF RACIAL, RELIGIOUS, SOCIAL, AND CULTURAL ISSUES. In these forms of conflict the specific issues themselves are often trivial, but tend to be symbolic of deeper ideological differences. Compromise is usually difficult, since in the minds of the people it would involve making concessions upon points of fundamental moral significance. Examples of such conflicts are the racial issue in the Union of South Africa and the religious split between Muslims and Hindus in India and Pakistan.

Hegemonic-Objective Conflict

This form of conflict has become synonymous with the power struggle between the United States and the Soviet Union in the era of the cold war. A single broad purpose illuminates an entire family of conflict issue whose crisis points lie along what has been called "the international shatter zone," where the main opposing forces are in direct contact. In its military aspect it takes the form of a tireless race for allies, raw mate-rials, bases, and armaments; in political terms it requires a constant search for "victory"; in psychic terms it calls for the pursuit of absolute hegemony over the adversary.

At present, on the periphery of the eastern and western camps, great power competition multiplies the zones of possible friction. Calculated pressures are heightened or relaxed according to circumstances, and are aimed less at winning a premature decision than at testing resistance and asserting the prestige and image of either party.

On the ideological plane, hegemonic-objective struggle gives rise to an enterprise of subversion which finds expression in a crusade by zealots. The mobilization of minds and psychological warfare support the politico-military effort. This form of tension leads to the centralization of governmental power in both major states and thrives on what becomes a conventionally high level of mass emotional stress. It produces general-ized anxiety, is prolific of myths, and generates self-justifying theorems that identify national objectives with the imperatives of an absolute ideology. The themes of provocation and inequality, developed with a rhythm of increasing "power," energize continued action and reaction in a climate of crisis.

Hegemonic-objective conflict requires long-term planning and must reckon with time. Given the present balance of forces, the more sensitive both sides are to the risk of total war, the greater the corresponding ten-dency for American-Soviet competition to establish itself as a way of life and to develop fixed patterns and practices.

The Tactics of Conflict

Certain elements of the intellectual process involved in conducting international conflict can usefully be reviewed here. At bottom, there are three sorts of decisions required of a policy-maker in the course of a struggle with another state: (1) when to begin the active phase of the conflict; (2) how to conduct his own part of the dispute; and (3) when to break off the controversy and resume normal relations.

The decision concerning the moment of beginning the active struggle is usually made by the state with the greater involvement of interest or the greater pressure for action. Once the crucial overt act has been per-formed, a certain power of decision remains with the second state, since it is not obliged to respond unless it wishes to. If the original provocation was above the threshold of tolerability, some conflict-oriented response is almost automatic. Lesser initiatives may often be ignored unless esca-lated or repeated. This general principle is more applicable to nonviolent moves than to military attack, since modern nationalistic states react without hesitation to direct military onslaught.

After being launched on open conflict, each side has further tactical decisions, depending on whether its approach is basically balancing or hegemonic. If initial considerations of intensity become relevant, how deeply will either side commit itself to this particular quarrel? Next, various operational decisions must be made. Will the state attempt to work changes in the general situational environment, or will its effort be expanded in attempting to preserve the status quo? Will neutralizing policies—if they are adopted—be in the form of direct head-to-head counters to initiatives from the other state, or will they be indirect counteroffensives? Will a defensive strategy remain defensive throughout the struggle, or will success lead to a magnification of objectives and acceptance of an unforeshadowed offensive program? Many such questions relate directly to how the state chooses to formulate policy and doctrine for the conflict.

Ending a conflict is frequently more difficult than beginning one. In principle, a state may escape from a dispute on any of four grounds: (1) achievement of its objective; (2) negotiation of an acceptable compromise that gives it adequate if incomplete satisfaction in return for its effort and involvement; (3) abandonment of the conflict as inevitably inconclusive; or (4) complete defeat. The first and fourth reasons are self-evident if the objective is explicit and the cost/risk factors kept well in mind. An acceptable compromise is often the most useful avenue of escape, but it is feasible only if both sides are fully aware of their respective notions of acceptability and their minimum requirements coincide. An inconclusive breakoff, usually occurring only if both sides decide that their objectives are beyond reach at a bearable cost and risk, is seldom made explicit; a broken-off conflict most often lapses quietly without fanfare or formal registry.

THE ADJUSTMENT OF CONFLICT

The existence of conflict in the international system requires that states develop techniques for the adjustment and settlement of their disputes. The choice of a particular method and its ultimate success or failure depends upon the purpose, skill, and interests of the contending parties.

Not every conflict or disagreement between states needs to be formally adjusted or settled. Many disputes settle themselves, particularly if they are left alone. However, when popular passions become increasingly inflamed, especially when the object of the conflict is a matter of great importance to the disputing states, a formal adjustment may become the only viable alternative to violence. Acceptable solutions to the more pressing and important disputes are usually the most difficult to find, because of the danger that both sides may have hopelessly involved their prestige. Unless both sides are able to preserve their self-respect, the substantive core of the problem may be beyond reach.

The methods developed over the centuries for the adjustment and settlement of international conflict may be classified into three general categories: methods of pacific settlement, coercive procedures short of war, and forcible procedures through war. Each of these has its strengths and weaknesses.

Pacific Settlement

The methods of pacific settlement make available a variety of peaceful substitutes for violence. In general terms they may be classified as diplomatic-political or judicial.

DIPLOMATIC AND POLITICAL METHODS. Diplomatic and political methods of adjusting conflict do not result in final judgments which the disputing states are obligated to accept, hence they are described as nondecisional or nonbinding. Settlement rests on mutual agreement, usually based on substantive compromise. Political disputes involving value judgments of environmental factors are particularly susceptible to diplomatic procedures.

Diplomatic methods of settlement can be attempted through direct negotiations, good offices, mediation, inquiry, and conciliation.

Direct negotiation may take the form of bilateral or multilateral diplomacy. Such negotiations may be conducted between heads of state (as in the presently common personal or summit diplomacy), directly through ambassadors and other accredited diplomats of the concerned parties, or through an international conference.

Good offices is the name given to a semidiplomatic contact through the intervention of a third party (a state, an international organization, or a prominent individual). It is frequently resorted to when the disputing parties have become deadlocked in their diplomatic negotiations. A third state offers its services as a go-between to expedite contacts between the disputants. Although negotiations proceed through the third party, this party is not empowered to suggest a solution, nor does it participate directly in the negotiations. Good offices, once accepted, usually lead to mediation. A famous example of good offices was the role played by President Theodore Roosevelt at the conclusion of the Russo-Japanese war in 1905.

Mediation is a procedure by which, in addition to good offices, a third party participates actively in the negotiations. It tries to reconcile the opposite claims and to appease mutual resentments developed by the contending parties. The mediator may not impose its own solutions on the dispute, but is expected to take a strong initiative in proposing formulas. The role of Dr. Ralph Bunche as United Nations mediator during the Arab-Israeli war in 1948 is a famous modern instance of the use of this technique.

Inquiry designates the settlement of a dispute through establishment of a commission of inquiry. Such a group, consisting of an equal number of members from each of the disputing parties plus one or more from a third state or states, acts to facilitate solution of the conflict. Article 33 of the Charter of the United Nations authorized the organization to create such a commission when appropriate.

The commission of inquiry does no more than elicit the facts of a dispute by means of impartial investigation. The theory of inquiry is based upon two assumptions. First, a basic obstacle to amicable settlement is the difficulty of establishing a statement of facts to which both parties agree. Second, this difficulty perpetuates itself by allowing passions to be aroused which obstruct agreement between the parties on points of principle.

An example of this form of settlement was the Commission of Inquiry which convened in Paris in 1905 to deal with the Anglo-Russian dispute over the action of a Russian fleet firing on English fishermen in the North Sea. The Commission's report of the facts led to speedy settlement of the controversy.

Conciliation is a procedure that combines inquiry and mediation. An individual or a commission (structured much like a commission of inquiry) may perform the functions of conciliation. Its functions thus extend to both determination of facts and presentation of formal recommendations for settlement.

The procedure of conciliation becomes appropriate because inquiry itself makes only a minimal contribution to the resolution of many conflicts. Conciliation multiplies the pacifying effects of both mediation and inquiry in the settlement of troublesome disputes. It is the most formalized of the diplomatic and political methods of settling international conflicts. It is peculiarly useful for serious political disputes, since its flexibility makes it more adaptable to varying circumstances than more rigid judicial or legislative procedures. Its object is always peace by compromise, not justice by law. The United Nations has used several conciliation commissions since 1945; perhaps the most famous is that for Palestine that oversees the truce arranged by Dr. Bunche.

It must be pointed out that neither inquiry nor conciliation provides a means of settling conflict unless the solution worked out is acceptable to the disputing parties. Usually it will command the assent of the contending parties only when it offers them terms sufficiently attractive to persuade all involved that they have gained enough in rewards to justify breaking off the struggle.

JUDICIAL METHODS. Judicial methods of settlement are an attempt to regularize the terms and procedures which form the basis of the disposal of disputes. The two judicial procedures are arbitration and adjudication. Solutions are reached on the basis of law—and in some cases equity— but they explicitly exclude political compromise, since only legal disputes can be judicially resolved. The awards of arbitration and the decisions of an international court are binding on the disputing parties, and hence these procedures are described as decisional or binding.

Arbitration is accomplished either by an ad hoc tribunal or by the Permanent Court of Arbitration at The Hague. Adjudication today is the exclusive province of the International Court of Justice, an organ of the United Nations system. With few relatively unimportant exceptions, submission of a dispute to either judicial procedure is a voluntary act of the states involved.

Judicial methods of settling disputes have certain advantages over any diplomatic method. Probably most important is that the conflict is taken almost entirely out of the hands of the disputing parties, thus avoiding prestige problems which might impede a settlement. The conflict is disposed of by reference to standards common to both parties and external to the dispute. Judicial settlement may depoliticize a dispute more completely than diplomatic methods of settlement, since it implies voluntary renunciation by the parties of their individual powers of decision, and submission to the impersonal criteria of law.

On the other hand, judicial settlement of disputes presents certain disadvantages. Relatively few of the important issues of international politics can be usefully cast in terms of a controversy that can be settled in a court of law. The more crucial the conflict is to the parties, the greater the likelihood that neither will be anxious for a settlement by any outside agency.

Arbitration may be defined as the settlement of international disputes through judges chosen by the parties. The first Hague Conference in 1899 established the Permanent Court of Arbitration. Since then this court has become the principal instrument of international arbitration. The Permanent Court consists of a panel of judges, four appointed for six-year terms by each member state.

Disputing parties wishing to use the Permanent Court of Arbitration must first negotiate an instrument called the *compromis d'arbitrage*. In this agreement, the procedures the tribunal will follow and the rules of law to be applied are stipulated. Each party then selects two judges from the panel, only one of whom can be its own national. These four judges choose a fifth member, called the "umpire." In their deliberations, the arbitrators can utilize only the rules of law which the contending states have agreed on in the *compromis*.

Adjudication has come to designate the settlement of an international dispute by the International Court of Justice of the United Nations. The court, established in 1945 as a successor to the Permanent Court of International Justice set up by the League of Nations, is also head-quartered at The Hague. It consists of 15 judges elected concurrently by the Security Council and the General Assembly of the United Nations for a term of nine years. Decisions of the court can be based on either law or the principle of *ex aequo et bono* (equity and justice).

All members of the United Nations are automatically parties to the Statute of the ICJ. In practice, however, states are not compelled to submit their disputes to the court, particularly since each state may qualify its adherence to the Court's Statute. A state not belonging to the United Nations may adhere to the court on conditions to be determined by the General Assembly on recommendations of the Security Council.

States which are parties to the Court's Statute may at any time declare that they recognize as compulsory, ipso facto and without special agreement, in relation to any state accepting the same obligation, the jurisdiction of the court in all legal disputes concerning: (1) interpretations of a treaty; (2) any question of international law; (3) the existence of any fact, which, if established, would constitute a breach of international obligation; and (4) the nature or extent of the reparation to be made for breach of an international obligation. States which thus choose to accept this compulsory jurisdiction may do so either unconditionally, on a basis of reciprocity, or for only a certain time.

The functions of arbitration and adjudication as methods of settling international conflict are narrow. Obstacles to the broadening of these functions spring directly from the nature of the state system and the eminently political character of the relations it engenders. Settlement of disputes between states is never comparable to settlement of disputes between individual persons.

For individuals, judicial settlement is the impersonal application of law, an expression of inculcated discipline embracing virtually the whole of social relations. This predisposes individuals to limit their claims to what is legally defensible and to formulate them in legal terms. The international system incorporates neither a hierarchic order embracing the totality of state interests and values, nor a single central power system that can control the play of competing forces. Law is therefore only peripheral to the real disputes of states, and can have no more than a random effect on their settlement.

Coercive Procedures Short of War

States turn to coercive but nonviolent methods of settling a dispute if pacific procedures fail to produce satisfaction. Most of these devices, although expressed in the mechanics of the diplomatic process, have their ultimate coercive effect in the psychological realm.

Among the leading nonviolent coercive techniques we may mention recall of diplomats, expulsion of diplomats of the other state, denial of recognition, rupture of diplomatic relations, and suspension of treaty obligations. Somewhat more obviously "unfriendly" (in the legal sense) is the class of actions involving "force short of war": blockade, boycott, embargo, reprisal, and retorsion (a technically complex form of retaliation).

Forcible Procedures: The Role of War

The *ultima ratio* of international politics, the final and unanswerable device for producing solutions to conflict, has always been the organized application of violence in the form of war. A nonregulatory social structure like the international system can have no final arbiter in a clash of wills except violence. Maturation of the international political process has resulted in a well-defined place for the institution of war. Statesmen have assumed a generic relationship between the dynamics of force and political antagonisms of states, and the interdependence of war and politics implied the rationality of force. Force was creative because it could be employed to resolve outstanding political issues between states. The scope and function of wars lent credence to the assumption of a complementarity of force and politics.

War is a distinct way of prosecuting conflict, not a special category of conflict. The disagreement between states that gives rise to armed combat lies in the policies or nationalist identifications of the adversaries, and the decision to fight is expediential. The principles of tactics that govern other types of conflict apply to war as well; for example, it is especially important to know when to initiate war, how to fight it, and when to stop.

Wars also partake of the general characteristics of conflict, in that they may be either balancing-objective or hegemonic-objective. In other words, a war may either be fought by tacit agreement within the terms of reference and restraint laid down by the international system and thus be related to the controlling equilibrium, or it may be potentially destructive of the system by threatening to alter relationships drastically, dysfunctionally, and permanently. The balancing-objective form of war is known today as "limited" war, while the hegemonic-objective type is the familiar "total" war.

Limited war—the form of war made classic by centuries of successful prosecution—is conceptually a method within the family of familiar policy techniques, a single enterprise aimed at achieving a single objective. The amount of violence employed is calculated to inflict no more damage than is necessary to gain "victory" in the form of the postulated goal. The end of such a war is theoretically marked by reestablishment of normal relations between the former enemies after political readjustments made necessary by the war have been consummated.

Such wars are supposed to culminate in a negotiated peace. Both sides, having fought their campaigns with partial commitments of power, thus retain bargaining capability when the struggle ends. The terms of peace reflect the continuing power relationship between them, as modified by the verdict of the battlefield.

THE RELATIONSHIP OF FORCE AND POLITICAL CONFLICT RESOLUTION

Radical changes in the quality of force and the nature of conflict explain the phenomenon of political antagonists eluding the dictates of war. Nationalism and technology—the two forces that have had a devastating effect on so much of international politics—have transformed the sophisticated notion of war as a regulating and adjusting device into a much simpler yet much more deadly form of action. While it was previously defined as the establishment of a balance, nationalism redefined war as the attainment of hegemony. Technology made it possible for wars to become struggles of annihilation between peoples rather than the resolution of single issue disputes between states.

The Changing Nature of Force

Discrimination in the use of force in total war has become extremely difficult. Greater military efficiency may be achieved by the new weapons of wholesale slaughter, so real victory must be total. The only conceivable forms of defeat are either utter destruction or abject submission in order to avoid such pulverization. No lesser margin of superiority will induce a people to surrender to a loathed enemy as long as they possess the capacity to fight on.

In logic, therefore, the only possible solutions of total war are absolute verdicts of dominance and submission. In the traditional course of international politics, questions demanding absolute answers have been relatively uncommon and dangerous, in that the consequences of a hegemonic decision are unpredictable. The so-called military dilemma of the contemporary era flows from the difficulty facing statesmen in developing a clear political (dispute settling or objective gaining) role for modern warfare.

It is incorrect to argue that total war cannot render a political decision; decisions are possible even in a thermonuclear war. But total war cannot provide the broad spectrum of possible outcomes that simpler warfare made available. It is inconceivable, for example, that anything resembling the traditional form of negotiated peace could emerge from a war initiated by a massive nuclear exchange. Solutions by total war are inevitably extreme; only two political outcomes are possible from an all-out struggle between nuclear powers. Such a war will either run its full course and result in the collapse, capitulation, or obliteration of one belligerent and a claim of victory for the other, or it will be abandoned by both as inconclusive and mutually devastating. An expensive and dangerous method that can produce only absolute answers or none at all is of only limited political usefulness. War is in no sense a widely applicable method of resolving conflict today.

The Changing Nature of Conflict

The nature of post-1945 political conflict has been analyzed on several levels. Some political theorists argue that the transition from the rational norms of the Enlightenment to the ideological forms of Communism, Fascism, or totalitarianism have torn the international system into irreconcilable camps. Divergences among these camps cannot be smoothed over by any conventional modes of statecraft, including force. Others have said, in a related vein, that the "anomic" condition of twentieth-century man has rendered him vulnerable to irreconcilable "isms." Twentieth-century political man is a true believer who expresses himself with selfish and irrational abandon on the international stage.

Advocates of such theses of present international political conflict fail to come to grips with the problem of linkages between their alleged causal factors, ideologies, and true believers, and the real international actors, governments. It is governments—not "isms" or true believers—that are the immediate sources of international political conflicts.

A more cogent analysis of the nature of present international conflict can be made by noting the interdependence of domestic and international policies of many governments. It is apparent that many governments now predicate their internal legitimacy—the maintenance of which is the primary goal of all governments—on the performance of external policies. The implication of this observation for the relationship of force to political conflict resolution in the present international system is evident. Since many governments justify their existence by reference to foreign policy commitments, these policies must be maintained despite forceful reversals. For a government to renounce its fundamental policies after military defeat would be to undermine its own internal legitimacy at the time of its gravest weakness. Hence, for many states, foreign policy is the dogmatic pursuit of fixed goals.

International antagonisms generated by these rigid and often irreconcilable foreign policies are not susceptible to political accommodation. Since only total defeat of a government's antagonist can allow it to terminate many frozen lines of policy, international conflicts—except in cases of total defeat of the enemy—remain impervious to the dynamics of force. This phenomenon is illustrated by the political conflicts outstanding between the Arab states and Israel, North and South Korea, and North and South Vietnam.

It is due primarily to the interdependence of domestic legitimacy and international commitments that many international political issues are not concluded today. Present political issues outstanding in the Middle East, Far East, and Southeast Asia defy the assumptions of traditional and limited war theorists who implied that force was a creative instrument for political conflict resolution. They also defy the assumptions of those who believed that, with the advent of the atomic bomb, the "unthinkable" nature of force would abolish wars in the modern world.

Due to the imperatives of internal legitimacy, many governments are engaged in conflicts which will terminate only with annihilation of the governments which oppose them. It is unfortunate but understandable that the norms of political conflict of one antagonist become socialized dialectically by other antagonists, and that these norms soon come to be accepted by many governments in the international system.

REFERENCES

* Aron, Raymond, *The Great Debate: Theories of Western Strategy.* Garden City, N.Y.: Doubleday & Company, Inc., 1965.

* Indicates paperback edition.

Bloomfield, Lincoln P., *Evolution or Revolution: The United Nations and the Problem of Peaceful Territorial Change.* Cambridge, Mass.: Harvard University Press, 1957.

* Boulding, Kenneth, *Conflict and Defense: A General Theory.* New York: Harper & Row, Publishers, 1962.

Coats, J. Wendell, *Armed Force as Power.* New York: Exposition Press, 1967.

Dunn, Frederick S., *War and the Minds of Men.* New York: The Macmillan Company, 1944.

* Etzioni, Amitai, *Winning Without War.* Garden City, N.Y.: Doubleday & Company, Inc., 1964.

* Griffith, William E., *Sino-Soviet Rift.* Cambridge, Mass.: The M.I.T. Press, 1964.

* ———, *Sino-Soviet Relations, 1964-1965.* Cambridge, Mass.: The M.I.T. Press, 1967.

* Hoffmann, Stanley, *The State of War: Essays on the Theory and Practice of International Politics.* New York: Frederick A. Praeger, Inc., 1965.

Langer, William L., *Diplomacy of Imperialism.* New York: Alfred A. Knopf, Inc., 1935.

Millis, Walter, *An End to Arms.* New York: Atheneum, 1965.

Salter, Leonard M., *Relations of International Conflict.* New York: Vintage Press, 1967.

* Schelling, Thomas C., *Strategy of Conflict.* Cambridge, Mass.: Harvard University Press, 1960.

* Simmel, George, *Conflict and the Web of Group Affiliations.* New York: The Free Press, 1955.

* Waltz, Kenneth N., *Man, the State and War.* New York: Columbia University Press, 1959.

* Indicates paperback edition.

EIGHT

Limitations
on State Action

In spite of the deceptively simple logic of sovereignty that derives complete freedom of state choice from the postulate of absolute power, the international system could not survive unless states accepted and acted upon a well-understood set of restraints. Limitations on state action, acknowledged by all governments as the price they pay for the continued viability of the international system, are only partially formulated. They rest to a large extent upon tacit agreement and the force of practice. To ignore these considerations, or to deduce a mechanistic doctrine of blind power as the energizing factor in international politics, is to condemn oneself to system-building in a vacuum. The limitations on the freedom of the state to act in international politics are not only as intrinsically important as that freedom itself, but also serve to give it form and direction.

In this chapter we shall examine three families of restraints that in some measure inhibit the choices that states make. Initially we shall consider the extent to which states are restrained by the teachings of morality. We shall next examine the role of international law in narrowing human choice in foreign policy to those actions that are legally sanctioned.

Finally, we shall briefly review the effect of the statesman's code of prudence in international politics. Although this three category list is by no means exhaustive, each restraint acts in its own fashion to reduce the effective range of state action beyond the implications of pure theory.

MORALITY AS A LIMITATION: WHAT IS A MORAL CONSENSUS?

The state is composed of human beings, all of whom accept and act upon a set of moral principles. All human action may be judged with varying degrees of accuracy and relevance in moral terms. These two factors—the moral base of government action in the international order, and the application of norms of morality to the behavior of states—constitute the basic elements of any discussion of morality as a limitation on international political action.

The Moral Problem in International Politics

Central to this perplexing issue is the intrinsic morality of the state and the relative claims of public purpose and private morality on the consciences of individuals. The foreign policy of any national state has no necessary nexus with any absolute or universal moral code. Whether the state is viewed as an amoral agent destined to function in an order beyond and irrelevant to moral codes, or as the architect of moral principles that are higher and more binding on individuals than private ethics, the result is the same. Individuals—particularly those subscribing to the Judeo-Christian code—are generally held to be disqualified from passing meaningful moral judgments on state action.

As long as the political sphere of human action does not impinge on private morality, such a duality raises few problems other than abstract ones. The moral issue becomes pertinent, however, when commands of the state to the individual represent a direct contradiction of what he has been taught to regard as right and good. The classic instance is the taking of human life. The Ten Commandments stipulate that "Thou shalt not kill," but killing enemies of the state on command of one's government is an act of highest patriotism.

Modern states have not felt seriously inhibited by this contradiction. Nationalist codes either emphasize that ordinary moral scruples do not apply to public purposes, or else assert that killing, stealing, or lying on behalf of the state are in themselves moral acts. Somewhat more sophisticated versions of these arguments suggest that moral principles might apply in ordinary circumstances, but the demonic nature of the enemy and the special sacredness of the national mission are ample reasons for individuals to suppress any personal qualms.

Theologians, philosophers, and psychologists of all schools of thought and methods of analysis have grappled with the problem of reconciling the requirements of foreign policy with the absolutes of personal morality, or at least reducing the clash between them to a bearable level. The public may be told that, since man is inherently sinful, he should not worry about committing what he might consider immoral acts for public reasons; a sufficiently worthy end justifies any expedient means. Morality and conscience are no more than semisuppressed guilt feelings, runs another argument, and "mental health" is attained by cheerful support of political leadership and performance of whatever tasks are assigned to the citizen.

The ingenuity of these arguments has not relieved many adherents of western cultural values from the dilemma in which they feel placed. Traditional morality contradicts the pretensions of the state at many points, and no completely satisfying rationale of reconciliation can be found. The enormity of the world crisis and the cataclysmic strategies adopted by many states have sharpened this acute sense of moral crisis.

The Rupture of the Moral Consensus

The problem of moral consensus, always inherent in international politics, has been exaggerated by the development trends of the state system in the past two centuries. Modern international politics was born in Europe in the aftermath of the universal moral code of the Middle Ages. The monarchs who played the game in its early stages operated within a clear moral consensus and a full set of principles of action. Czar Alexander's "Holy Alliance" of 1815, which proposed joint action by the rulers of Europe in a spirit of Christian brotherhood, was startlingly inappropriate for its age. In another sense, it was no more than a platitudinous advocation of the implicit assumptions of international politics a century earlier.

The moral consensus that served to restrain international politics in the seventeenth and eighteenth centuries no longer exists, due to two related historic forces—nationalism and universal ideology. Modern nationalism, born in the era of the French Revolution, replaced "mankind" or "Christendom" as the supreme moral unit with the concept of the "nation." The national group was invested with the special moral superiority and sacred mission that had formerly been widely dispersed. From this atomization of a once universal moral code came an aggregation of differing political moralities, all phrased in absolute terms but each incorporating a distinct national point of view on questions of good and evil. Contemporary universal ideologies stem from a particular world view unique to each, and develop much more sweeping interpretations of human action than do nationalist exegeses, but their effect is even more divisive. While nationalism proceeds from a moral base, but has a generous admixture of crass and concrete calculation, modern ideologies fit all human experience within a moralistic framework and deduce action programs from rigid postulates about the moral nature of man.

Therefore, two additional sets of moral codes currently vie with traditional western morality for the allegiance of individuals. Nationalist morality and ideological morality often join forces—as in the case of communist states—but as often conflict. Judeo-Christian principles with clear universalist implications are commonly modified, stretched, or even perverted to serve one of the newer moralities. The political consequences of this moral pluralism are obvious.

No state admits publicly that its policy has any but a moral base. Political conflict between mature states has an inescapable, if futile, moral dimension, as both sets of participants insist that their goals are the achievement of the highest good. However, only rarely does a moral argument advanced by one side receive even a hearing, let alone acceptance, by the other. The international order today is suffering not from too few moral referents, but from too many.

Morality and Foreign Policy

The ubiquity of moral discourse has an immediate effect on the choices made by states. Decision-making goes on in a social context, a large portion of which flows from the moral orientation of the society. The objectives of policy are derived from social values with a self-evident moral basis. A moral code generates a world-view, a way of observing, classifying, and giving meaning to phenomena in the real world. Thus what we have called situational analysis is obviously limited by the prevailing moral predispositions of the society. The tactics of policy are clearly affected by social considerations of what public actions are right (permissible) and wrong (prohibited). At every turn, internal morality guides and inhibits the policy-maker.

If policy is developed by men who take note of the consensus, and if it is commensurate with public interpretations of absolute good, its implementation is greatly strengthened. Any contradiction of mass moral expectations raises the prospect of internal divisions or reduced public vigor and zeal. Such matters as nuclear testing, espionage, strategic bombardment, and compromise bargaining with communists have spawned serious moral problems for Americans in the past few years.

Two questionable dichotomies have plagued the discussion and analysis of moral issues in international politics, especially within the orbit of western culture. The first draws a distinction between morality and national interest, the second between morality and power. Although these conflicts are far too complex to detail or solve here, some observations seem suitable.

The alleged clash between morality and national interest would appear to be false, since there is no reason why the teachings of any moral code and the formulation of any state's national interest should conflict. National interest is based on a controlling value system. A state's choosing to make advancement of moral principles its highest political value does not make its national interest any less valid a criterion. Those who profess to discover such a contradiction are often in reality pressing a particular policy in the face of opposition and—especially in the United States—are convinced that their case is strengthened by casting aspersions on "idealists" who advance moral principles in support of different policy prescriptions.

Morality and power constitute a more formidable contrast. Power in this sense is understood to be brute force, often alleged to be a manifestation of man's inherent sinfulness, thus depriving it of moral neutrality and instrumental character and elevating it to a positive factor in a moral equation. A state, it is alleged, can be either moral and therefore ineffective in a power-dominated world, or powerful and effective. Such an embrace of power is a compromise with strict morality, to be justified only on the basis of the duality of man's nature. Absolute moral solutions cannot be found in an amoral (often immoral) system, so men are urged, albeit sometimes regretfully, to eschew strict moral principles in the interest of effective use of power.

Analytically, this position is illogical and indefensible, there being no reason to equate power with force or to strip it of moral content. A state is concerned with winning international consensus in support of its purposes. It is not difficult to cite many examples of cases in which moral principles have proved important to the achievement of that consent. In this sense, morality becomes a part of power—or, more accurately, of capability. The role of morality in strengthening or weakening a state's international competence is therefore a function of particular situations, and not subject to generalizations in advance of action in a concrete context.

Neither as a basis for calculating capability nor as a pretext for suspending individual moral scruples is the distinction between morality and power meaningful. Power may be used for immoral or moral purposes. Morality may be exterior to capability or one of its key components. Lack of absolute moral solutions to international problems does not free man from his responsibility to remain a moral being, even when considering questions of foreign policy. Power and morality are concepts that belong in different analytical frames of reference and cannot be joined in any prescriptive way.

The Rise of International Morality

A dream that has energized the efforts of many would-be reformers of international politics is that of a rebirth of an international moral consensus. If some way could be discovered to recreate the common moral ground rules that governed the course of international politics prior to the birth of modern nationalism, the political system and mankind itself would be enormously better off. The danger that differing but equally passionate moral outlooks might precipitate catastrophe would be sharply reduced, and the possibilities for finding common ground for mutually acceptable solutions to important problems would be correspondingly increased. Some such idea of what was called in the nineteenth century a "natural harmony of interest" among all men motivated much of the effort that culminated first in the League of Nations and later in the United Nations.

An international moral consensus is a prerequisite to an orderly and stabilized world. More efficient international organizations and safer international politics must remain illusory hopes so long as the human species, bound into a constricted political space by an inexorable technology, continues to break into quarrelsome and mutually exclusive factions on moral issues. Men must reach some agreement on their basic moral terms of reference before there can be any significant improvement in the tension climate of world affairs.

Put this way, the proposition has been traditionally felt to be self-cancelling; a world divided into a set of sovereign states, each busily perfecting and promoting its own nationalistic morality, has long been held incapable of mustering adequate agreement on any set of propositions broad enough to permit formulation of "international morality." Ideologies, cutting across national and ethical lines, provide a broader base of moral action than state morality, but ideological conflict represents movement away from consensus rather than toward it. The failure of Woodrow Wilson's dream of the "Parliament of Man," as epitomized in the League of Nations and the deep and bitter divisions of the cold war era, seems conclusive proof of the unattainability of international moral consensus.

But patterns of contemporary international politics are developing in such a way as to throw doubt on this long-standing generalization. The technology that has made war so destructive has also brought nations into closer physical contact with each other. Especially in the United Nations, but in all manner of conferences, meetings, and assemblies, men and governments are jointly exploring the larger issues of the age and discovering, often to their surprise, that their moral judgments are astonishingly similar. From this new awareness of a common interest in a single destiny has emerged the beginnings of a true international morality.

Its root is, of course, expediential—the urge to survive in a world of great danger. No moral code makes a senseless death morally justifiable, and sanity argues that the continued existence of the human species is a highly desirable goal. Sheer biological survival is not, however, the crux of this new moral outlook. If men are to die, they insist that they die for a *cause* which is in some way advanced or defended by death. The new morality is slowly proceeding beyond this fundamental moral judgment to develop a more elaborate rationale on which to base state behavior in a less political world.

Any international morality must inevitably weaken the monistic bonds of nationalism. Although this is still a highly nationalistic age, the character of mass national identifications is perceptibly changing. In some areas a clear decline has set in, in others nationalism is still seeking a new direction, and in still others it continues to seek larger units of loyalty. Only a few states espouse the old, militant, integrating impacts of nationalism. Similarly, the decline in the impact of ideologies on the behavior patterns of mass man, detectable only in recent years, is a hopeful sign.

The Restraining Effect of Moral Consensus

The new, and as yet peripheral, force of international morality is given form by means of an international consensus. Whether expressed formally in the General Assembly of the United Nations or informally by the intangible of "world opinion," collective moral judgment is now a situational factor with which all policy-makers must reckon.

International moral restraint is, of course, powerless to prevent a great power from taking a single overt step or even from launching a particular policy. It probably never will be an instrument for casting an effective vote on a unique event. Its role up to the present has been to help condition the climate of decision for both large and small states by developing clearer and more restrictive parameters within which the state system can move. Nor is it likely that its negative restraining function will ever be overtaken in importance by a positive and goal-postulating role. Morality may define the permissible for states, but not the mandatory.

However, the logic of technology and the evolving mutual awareness of men have combined to make moral judgments again relevant to the course of international politics. A newly-born supranational and suprastate criterion of evaluation is available to men everywhere. Its usefulness to this point, although admittedly limited, argues for its continued and more extensive application. Morality, international as well as internal, will continue to be a limitation on state action, difficult to define but impossible to ignore.

INTERNATIONAL LAW

Whether international law is "law" in the true sense has been a subject of constant debate among jurists. Certain theoretical aspects of the nature of law must be understood in order to grasp the significance of this problem.

Law in the abstract suggests a fixed relationship between or among certain entities. Two types of law may be distinguished in terms of their subjects: natural law (in the technical sense) and human law. Natural law is the law of natural causes of human or nonhuman phenomena and thus contains no element of volition. In human relations, however, volition is omnipresent. Human law covers the relations among persons or groups governed by rules to which the subjects have explicitly or tacitly agreed to conform, subject to official demands for obedience. Human law rests ultimately on agreement.

International law is a branch of human law. In spite of the implications of sovereignty to the international behavior of states, the international system is generally regarded by all its members as having a legal base resting on the consent (theoretically explicit) of all states bound by the law. International law is a product of the operation of the international system. Its growth is almost accidental in that it seldom is the result of deliberate planning, but instead develops slowly from international practice. A rule has often attained near-maturity before statesmen appreciate that there has been an addition to the total corpus of the law.

Probably the greatest inspiration for the continued historical growth of international law has been the demands of states for reciprocity, uniformity, and equality of treatment. In international practice this demand approximates the ideal of "justice," in that each state expects its due from the law. The legal rights a state may enjoy (apart from the freedom of action to influence or coerce other states) depend upon the willingness of other states to recognize these rights in practice. The divergence between this idea of justice and the working principles of international intercourse may be bridged only by effective application of the rule of consent.

The Subject Matter of International Law

The considerable dimensions of international law can be reduced to three general areas: the acquisition and meaning of statehood, the rules and procedures of peaceful international intercourse, and the rules and procedures of war.

THE LAW OF STATEHOOD. This deals with the legal personality of the state and its rights, duties, and privileges. It covers such subjects as assumption of statehood through recognition, state succession, and loss of international personality. It delineates the methods of acquiring and losing territory, and defines the status of equality of states and the responsibility of a state for events on its territory and actions by its nationals abroad. It distinguishes the territorial jurisdiction over air, land, and sea. It also covers state jurisdiction over persons, including the broad ground of nationality, citizenship, and the rights of resident or transitory aliens in its territory.

THE RULES AND PROCEDURES OF PEACEFUL INTERNATIONAL INTERCOURSE. These include the law of diplomacy, the law of treaties, and the law of pacific settlement of international disputes. The law of diplomacy prescribes the powers and privileges of diplomats and establishes the protocol affecting the conduct of diplomatic business. The law of treaties, one of the most important aspects of international law, designates the methods of negotiation, tests of validity, rules of interpretation, and processes of termination of a treaty. The law regulating the pacific settlement of international disputes controls the various procedures utilized to settle international conflicts short of war, and the rights of parties to such procedures.

THE LAW OF WAR. This deals initially with the legal concepts of belligerency and neutrality. In traditional international law, belligerency grants a state many legal rights it does not enjoy when at peace, while depriving it of others. It also requires a state to obey the laws governing the conduct of warfare. Neutrality confers certain special rights upon a neutral state, such as the maximum immunity practicable from the effects of the war. In return, it imposes certain obligations on the neutral state, such as abstention from specific unneutral acts and preservation of strict impartiality. In addition, the law of war covers rules for the conduct of warfare relating to population, prisoners of war, prohibition of certain weapons, and similar matters.

Political Conception of International Law

International law reveals most sharply the contrast between domestic and international political systems. While the former can be identified with "vertical" law, the latter approximates a "horizontal" legal order, which is decentralized, resting upon the reciprocal discharge of functions by national states which are technically equal. By contrast, a "vertical" order includes a centralized hierarchy of institutionalized decision-makers ranging from the minor political official to the head of a state.

State officials acknowledge the obligatory character of international law as a body of rules, but reserve to themselves determination of the rules, how they apply to specific situations, and the nature of their administration. Such a decentralized system is not utterly chaotic, and state officials do not have unlimited discretion to act abritrarily. They are deterred from doing so by a number of considerations: the general need for order and stability, the reciprocal advantage of many rules, and the desire not to offend other states for a variety of reasons, including the possibility of incurring various sanctions.

Several basic points apply in assessing the relevance of international law to the control of force. First, a state is prohibited from using force except for individual or collective self-defense against a prior armed attack. Second, there is no generally accepted definition of what constitutes either "aggression" or "self-defense." Third, much controversy surrounds the limits of authorization for the use of force by, or under the auspices of, the United Nations. Fourth, allocation of legal authority among the Security Council, the General Assembly, and the International Court of Justice has not been settled. Fifth, no clear doctrine governs either the limits of force permissible by a regional security organization like the Organization of American States, or by the UN against a nonmember state.

However, international law influences national behavior in three separate ways: (1) the formulation of standards of behavior; (2) the pro-

ERRATA

For the section "Political Conception of International Law" on pp. 170ff. the author is greatly indebted to the discussion of international law in K. J. Holsti, *International Politics* (Englewood Cliffs, N.J.: Prentice-Hall, Inc., 1967).

For the section "Impact of Cultural Traditions on International Law" on pp. 174ff. the author drew upon the insights of O. J. Lissitzyn, "The Less Developed Nations," in R. A. Falk and S. H. Mendlovitz, eds., *The Strategy of World Order*, Vol. 2 (New York: World Law Fund, 1966).

Concepts Of International Politics, 2nd Edition

cedures available for interpretation of these standards; and (3) the procedures available to implement the interpretations. Prohibitions on the use of force are abstract and vague. Each state claims to be acting in self-defense, even when it undertakes an aggressive policy. If force is used in a state-to-state relationship, the most authoritative decision-makers are the national officials of the states concerned. If a regional organization or an organ of the United Nations becomes involved, the decision is made in the light of a supranational consensus. However, it may be unclear whether this consensus reflects the political preferences of the voting states, or their attempt at impartial interpretation of the legal norms. Enforcing an authoritative consensus is a problem, since there is no regularly constituted police force available to the UN. Hence, enforcement depends upon the ability and willingness of states favoring the consensus to make it effective.

Any obligation is a limitation on a government's freedom of action. Certain rules of international law define what states may or must do; others point out what states must not do; additional rules or norms attempt to define the situations in which positive or negative obligations become operational. Policy-makers must always consider whether their actions or proposed responses to actions conform with these obligations and standards of conduct. If governments meet these obligations, even at the expense of their interests or foreign policy, the rules have acted as effective restraints. If, in other circumstances, governments interpret the rules in an arbitrary fashion, or violate their permissive, positive, or negative obligations, we must conclude that other values and interests were more important. A common view of international politics holds that governments are not restrained by international legal norms, except perhaps in technical and commercial matters. Despite numerous treaties, international organizations, and charters which attempt to restrict the use and threat of force as a means of resolving conflicts and achieving objectives, effective control over military capabilities still rests with the independent political units making up the international system. Decisions to employ force seem more closely related to perceptions of threat and calculations of military and political risks and costs than to considerations of legality.

Some of these treaties and charters are not entirely clear in details, but this should not suggest that more and better treaties or international institutions will solve the problem of conflict. Relatively few disputes and conflicts of objectives arise out of differing interpretations of law. Since international law involves, in addition to collaboration and competitive relationships, the problems and processes of adjusting conflicts arising from more or less incompatible collective objectives, the law would not be observed in all instances, no matter how clear, precise, and logical it might be.

In those areas of international politics involving conflicts between important collective objectives, the role of law in prescribing the limits of action is unpredictable. Whether legal rules are a major consideration in framing policies in a conflict situation probably depends upon the general climate of relations between two countries, their mutual responsiveness, and the degree of incompatibility between their objectives. If a serious conflict arises between allies with a tradition of responsiveness to each other's needs and interests, legal rules may well set the limits to the policies used to resolve the conflict or to change the behavior and attitudes of the other state.

Legal norms are also likely to restrain behavior or permit observance of obligations if both sides perceive that their prestige might be lowered by flagrant violations of accepted international practice or of treaties. Certainly, most governments are sensitive to the violation of treaties.

Disregard for treaty commitments and general principles of international law is often displayed when: (1) two or more states have incompatible objectives which can be achieved only at each other's expense; (2) the level of involvement between them is high; (3) there is no tradition of mutual needs or responsiveness; and (4) one side has already established a precedent by undertaking actions in violation of the law. When these circumstances combine, adherence to treaty obligations or norms prohibiting certain instruments of inducement is often sacrificed in order to defend or achieve an objective with higher value. Conflicts in this kind of relationship are seldom resolved by recourse to legal rule and procedures, because much more important values are at stake.

The effectiveness of legal norms in restraining types of behavior in a conflict situation depends on an assessment by policy-makers of the value of observing legal norms versus the value of achieving or defending the stated objectives of the government. In relationships typified by great hostility and incompatibility of objectives, no statesman could be expected to attach absolute value to law observance if this would sacrifice all his other objectives, including the security of his country. Even the most legally minded statesman would use whatever techniques of statecraft or action are necessary to achieve or defend stated objectives, although fully aware that to do so involves deliberate violation of treaties or legal principles.

Non-Western Attitudes toward International Law

The emergence of non-western states has had an undeniable, though not easily measurable, impact on international law. Their interpretation of international legal norms differs from traditional western views and reveals an apparently revolutionary temper. They consider many of the sanctified values of international law irrelevant to their concerns and aspirations.

The non-western states acknowledge the binding force of international law, all of them having invoked its norms in disputes with other states and in debates in international organizations. Yet non-western spokesmen often stress the need for further development of international law to reflect their values and interests in such areas as nationalization, territorial sea, treaties, and sovereign immunity.

A generally accepted "international standard" in traditional international law governs state responsibility for the treatment of aliens, as regards both their person and their property. In case of expropriating or nationalization, the international standard has required payment of "prompt, adequate, and effective" compensation. The western states uphold this traditional standard, whereas the non-West favors the doctrine of "equality of treatment," providing for compensation to aliens in accordance with the local laws of the expropriating state.

With regard to the law of the sea, most of the non-western states are against the traditional three-mile doctrine of width of the territorial sea which is still upheld by leading maritime powers of the West. At the 1958 and 1960 Geneva Conferences on the Law of the Sea, coalitions of most of the non-western states with the Soviet bloc frustrated the prospects for reaffirmation of the three-mile limit.

In the law of treaties, the non-western states have tended to oppose the "unanimity doctrine" of the admissibility and effect of reservations to multilateral conventions. They show preference for the Pan American Rule, developed by the Latin American nations, in accordance with which the reserving state becomes a party to the treaty with respect to other parties that do not object to the reservation.

On the issue of sovereign immunity, the non-western states favor the "restrictive" doctrine (the view that a state is not entitled to immunity from suit in the courts of another state with regard to claims arising out of its commercial activities). This view is gaining increasing support in Western Europe and the U.S. The Soviet Union, on the other hand, upholds the "absolute" immunity doctrine.

Assertions that the newly-independent states are not bound by old norms do not imply wholesale rejection of traditional international law; rather, they must be regarded as an expression of the resentment still felt by newly-independent states over their colonial past, and as an assertion of their sovereignty and equality. They also serve to remind the older states that the views of the newcomers are not to be disregarded in the formulation and further development of international laws. Nevertheless such an assertion is a departure from the principle that, upon being admitted into the international community, a new state is automatically bound by the preexisting norms of general international law. In the older and previously dominant part of the international community, it cannot but cause a disquieting sense of uncertainty and instability.

There is resentment among Asians, Africans, and some Latin Americans against what appears to them a double standard—reliance by the more advanced states on the arrangement obtained by force or pressure during the colonial era, and their simultaneous denial of the lawfulness of the use of force by non-western states to uproot these fruits of past aggressions. In the attempt to provide legal justification for their efforts to change the status quo, the non-western states rely increasingly on the argument that "unequal" or "inequitable" treaties, and treaties imposed by duress, are invalid *ab initio*.

Only a few non-western states have accepted the compulsory jurisdiction of the International Court of Justice under the optional clause of Article 36 of the Court's statute. This may stem from fear that the Court might apply norms of international law rejected by the non-western states, or might uphold the legal rights of western states against attempts to change the status quo inherited from the colonial era. There have been, moreover, very few African and Asian judges on the Court, which may well be a factor in the cautious attitude of many newly-independent states toward the Court.

Impact of Cultural Traditions on International Law

Does the non-western cultural background of the new states lead them to attitudes toward international law which are different from those of the western nations? The evidence indicates that national interest, rather than cultural tradition, has been the immediate decisive factor. For example, states of widely different cultural backgrounds have been united in opposition to the traditional norms on expropriation of foreign property and width of the territorial sea.

Differences in levels of economic and political development lie behind the more extreme differences between legal institutions. Much of international law has developed in response to the requirement of western industrial civilization. As non-western states move toward fuller participation in present-day economic and political life, they realize that many of their legal traditions are no longer adequate to their needs. Most of these countries are adopting, in varying degrees, modern institutions, largely derived from those of the West; reception of western law has already reached an advanced stage in some of these states. In the West itself, law does not stand still. The effects on law of greater state participation in economic life and the rise of the "welfare state" are likely to be worldwide. This factor should ultimately serve to reduce differences in attitudes toward international law.

It has been suggested that non-western cultural traditions must be introduced into the fabric of international law to make the system acceptable to the new states; such a synthesis would extend the cultural base of international law beyond its western origins to include Hindu, Moslem, Confucian, and Buddhist elements. Another contention is that the critical element in the attitudes of the non-western states is their ability to perceive their national interest. The perception of the new states is not distorted by cultural outlook, but is shaped primarily by economic considerations and the pursuit of political power. Thus, they desire an international law that will facilitate economic development at home and accord them maximum influence abroad.

To confuse policies born of changing positions of interest with religious, cultural, and other values inherent in the culture pattern of the people can lead to grave distortion of the real problems of contemporary international law. Just as the relative positions of Britain, France, the U.S., and other countries in the western world changed with alterations in their political and economic status, so the positions of the non-western states will be affected by their development. It can be predicted that as countries such as India or Brazil attain an economic position comparable to that of the developed industrial countries and become exporters of capital, goods, and skills, their legal theory will move closer to that of the developed countries.

Some diversity in attitude toward international law is bound to remain in the non-western world, as it has in the West. But as non-western states find their place in the international system, there should be less reason to fear that differences of cultural heritage will produce an unbridgeable gap between western and non-western attitudes toward international law. The long-range trend is in the direction of greater uniformity of legal systems and traditions.

Recent Trends in International Law

Contemporary trends in international law demonstrate a closer link with international politics. It has proved impossible to adjust life to law, so the controlling emphasis is upon the adjustment of law to life. International law of the nineteenth and earlier centuries assumed the sovereignty of states. Its object was not to eliminate war, but to restrict it in time, place, and method, and hence establish an equilibrium of power. Twentieth-century international law has acquired the goal of establishing an equilibrium of justice, and assumes the interdependence of states and the integration of power.

The technological revolution has produced both positive and negative effects on international law. Progressive development of the positivist view, which heightened the role of power by making it more difficult to subject states to rules of law, secularized the entire concept of international law and weakened its moral foundations. Law in a power-oriented society maintains the supremacy of force and hierarchies established on the basis of power, and gives legal respectability and sanctity to the system. Many new states which have joined the international system in recent years do not share in the historic tradition of international law. Hence, they are not inclined to limit their claims to what is legally defensible under the old system, a system that they feel is biased in favor of older, more developed, and more powerful states. In this sense, modern trends already have begun to weaken the universality of law.

On the other hand, the logic of the technological revolution and its by-products compels states to establish a better balance between law and politics in order to form a more cohesive international system. International law today is formulating these demands in terms of new standards of justice. The relationship between international law and the dynamics of the international political system is more apparent today than at any time in history. Law and social organization operate upon each other reciprocally: law sets limits to the structure, functions, and effectiveness of a social system, while the organizational dynamics of a society control the development, formulation, and application of legal rules. Modern technology, by clarifying this two-way relationship and demonstrating the necessity for greater cohesiveness in the international order, emerges as a positive force for the elaborations of international law. A more effective legal system in interstate relations will be an automatic function of an increasingly interdependent world society.

THE CALCULUS OF PRUDENCE IN STATECRAFT

Our analysis of the foreign policy process in Part I pointed out that strategy in foreign policy or in war is a very conservative enterprise. The inexorabilities of cost and risk in an intrinsically unstable action system combine to inhibit decision and limit implementation. Under such circumstances, perhaps the most powerful and certainly the most widely applicable restraint on state freedom of choice is the code of prudence that governs rational policy-making.

Rationality and Prudence in Statecraft

Operationally, there is no reason why all statesmen should be sane; a lunatic, if he were capable of issuing coherent orders, would be as qualified to operate the controls of government as a philosopher-king. But sanity and rationality are assumed to be requisite qualities in a foreign policy-maker because only men marked by these traits can anticipate the probable results of their actions and govern their decisions in response to these calculations. The rational statesman is the prudent statesman.

An analytical and rational approach to foreign policy must be marked by caution because of a number of factors to which we have alluded, including incompleteness of information, possibility of accident or pure chance, and perverseness of the human personality. If every decision takes account of these limitations on the accuracy and validity of choice, a generous margin of error is inevitably built into policy. Game theory teaches that the primary responsibility of the player is to ensure his continued participation in the game; no more graphic summary could be made of the task of the statesman who invests his nation's survival in his ability to match strategies with his fellow policy-makers.

The Role of Probability

Policy-making requires the application of probability theory. Every statesman accepts that nothing in international politics is either inevitable or impossible—or at least that the determination of inevitabilities or impossibilities is beyond the scope of his analytical techniques. He is therefore forced to determine the relative probability of the various possible outcomes of each problem he faces. He must base his action decisions upon the greater probability of one outcome, with the necessary margin for error provided by his conclusion as to how much more probable one alternative is than others.

One psychiatric interpretation of this situation asserts that to ignore relative probabilities in favor of a fixation on the possibilities inherent in a situation is a mark of paranoia. A statesman may on occasion—as did Adolf Hitler in trusting to his "intuition" that the Nazi armies would defeat the Soviet forces in World War II—conclude that a certain eventuality is cosmically inevitable, and pay for his error with his head. Much more common, however, is the opposite failure: to conclude that a desired result is impossible, and thereby miss a real opportunity for meaningful action. Whether or not statesmen who commit these blunders are actually paranoid, they are certainly performing at a level far below the optimum, and their respective nations bear the cost of their failures.

The Virtues of Half a Loaf

A further manifestation of the ubiquity of prudential calculation is the strong preference of statesmen for partial successes achieved at minimum risk over all-or-nothing choices. With continued survival as the prime consideration in statecraft, rational policy-makers strive to gain such prizes as can be won without endangering their self-preservation or security. This has contributed to what we have noted as a characteristic pattern of interstate conflict: the struggle for small victories with only partial commitments of capability. Each state involved in such a contest can accept defeat with only minimum disturbance, since it knows in advance that even the most unfavorable outcome will leave it in a viable position for further action.

The cost/risk calculation requires that the analyst never gives himself the benefit of any major doubts, and that he be prepared to pay the maximum probable cost for his objective. Since the individual decision-maker has only a limited ability to reduce cost factors in a situation over which he has only minimal control, the only way he can rationalize an unfavorable cost/risk computation is by scaling his objective down to one he can afford. Once again prudence dictates restraint on decision.

The Relativism of Decision

Absolute calculations and absolute decisions have no place in rational policy-making. A high degree of relativity in all phases of decision and action is a characteristic of the skillful and successful statesman.

Success is the only absolute criterion of value in foreign policy to which all states render homage. A foreign policy is "good" or "bad" only in the extent to which the state moves toward its objectives and in behalf of its national interest. Since the objectives themselves, and even the basic postulates of interest, change in response to shifts in mass preferences and situational dynamics, policy-making is a constant exercise in relating many variables to one another. There is no room for fixed and absolute generalizations about the nature of the political world, the nature of the problems facing the state, or the substance or methods of the responses the state must make.

Were all policy-makers equally prudent, international politics would remain confined within parameters of safety and would never approach or surpass the boiling point. But history points out many overoptimistic leaders who misread the probabilities of a situation, and some who were persuaded that they had the key to the final significance of history and could reshape the destiny of man. The international political system could tolerate such leaders in a simpler day, when failure was confined to the offending state.

Today, however, mankind is the loser each time imprudence takes command of the policy machine of a state. The best most of us can hope for is that prudence will continue to shackle the hand of recklessness and adventure; the stakes are too high to permit any but the cautious to play the game of survival in an age of thermonuclear bombs.

REFERENCES

Brierly, J. L., *Law of Nations: An Introduction to the International Law of Peace* (6th ed.). London: Oxford University Press, 1963.

Butterfield, Herbert, *Christianity, Diplomacy and War: An Introduction to International Politics*. New York: Abingdon-Cokesbury Press, 1951.

* Carr, Edward H., *Twenty Years' Crisis, 1919-1939: An Introduction to the Study of International Relations* (2nd ed.). New York: St. Martin's Press, Inc., 1946.

* Coplin, William D., *The Functions of International Law*. Skokie, Ill.: Rand McNally & Co., 1966.

Corbett, Percy E., *Law and Society in the Relations of States*. New York: Harcourt, Brace & World, Inc., 1951.

————, *Morals, Laws and Power in International Relations*. Los Angeles: The John Randolph Hayes and Dora Hayes Foundations, 1956.

Davis, Harry R., and Robert C. Good, eds., *Reinhold Niebuhr on Politics*. New York: Charles Scribner's Sons, 1968.

De Visscher, Charles, *Theory and Reality in Public International Law*. Princeton, N.J.: Princeton University Press, 1966.

Falk, Richard A., and Wolfram F. Hanrieder, *International Law and Organization*. Philadelphia: J. B. Lippincott Co., 1968.

Falk, Richard A., and Saul Mendlovitz, eds., *The Strategy of World Order: International Law*. New York: World Law Fund, 1966.

Friedmann, Wolfgang, *The Changing Structure of International Law*. New York: Columbia University Press, 1964.

Kelson, Hans, *Principles of International Law* (2nd ed.). New York: Holt, Rinehart & Winston, Inc., 1966.

Mangone, Gerald J., *The Elements of International Law* (rev. ed.). Homewood, Ill.: Richard D. Irwin, Inc., and The Dorsey Press, 1968.

* Niebuhr, Reinhold, *Moral Man and Immoral Society*. New York: Charles Scribner's Sons, 1960.

* Indicates paperback edition.

Nussbaum, A., *Concise History of the Law of Nations* (rev. ed.). New York: The Macmillan Company, 1947.

Stone, Julius, *International Conflict in the Twentieth Century: A Christian View*. New York: Harper & Row, Publishers, 1960.

* Thompson, Kenneth, *Political Realism and the Crisis of World Politics*. New York: Science Editions, John Wiley & Sons, Inc., 1960.

* Wright, Quincy, *Contemporary International Law* (rev. ed.). New York: Random House, Inc., 1961.

* Indicates paperback edition.

part III

THE SUBSTANCE
OF POLITICS:
MAJOR PROBLEMS
OF THE AGE

NINE

War in
the Modern World

In Parts I and II, we analyzed the rationale of foreign policy as conceived and executed by individual states, and examined the general characteristics of the international political system within which states move. One primary consideration has affected everything we said in both discussions: under the standardized condition of interstate life, it is impossible for a state to operate and for the system to function except on the fundamental basis of physical coercion or violence most clearly expressed in war. We cannot avoid the analytical and practical centrality of military judgments; the system as we know it today is postulated on the right and capacity of states to work their will by force if they so desire.

However, the process of international politics is in the grip of a strange paralysis. Foreign policies, particularly those of major powers, do not receive the vigorous and powerful implementation one would expect; interstate disputes seldom reach the resolution in power terms that the system would seem to demand. Small states display unwonted independence of choice and action, while great powers cast about (with indifferent success) for ways to make their putative dominance again a reality. To a great extent the political world has been, if not turned completely upside down, at least knocked off balance.

The major reason for this unprecedented state of affairs is the blighting effect of new theories of warfare on interstate political relations, and the weapons that have given birth to these theories. Statesmen from the major powers wrestle with the problem of fitting modern military doctrines and techniques within the framework of foreign policy and international politics. They have not yet succeeded; the old ways of war are outmoded, and the new warfare has not yet found its political niche. Paralleling the international power paralysis of the super powers has been the increasing incidence of internal war, or armed conflict used to achieve revolutionary aims within nations. If any development of the last half of the twentieth century approximates the traditional role of force as a coercive agent of change, it is its use by competing groups *within* nations, rather than across international boundaries. Internal wars have placed greater emphasis upon the political effects of military action than upon the military outcomes per se, a development which has further obscured the conventional relationship between military and political objectives observed by the major powers.

In this chapter we shall examine the nature of the military dilemma, in terms of both its own components and its impact on the political process. Recent years have seen a great increase in emphasis given to military matters in the study and teaching of international politics. While this chapter cän only skim the surface of the vast subject of military science, it is designed to acquaint the student with at least the basic vocabulary of contemporary military discussion, and to relate these concepts to the larger context of international political affairs.

TOTAL WAR AND THE STATE SYSTEM

What have been the specific effects of total war upon the state system? How has the new warfare affected the general pattern of international politics? We have already answered both questions in general terms, but certain basic considerations merit further consideration.

The Possibility of Catastrophe

War became a normal aspect of international politics because it provided a final answer to problems *within the system itself;* i.e., war balanced the political process but never endangered it. Even World War II, with all its destructive and disruptive results, nevertheless ended with a recognizable political system still in existence. Modern total war, with nuclear missiles and other technological niceties, raises the grim possibility of destruction of the political system and perhaps of civilized existence itself.

Advocating a technique for resolution of an international dispute that might effect complete disaster for mankind is like recommending decapitation as a cure for headache. No purely political goal is so important as to justify risking survival. It would seem that considerations of risk—assuming an optimistic cost calculation—would be absolutely prohibitive of a decision for total war. This has been the factor restraining all statesmen who have faced the choice since the dawn of the nuclear era.

There are, of course, many persuasive arguments that total war would not obliterate mankind or the monuments of his civilization, but rather that the recuperative capacity of industrial society would permit relatively rapid recovery from a thermonuclear holocaust. These contentions receive a moderately sympathetic hearing as long as they remain no more than intellectual speculation. No government, however, has been willing to gamble its existence (and that of the entire world) on the validity of these hypotheses. The possibility of utter catastrophe looms large in all military calculations today.

The Invalidation of "Victory"

With the constant possibility of utter debacle, and with the certainty of monumental devastation no matter what the course of the war, the classic military objective of "victory" has been substantially stripped of meaning. Victory in battle has always meant submission of the enemy; victory in war has always meant achievement of the positive or negative goal for which the war was fought. These classifications are almost meaningless with respect to total war.

The destructiveness of thermonuclear war is beyond belief. If one state loses 75 per cent of its people and 90 per cent of its productive capacity, will the survivors be consoled by realizing that the enemy lost 85 per cent of its people and all its productive capacity? Will victory in such a case be sweet or—in the words of a leading theorist of nuclear war —"will the living envy the dead?"

One possible manner of achieving victory continues to tantalize military theorists. If a state can gain enough initial striking power to eliminate in one blow an enemy's capacity to retaliate, perfect dominance will have been achieved with no damage in return. But (as our discussion of the arms race will show) this margin of superiority is so difficult to acquire, and its employment so contingent upon absolute surprise, that it remains an illusory goal.

Victory in total war today is a notion without content, a fact that exercises an inhibiting effect. With no likelihood of bringing about a real triumph, a statesman's urge to begin combat never grows very strong. Total war is unattractive at best; without victory to give it point, it finds no political justification today.

The Rethinking of Political Values

The motive force of international politics has long depended on the primacy of political values over all competing notions of good. Men were expected to support the state's efforts at whatever cost to themselves, even to sacrificing their lives. Now that total war may have lost its point, the justification for patriotic death is no longer self-evident. Men might die for God or for posterity, but to die knowing that only nothingness will follow has thrown the entire process of mental and emotional commitment out of plumb.

A serious rethinking of political values has been launched in much of the world. With the greatest sacrifice a man can make for his state, his life, reduced to a mockery, many once self-evident truths about the purpose of foreign policy are undergoing reanalysis, and drastically different answers are being advanced to old questions. Some men are suggesting that the content of political life needs overhauling in order to make it more directly responsible to individual needs and aspirations. Although it is small at the present time, this trend could conceivably develop and sweep away many of the underpinnings of traditional international politics. Internal wars, "proxy" wars, and well-circumscribed wars between "mini powers" employing conventional weapons remain exceptions to this evolution of political values. In these conflagrations patriotic death has lost neither its meaning nor its allure. Men, even nations, have demonstrated that they remain quite willing to sacrifice their lives for political, religious, or social goals. Conflicts of this kind, usually labelled "limited wars," are limited only in the eyes of the major nuclear powers; to small nations such as Israel and Pakistan, and to countries in the throes of revolution, these wars are *absolute*. In this sense, such low-level conflicts, and their persistence in the nuclear age, have restored the efficacy of war as an instrument of political policy, albeit as a mutation of the pre-World War II variety.

The Disappearance of Decision

With war no longer a good foreign policy investment, the state system is deprived of its only effective method of reaching a clear decision in a direct confrontation between states. Smaller states, although not risking nuclear incineration if they fight, operate in an environment severely constrained by the probability of great power intervention and the fear of consequent expansion to total war. States repeatedly become involved in positions from which only a successful war could extricate them, but inhibitions on warfare prevent them from taking the critical step. Unable to go forward and unwilling to retreat, the contestants remain locked in an uneasy stalemate, and issues remain unresolved. In "micro" wars between or within small states, great powers, spurred by fears of the eventual ultimate confrontation, have usually intervened prior to the achievement of a permanent political or military resolution. Although the small nations have fought, the issues have tended to remain undecided.

International politics since the end of World War II has seen a succession of great power issues go to the point of maximum bearable reciprocal pressure and then remain hanging in unrewarding suspension. Cultural lag prevents most states from recognizing and acting on the implication of loss of decision capability in the system. They persist in embarking on policies whose full fruition might require war, and express baffled annoyance when they feel themselves trapped. Some smaller states, recognizing both the opportunities and limitations inherent in such an era, have had great success in pursuing active policies cast in a frame of implementation that excluded high probability of war. With increasing frequency in the past five years, they have enlarged that frame of execution to include war itself.

Decision by Consensus

With war stripped of its role as ultima ratio—ultima it may be today, but never ratio—some effective substitute is necessary if the international political system is not to collapse from malnutrition. The most broadly applicable alternative to war has been the institutionalization of consensus. Speaking primarily through the General Assembly of the United Nations, but on occasion through special conferences or other ad hoc instrumentalities, a cohesive and articulate body of supranational consensus has sometimes exercised a controlling effect on crisis situations. If development of such international consensus goes to completion, displacing military power as final arbiter, the international political system will become a vastly different phenomenon than it was for three centuries.

POLITICAL EFFECTS OF THE NEW WARFARE

We have considered some of the effects of total war on the operation of the state system. Equally important to an understanding of the impact of military technology are the influences to which it subjects the statesman engaged in a policy decision on behalf of his own state.

The "Balance of Terror"

Probably the most important consideration affecting foreign policy decisions by both large and small states is the so-called "balance of terror." This situation stems from the present distribution of military capability in the world: two great states have built up arsenals of new weapons that far outclass all other states, yet each remains incapable of mounting adequate superiority over the other. This allocation of military power inhibits everyone to the same extent, if not in exactly the same way.

Since each of the great powers is unable to contemplate unleashing war on the other, both the United States and the U.S.S.R. have a vested interest in avoiding war. There is little philanthropy or charity in this self-restraint, only elementary calculations of the prospects for survival on the cost/risk scale.

Furthermore, neither is safe in making indiscriminate use of its great military power against lesser states. A large proportion of the smaller powers are under the protection of one or the other of the giants, and any overt pressure on these proxies or "demiproxies" would bring their great power patron into the dispute. Although the concept of neutrality has changed, and the post-World War II notion of cold war is becoming an oversimplified anachronism, small unaligned states are as well-protected as when their status was preserved by the cold war counterweights of the major bloc leaders. However, the prevalence of internal conflicts, externally supported in many cases by major powers or their proxies, has encouraged great power counteractivity in these "unaligned" nations and the inevitable political-military polarization of the particular regions. If the polarization continues, spurred by the seemingly irreversible trend toward internal violence, the concepts of neutrality and unaligned in the old cold war context will probably disappear altogether. Any attempt by either cold war camp to exert military coercion on almost any neutral would also bring in the opposite bloc and once again polarize the military situation.

If the nuclear giants are inhibited by the balance of terror, so are the smaller states. Neither nuclear leader can view calmly an outbreak of war anywhere, so both deny smaller powers the capability to reach decisions by the violence which they themselves are denied. Their reasons for preferring peace are the same as those governing their direct confrontation: a war which cannot be won, or in which the prospects of real victory are remote and difficult to visualize, is of no value to them. A small war may spread and involve either or both in massive risk for small possible profit. Even here the influence of the nuclear stand-off is paradoxical, since control of conflict may require the active great power intervention the nuclear nations seek to avoid.

The small war belligerents have exploited the operational freedom afforded by this dilemma. When the super powers have chosen restraint, combat has been pursued to exhaustion or completion; when some intervention was exercised, the small nations have skillfully manipulated their bargaining position between the powers. The significant dual developments of great power preoccupation with conflict control and the demise of the bipolar system have afforded the small powers an unexpected amount of freedom in employment of military force. Thus it may be said that modern weaponry, as long as it remains narrowly distributed, is a poor way to fight a war but a remarkably effective device for preventing one. The continuing proliferation of nuclear weapons promises to upset commonly accepted views about their deterrent effects. New nuclear nations such as Communist China and France, although attaining only a marginal increase in military "power" vis-à-vis the United States and the Soviet Union, have greatly enhanced their prestige and created serious political repercussions within their military blocs and geographic regions.

Such nonnuclear nations as West Germany and Japan, potentially facing an intransigent nuclear-armed opponent, have deliberately retained the technological options necessary to achieve nuclear capability at manageable cost within two to five years. Sixteen other nations, including such volatile combinations as Egypt and Israel and India and Pakistan, could produce nuclear weapons in a relatively short period, but most would suffer the political cost of violating the 1968 Non-Proliferation Treaty and be forced, for the development period, to focus all of their national resources on the project.

Whatever the reasons nations seek nuclear arms, the uncertainties of proliferation and its strategic consequences will probably continue; as ownership of nuclear weapons expands, the mathematical probability of their use increases. The more crucial political and military pressures demanding their use are less proportionate, but quite as predictable. Whether these influences will be balanced by the deterrent effect of the "balance of terror" and the responsible awareness of "nuclearhood" remains a major uncertainty in the late twentieth-century nuclear environment.

The Declining Credibility of Military Force

The balance of terror not only makes war irrelevant to policy, but also deprives military power of much of its credibility as a coercive or persuasive technique in the course of ordinary political confrontation. The credibility of the threat of violence as a tool of policy is no more than a partial function of the threat; of even greater importance today is the likelihood of its being made a reality. The sheer enormity of contemporary threats, especially those mounted by nuclear states, is greater than at any earlier period of history. Their impact on affairs, however, is almost negligible, since it is so unlikely that the threatening state will make good its menace.

We see the consequences of this development at every turn. Threats of dire consequences made by nuclear states against lesser opponents are dismissed as empty bluster and casually disregarded. Even great power confrontations find the nuclear giants searching for conventional military forces to implement a "nuclear" strategy they are neither spiritually nor politically prepared to use. Among nonnuclear powers, where more traditional calculations might be expected to hold sway, the variety of restraints vitiate once dominant military superiorities. However, as the nuclear powers have become accustomed to the environment of mutual annihilation, they have edged with increasing temerity away from the bipolar operative range of military force which existed in the middle to late fifties. The great powers, either directly or through their proxies, have abandoned the concepts which limited use of military power to extremes of either total war or paralysis, and, as in Vietnam and the Sinai, have begun to operate once again in the gradations of force between the poles.

The End of Status

The disappearing credibility of military power has threatened to erode (but not eliminate) the status system that regulated the relations of states. The old classification of states into categories of rank and privilege based upon their respective military capabilities has been substantially invalidated. Great powers could not receive deference if they could not act in the way expected of great powers. The result has been a new and potentially devastating sense of what we might call international egalitarianism that promised to spread widely once the balance of terror began to exert its influence.

States of all military levels approach each other on an a priori basis of substantial status equality. The deference and privilege enjoyed by each in a particular relationship is a function of the specific situation and their respective range of capabilities, and cannot be inferred in advance from any generalized characteristics or self-image. The essence of a status or class system is a fixed stratification of groups, and military capacity long functioned as the determinant of a state's level. No universally accepted criterion of rank has arisen to replace military power, and the international social system is more fluid and less structured today than it has been since its inception. There are no accepted "leaders," no "inner circle" of dominant powers that give shape to the patterns of world politics—except insofar as the nuclear states can keep attention riveted on themselves by virtue of the destructive capacity they control.

The Utility of Military Force Today

Are we arguing that military force and the institution of organized armed conflict has lost all relevance to contemporary world politics? In strict conceptual terms, the temptation toward that position is strong, but a glance at the world of reality suggests that military power retains much of its capacity to render a decision in an increasing number of special cases. A brief catalogue of these instances will not only measure the relevance of war today, but also vignette some salient characteristics of the contemporary political world.

The first present-day situation in which military force is useful is one in which a leader of a major bloc uses armed force to subdue a rebellious or recalcitrant satellite; classic instances were Soviet intervention in Hungary in 1956 and in Czechoslovakia in 1968. With the threat of violent intervention thus validated, armed forces may be used by bloc leaders to coerce maverick satellites, with the contingent mission of reinforcing indigenous bloc forces if violence flares. The rigidity of the bloc's international position effectively inhibits the likelihood of an attempt at penetration from any outside source, specifically from the other bloc.

A second situation, illustrated by the 1961 Indian invasion and capture of the Portuguese enclave, Goa, is action by an anticolonial state against a (usually small and isolated) remnant of a colonial empire. Here the military state has the protection of anticolonialist ideology, with a considerable preformed consensus supporting its action. If its military venture is rapid and clean, opposition and resistance develop so slowly that the entire operation is over before anything can be done about it. However, if the move is not made quickly and crowned by success, international complications may serve to vitiate its effect. Realistically, the world is increasingly barren of these "quick and clean" opportunities; those which appear so superficially carry promise of deeper complications. Such opportunities have traditionally been no more than indirect applications of military power, usually confined to the supply of materiel, economic, and political support rather than overt commitment of military manpower. In many cases this remains so; however, a new range of variants of these essentially "proxy wars" has materialized. Proxy-patron relationships have assumed a surprising degree of complexity and unpredictability on all levels.

Probably the most conspicuous example of one form of this device was the extensive Communist support given North Korea during the Korean War of 1950–1953. The pattern there of proxy vs. great power multilateral force was altered by the appearance of Red Chinese "volunteers" who fought a large part of the battle.

The Sino-Indian conflict of 1962 provides a variant to the proxy typology; in this case, another China bloc power (albeit an increasingly intransigent one) fought a "demi-proxy" of the two major bloc powers, the United States and the U.S.S.R. Indian reaction to this conflict, which expressed itself in increasing political-military reliance upon the United States, set the stage for the complex and confusing proxy war between India and Pakistan in 1965.

Pakistan, a treaty ally of the United States, calculated that military aid from both blocs seriously upset the regional military balance. The resulting conflict spawned puzzling dilemmas for both blocs: the United States was caught in a conflict in which both combatants were proxies, while the U.S.S.R. was supporting a demi-proxy, India, against a strategically important neighbor, Pakistan, which was wavering toward the Chinese side. Under such confusing circumstances, the haste of the great powers to achieve some kind of "peace" is understandable.

The Arab-Israeli conflict of 1967 illustrates yet another kind of proxy war, but one on three levels, in which one bloc leader, the United States, played patron to segments of both sides. The United States resisted the Soviet drive to polarize the region into the Arab-U.S.S.R. and U.S.-Israeli blocs by keeping a foot in both camps—supporting liberal Arabs such as Hussein while avoiding total support of Israel. Israeli success of arms postponed what could have become a serious dilemma for the United States.

The emergence of "liberation wars" in the less developed states has lent still another aspect to the texture of proxy wars in this decade. They have provided ideological justification as well as practical opportunities to play out the great power conflicts through proxies in the "third world." Less extreme involvements in recent years have included Soviet-Chinese support of the Pathet Lao in Laos, the Antoine Gizenga group in the Congo, the FLN rebels in Algeria, and the Viet Cong in Vietnam.

Vietnam illustrates the dynamic quality of these conflicts; their character changes as the great power proxy relationships shift. From its origins as a civil-internal guerrilla war with outside support originating in both blocs, it evolved, with the massive U.S. assistance which energized U.S.S.R.-North Vietnamese reaction, into an international war much like the Korean conflict. The relationship of the combatants, with a major power fighting a proxy of another (or others), and the nature of the fighting are very similar to the earlier Asian conflict. Thus the conflict has moved from the guerrilla-internal war side of the spectrum toward conventional war-direct great power involvement, a development which belies the notion that great powers will not engage in "limited" conventional military actions in the nuclear age.

Another example of the use of military force which may become more prevalent, especially if major power intervention in "small wars" persists in being as unsatisfactory as the recent U.S. experience in Vietnam, is in conventional combat between small nations. Wars in sub-Saharan Africa or South and Latin America may not invite great power participation because the costs outweigh the benefits of their intervening. Mutual indifference will also deter interference, although political and military developments, possibly instigated by a third power, may change the calculations of the major powers. Intervention in these cases would not be unlike proxy war situations. Great powers may also refrain from intervening in small nation wars because they fear escalation to the nuclear level, although this constraint seems less compelling now than a decade earlier.

Significantly, modern experience has indicated that military power may be used to obtain political decisions by groups of small states acting under authority given by the United Nations. The two most successful of these applications of military power have been the United Nations interventions in the Suez Canal Zone in 1956 and in the Congo crisis in 1960. In both cases, the collective nature of the action, the relatively small and weak (and therefore nondisturbing) nature of the states involved, and the general disinterested air evoked by the combination of small powers and the United Nations, contributed directly to the accomplishment of the military mission and its political goal. In Suez, the

UNEF did no fighting; in the Congo, the force was committed to direct and successful (but sharply limited) operations against the secessionist regime of Katanga province.

Nevertheless, United Nations peacekeeping was intended to be the direct product of great power unanimity, cooperation, and concerted action, and these two examples were organized under unusual circumstances for the great powers. When ONUC and even UNEF operations became adverse to the interests of one or more of the great powers, the financial crisis of 1963–64, which indicated a deeper consensual issue, gripped the organization and threatened to destroy it. A realistic appraisal of United Nations peacekeeping in the nuclear age would conclude that little can be done in the face of great power intransigence, although this very opposition (or the possibility of it) has spurred innovative approaches to peacekeeping (such as the Cyprus operation) which may yet prove the most efficacious.

Even in these instances, however, the range of effective military action is quite narrow. At super power level, the problem of relating contemporary military capability to foreign policy objectives will continue to defy solution until military specialists and political leaders learn more about the implications of modern technology as applied to war. Smaller powers are also faced with the problem of understanding and handling the use of military force within an uncertain and dynamic great power milieu which provides no safe or predictable frame of reference for their operations.

NEW DOCTRINES AND THE MILITARY DILEMMA

We must not suppose that military experts have remained suspended in bemusement at the massive effect of the new technology of warfare on their profession. On the contrary, military and civilian analysts in all countries have been devoting great effort to coming to terms with the changed conditions of war. Out of this enterprise has come a spate of new doctrines and concepts, covering a broad gamut of situations, but analogous in their attempt to develop an intellectual base for warfare in the modern world.

The Importance of Military Doctrine

The scope of modern warfare is so vast and its instruments so complex that it would be impossible to conduct a campaign without a doctrine governing the military process. A military doctrine spells out a series of assumptions about the nature and conditions of combat and the calculations controlling its initiation, prosecution, and termination. Military doctrine also resolves in advance the dilemmas inherent in battlefield operations: the relative importance of conserving materiel compared with conserving life, the respective roles of position and maneuver, the concept of "firepower" as opposed to that of occupation of territory, and so on. Military doctrine, by developing a mental framework within which operational decisions can be made, makes the task of modern commanders manageable.

Military doctrine occupies a central place in the capability judgments of a state. Since it governs the makeup of the military machine, the principles that will affect its employment, and the point of view and professional orientation of its officer corps, doctrine is one of the filters through which raw military potential must pass before a sophisticated evaluation can be made of a nation's real military capacity. American military doctrine has always emphasized fire and maneuver as the ingredients of victory, and has always argued that the offensive was both less costly and more productive than a defensive posture. Preservation of manpower has always ranked higher than the husbanding of materiel. The maintenance at all times of a force ready to fight is another standard American tenet, although one developed only since World War II. These principles contrast with the relatively low rank given by Chinese military thought to the conservation of life, and the emphasis on small-group irregular tactics developed by Mao Tse-tung. Russian doctrine emphasizes massed firepower and places less emphasis on maneuver and mobility. All of these considerations (to which analogues could be found in the military doctrine of all states) have a significant effect on the way the nation's armed forces are constructed and used. They are important to both the foreign policy planner contemplating military action and the statesman evaluating the potential of another state.

The Doctrinal Crisis: Is This a New Era?

The great crisis currently facing scholars of military doctrine involves an estimate of the impact of the new technology on the classic principles of warfare. Do these rules of strategy and tactics, evolved over the centuries and absorbing earlier technological advances from the bow and arrow to the tank, the "blockbuster" aerial bomb, and the technique of "vertical envelopment" by airborne forces, still apply in the era of thermonuclear warheads on intercontinental ballistic missiles? One school of thought argues that changes in warfare are entirely quantitative and not qualitative, and the historic doctrines of warfare need only adapt to new conditions. Another group contends that modern weaponry has breached the parameters of warfare, and entirely new concepts are needed before men can exploit this as yet untried range of capability.

Traditionalists argue that the new weapons are no more than advanced versions of classic types. A thermonuclear bomb has the explosive potential of 50 million tons of TNT; although a frightening figure, this comparison suggests that it would be possible to duplicate the blast of a hydrogen bomb by traditional means. Missiles are no more than improved delivery systems; the entire history of warfare involves gradual advance in delivery techniques, from the individual foot soldier carrying his spear, through rifleman, cavalryman, tanker, airplane pilot, and now the missileman. Each advance, although not eliminating the human element, has involved increases in both the speed and reliability of the delivery of a weapon to its target. Thus, the argument goes, there is no conceptual difference between the doctrines of Caesar's legions and those of contemporary ICBM squadrons; only the technical details of mobilizing and employing the manpower and materiel are new.

The opposite position stems from the belief that destructive capabilities, such as those of hydrogen bombs and delivery systems using fractional orbits and multiple independently retargetable warheads, have made a travesty of the established doctrines of warfare. Not only have modern weapons endangered the survival of the political system that they are supposed to regulate, but they have also made war a cruel deception and a recipe for holocaust.

Advocates of new doctrines go in two different directions from this basic premise. One school contends that a new theory of total war must be developed, founded on principles different from historic practice and emphasizing the major characteristics of the new weapons: destructiveness and rapidity of delivery. The other group contends that war has been rendered obsolete, and that the principal military mission of the future will be to prevent recurrence of combat rather than to win a war.

The doctrinal dispute wages unabated, and statesmen remain suspended between passivity and recklessness while the experts wrangle. There seems little likelihood that any normally prudent policy-maker will take the risk intrinsic to modern war until he has resolved the doctrinal dilemma to his own satisfaction. So long as military specialists continue to deepen the gaps between the several schools of thought, the use of armed force on an organized basis by any major state remains only a remote possibility.

Doctrines of Total War

DETERRENCE.   Deterrence—the capacity of modern weapons to deter another state from initiating warfare—is one of the pervasive doctrines of the new military era. This notion has always been part of military lore, but the peculiar qualities of the new techniques make deterrence more significant than ever before.

Much thought has gone into the ramifications of the deterrent mission of modern military establishments. In the United States, two rival theories of deterrence have been voiced. One, called the "finite deterrent," argues that a nation's retaliatory capacity should be increased to such a point that, regardless of the damage inflicted by an initial strike, the enemy would immediately receive an unacceptable amount of return damage on his cities, his industrial capacity, and his clusters of population. This so-called "city-busting" theory (also called "countersociety" or "countervalue") has been opposed by the "counterforce" concept that bases deterrence on the development of capability sufficiently well-aimed to destroy the enemy's military capacity while leaving his cities and population relatively intact. In practice, all states with adequate productive capability have attempted a policy that partakes of both points of view. The ultimate deterrent, regardless of the counterforce-countervalue mix, remains the ability of a nation to assure an unacceptable level of damage to another nation's society.

Deterrence is the mission for which modern weapons are extremely appropriate. Their indiscriminate and uncertain effect, and the fact that the "new generation" of weaponry has never been used in combat, make policy-makers extremely cautious and susceptible to being deterred. It is paradoxical that such refined and sophisticated military technology has proved best suited for making war an unwise gamble, rather than for winning it.

THE NATURE OF RESPONSE.   Conceptually part of the deterrent concept, but a considerable doctrinal issue in itself, is the question of the response a state should take to a military-political provocation. As in deterrence, several different approaches have been developed. We shall look at the way the controversy has been prosecuted in the United States, although all major states are seized by the issue.

One school of thought, now in disrepute, favors "instantaneous response," more popularly known as "massive retaliation." Americans advancing this argument have contended that any direct Soviet-American armed conflict is inevitably a total war, and urge that whatever strategic advantage lies in the first strike should be retained by the United States. The theory of response, therefore, is that the moment a Soviet provocation crosses the threshold of tolerability, the full weight of American nuclear capability is to be unleashed on the entire spectrum of targets in the U.S.S.R. Its advocates insist that this doctrine not only ensures the optimum basis for accepting total war, but also contributes to the efficacy of deterrent dispositions. No aggressor, certain that total war would result, will risk breaching an admittedly unclear line of tolerance.

The contradictory position was originally identified with the doctrines of limited war, which shall be examined in the next section. Recently, however, a more sophisticated position known generally as "flexible response" has been developed. Its basic rationale is that the United States should not commit itself to an all-out immediate response to a challenge, but should allow itself a "pause for decision" before taking action, and then respond only at a level adequate to neutralize the immediate threat. Responsibility for escalating the conflict will rest upon the enemy, and the United States will be free from the danger of initiating an unnecessary total war.

American policy, long officially committed to instantaneous response, has shifted to a version of flexible response, with a wide range of force capabilities that provide multiple response options across the force continuum. Although this has been hailed as a basic doctrinal overhaul, the United States still overtly retains the right to initiate nuclear warfare in the event of an unbearable but nonnuclear provocation from the Soviet Union. This proviso, built into the doctrine, furnishes the doctrinal and tactical link between past and present policy.

"First Strike" or "Second Strike." Another doctrinal issue of great importance concerns the relative merits of the "first strike" as opposed to the retaliatory or "second strike" posture. It is generally conceded that there is not yet any reliable defense against nuclear attack, and the only deterrent is assured destruction. The doctrinal issue is whether a nation, in view of this dangerous situation, can safely adopt a second strike strategy.

The United States has done so, and there has been intense controversy over whether this decision was wise. Opponents of the American willingness to "give the enemy the first blow" contend that the enemy might, in one assault, cripple either the nation's will to fight or its capacity to strike back; this, they say, is too great a risk to take, and a revised American doctrine should permit the United States to strike first in a preemptive or preventive way. Defenders of the established American position point to the increasing invulnerability of the retaliatory United States weapons systems—such as the *Polaris*-carrying nuclear submarine fleet and Minuteman missiles in underground silos—and argue that any change in the American doctrine would be viewed by the Soviets as a dangerously provocative move. The dilemma has been partly resolved by the decreasing military feasibility of a first strike. The U.S.S.R. has also developed weapons systems with low vulnerabilities, giving it essentially the same second strike destruction capability as the United States. Mutual invulnerability and the low success probability of a first strike have, in the eyes of many, stabilized the nuclear deterrence environment.

For a status quo state like the United States, the first strike argument is a difficult one. Since the United States is strategically more interested in deterrence than in initiating war, it must maintain great retaliatory capability and yet avoid increasing tension and the probability of war. However, if deterrence fails, it must be capable of winning the war that has been forced upon it, and dare not forego the advantage of the first strike. American second strike strategy is more an optimistic verdict on the probability of successful deterrence than it is a rationalized theory for fighting total war. Nevertheless, as the major powers have reached the state of "saturation parity," they have come to view additional weapons systems and upgraded capabilities in terms of limiting damage, war fighting, and war termination, should deterrence fail. Damage limiting, although secondary, is one of the two basic capabilities the United States has repeatedly sought in its general war forces, and such thinking has generated new targeting and employment concepts throughout the military establishment.

DEFENSE AND SURVIVAL.   Estimates of the casualities that would be produced by a nuclear attack on an urbanized state are uncertain, since nobody knows what would actually happen; but all are terribly high. The prohibitive cost in human life has produced considerable doctrinal effort in the areas of passive defense to nuclear attack and prospects for national survival after a major blow.

The discussions cluster around two major points. One concerns the defensive measures civilian populations might take, including evacuation, shelter, permanent underground installations, and fallout and radiation protection. The entire subject suffers from a number of conceptual and practical difficulties; since there is no reliable experience on which to build, the extent to which the theorists and responsible officials are themselves persuaded of the utility of their measures is debatable, and public fatalism and widespread apathy reflect a profound belief that initiation of nuclear war is simply the end of everything. No major nation has more than scratched the surface in the field of passive defense.

Theorists of recuperation also have little evidence to support their dogmas. Their usual criterion is the rapidity with which the attacked state might be expected to restore its productive plant to preattack levels, and estimates vary according to the optimism of the analyst and his evaluations of his opponent's strategy, and in response to current political exigencies. Only a few students have addressed the question of human response to a destructive attack, and have inquired into the extent to which a battered remnant of survivors would perform public reconstruction after their private lives had been shattered. It is generally agreed that a nuclear onslaught would destroy political democracy and individual freedom. How would a population accustomed to an open society respond to the imposition of an authoritarian regime in the midst of smoking ruins and wholesale death?

The problems of defense, survival, and reconstruction have not yet received their definitive doctrinal formulation. Students will continue to wrestle with them, for they are inescapable as long as total war remains a possibility. Until they are solved, initiation of total war will remain a risk of unpredictable dimensions.

Doctrines of Limited War

"CONVENTIONAL WAR." We have scrutinized the doctrines advanced and developed by theorists of total war. Other doctrinal positions have been developed by analysts who challenge the ubiquitous destruction of all-out nuclear conflict, and contend that the balance of terror and reciprocal deterrence allow a place for politically relevant warfare that is less than total. This is the province of the theorists of limited war.

Limited war doctrines accept the deterrent implications of the nuclear absolutes, but challenge their universal effect. Adherents of this position generally argue that nuclear weapons can deter a nuclear attack, but that no nation will ever unleash an all-out response to a relatively minor provocation. They contend that subnuclear challenges can best be met by subnuclear responses, with the ensuing conflicts fought to a political decision without escalating into an apocalyptic conflagration.

The most common formulation of the limited war position is cast in terms of so-called "conventional war"—war fought with high explosive rather than nuclear weapons. The traditional division between conventional war and nuclear war is blurred by the introduction of "tactical" nuclear warheads, some with yields in the high explosive range. Debate over the advisability of employing any nuclear weapons, even in a limited role, persists. Most analysts agree that when the nuclear "firebreak" is crossed, the complex relationship among the stationing of the tactical systems, their ranges, their basic nature (aircraft, artillery, missile), and the strategies under which they are employed may lead to a rapid self-propelling jump to total war. Contrary arguments are possible, but the great uncertainties associated with the introduction of tactical nuclear weapons to the battlefield generally exclude them from the range of attractive military options in "limited war," and they have been relegated to a deterrent role (as in Europe) or to the status of additional help if deterrence fails. This argument suggests that the balance of deterrence is absolute, and that conventional and traditional military calculations can proceed almost as if nuclear weapons had never been invented. The notion has obvious appeal to all traditionally-minded military thinkers, particularly to those branches of service—such as the army ground forces —which fear eventual displacement by modern gadgetry.

Conventional warriors in the western world have pressed their case with skill and determination, but the Soviet line has not been encouraging to their position. Recent Soviet pronouncements have suggested that Moscow feels that any direct Soviet-western conflict would escalate into all-out nuclear exchange, and that conventional military doctrines cannot provide any rationale for such a struggle. It is possible that this Soviet position is part of Moscow's own deterrent strategy, and perhaps the limited war theorists are correct. In the face of such a grim warning, however, few western leaders are willing to gamble survival on their ability to keep an open clash with Moscow from becoming a total war.

The conventional war theory suffers from two practical inhibitions. First, the task of developing a situation to test its validity has proved extremely difficult. However convincing its rhetoric, no doctrine has any functional utility unless it is applicable in the real world on a bearable cost/risk basis. Second, the record of the cold war period indicates that the West can meet Communists on the battlefield without the war becoming total, as shown by the experience in Korea, Vietnam, and certain other crisis points. But a war between nuclear powers can be kept at a subnuclear level only at the price of virtually abandoning the possibility of a political victory. This lesson was learned in Korea and relearned (with variations) in Vietnam. The Vietnam war has demonstrated the application of military power as "force"—to gain military-political objectives in South Vietnam (as in the Arab-Israeli conflict of 1967) and the bombing campaign in North Vietnam—and to produce "violence"—pain and suffering. Once the military "force" utility of the bombing became marginal, it continued to be valuable in the bargaining and negotiating role. Since limited war seems feasible only if allowed to deteriorate into a stalemate, it is difficult to see why it should win the sympathy of success-minded statesmen.

Guerrilla Warfare. A second line of attack of the limited war theorists is represented by doctrines of guerrilla warfare and other irregular and "paramilitary" (sometimes called counterinsurgent) techniques. If limited conventional war carries too many risks, paramilitary techniques may well provide a safe way to apply force to the accomplishment of political ends.

Modern theories of guerrilla warfare are products of Communist thought. The most widely read treatises on the subject today were written by Mao Tsetung.[1] The obvious success of Communist action groups using guerrilla tactics in southeast Asia and other trouble spots has awakened much western interest as nuclear deterrence and the risks of conventional warfare have closed the more familiar avenues for exercise of military power. The principles of small-group action, irregular formations, hit-and-run tactics, and a long-term war of attrition have become familiar to western military analysts.

The current enthusiasm for paramilitary techniques should not blind military thinkers to the fact that guerrilla warfare is not a technique of war, but of revolution. It is a political, not a military, procedure. As a form of strategy it is not applicable under a great variety of conditions, but only in those special situations where the basic ingredients are present: a population alienated from its government and gripped by widespread disaffection, and a government that lacks energy and efficiency in dealing with both the guerrilla threat and the socio-economic-political conditions that spawned the revolution itself. It is of limited relevance to those states, including most leaders of the western bloc, whose interest lies less in overturning governments and promoting revolution than in stabilizing and harmonizing relationships. Counterguerrilla activity—strategically a doctrine of defense rather than attack—has an unquestionable military dimension, but just as the guerrilla problem has its roots in social unrest, so campaigns against guerrillas must be based on social reform, and use military operations as a fringe effort rather than as their ideological and operational center.

THE ARMS RACE AND DISARMAMENT

With the logic of military action so subject to question under contemporary conditions, it is not surprising that states have been pursuing the issue of securing some release from the grim pressure of potential destruction. Two interacting political trends have accompanied the doctrinal and conceptual discussion of military matters since the dawn of the nuclear era. The major military powers have embarked on a massive arms race conducted primarily in the categories of new weapons and delivery systems. At the same time, significant efforts have been made to discover workable formulas for arms reduction, arms control, and—at least in principle—eventual total disarmament.

Each of these enterprises is really an almost instinctive attempt by governments to develop a larger margin of relative security in a world grown more dangerous. Both are understandable and merit sympathetic analysis, yet each tends to cancel out the other and leave the system as it would have been. Neither the arms race nor disarmament has made the world any more secure.

The Arms Race

The arms race between the communist world and the western bloc, essentially a technical rather than a military contest, has been in effect for more than a decade. Each side seeks advances in quality rather than in quantity of weapons. The major categories of effort include the increase in explosive "yield" of large nuclear bombs, the miniaturization of nuclear warheads for tactical purposes, the improvement in delivery systems—primarily in longer-range but more accurate missiles—and the development of detection and antimissile systems.

The most apparent dimensions of the arms race have been the series of subterranean, surface, and atmospheric tests nuclear powers have undertaken to prove the effectiveness of their new weapons. As weapons have grown larger and yields increased, the psychological and physiological resentment of nonnuclear powers and well-organized groups of private citizens has grown. Between 1958 and 1961 the United States and the Soviet Union maintained an informal moratorium on nuclear testing that remained unbroken even when France began to test in the Sahara Desert. Late in 1961 the U.S.S.R. abruptly resumed testing, and the United States shortly followed suit. Finally, in 1963, both nations, in the words of President Kennedy, "put the genie back into the bottle" with the Nuclear Test Ban Treaty barring atmospheric or exoatmospheric testing. Since then, nuclear tests have been confined to underground explosions, with the exception of those conducted by France and, more recently, Communist China.

The Logic of the Arms Race

The rationale of the arms race is devastatingly simple. Although military theorists question whether either side can ever gain a meaningful advantage, neither dares to relax its effort lest the other succeed in achieving a technological and military breakthrough. Each new move brings its inevitable riposte, which in turn triggers another step, and so on.

Ample military and scientific arguments exist to justify indefinite prolongation of the race. There is much that the experts can accomplish in the improvement of old weapons and the development of newer and more sophisticated devices, so in this sense the arms race is actually a productive enterprise. In addition, every new move that makes weapons more effective and war more horrible also augments the deterrent effect of military power. A persuasive case can even be made for the arms race as a force for peace, in that it progressively narrows the range of military action enjoyed by states.

Yet there would seem to be a point of vanishing returns. When each side has developed a truly finite deterrent (possessing the capacity to destroy the other completely), any further refinement becomes merely "conspicuous consumption." The stakes become no more than a meretricious factor of prestige, with faint possibility of achieving any meaningful psychological advantage over the other contestant. However, as in the 1967–1968 anti-ballistic missile (ABM) debate, there has occasionally arisen a technological possibility which threatens to upset the precarious balance. In this case, there was danger that one major power, the Soviet Union, could so degrade the assured destruction capability of the other that mutual deterrence would be eroded to the point of dangerous instability. Part of the debate revolved around which measures to take—offensive or defensive—if the Soviet ABM was indeed effective. It was apparently technologically feasible to overwhelm the ABM offensively (through pure saturation and sophisticated tactics), possibly restoring the deterrent balance, but at the great additional cost always attending massive increases in total weapons systems. This grim prospect of a costly arms spiral upward with no prospective increase in security convinced the major powers that they should explore new ways to limit the arms race. By early 1968 the U.S. and the U.S.S.R. were engaged in conversations directed toward that end, and both had markedly slowed ABM development and installation. Nevertheless, one need not be a philosopher or humanitarian to wonder if the rewards that seem to justify the effort of continuing the arms race are negligible.

The Failure of Disarmament

A dismal page in the history of international politics between 1945–1961 was the utter failure of any attempts to reach an agreement on arms reduction or arms control. All the abortive projects, different only in detail, shared the same fate. Plans were advanced for elimination of nuclear weapons, reduction of conventional armaments, cessation of nuclear testing, and various inspection schemes to reduce the probability of cheating or surprise attack. All came to inglorious ends, and the arms race appeared to have been accepted by the major powers as an acceptable substitute for arms control.

Yet both East and West had embraced the principle that general and complete disarmament, except for internal security forces, was the goal for which all must strive. Progress was halted, not on matters of principle, but on the nature and sequence of steps to be taken to achieve the eventual end. Each side had an initial *sine qua non* on which it has insisted in full knowledge that the other would reject it: the U.S.S.R. demanded nuclear parity and abolition of nuclear weapons by treaty before it would consider any implementing steps, while the United States demanded full acceptance of a "control and inspection" system as a prerequisite to any consideration of the substance of disarmament. No negotiations were able to pass over this initial hurdle, and all broke off in mutual recriminations. The Soviets claimed American concern with inspection was a cloak for espionage, while the United States found the Soviet attempt to forbid use of nuclear weapons in war a sinister plot to undermine American security. With the advent of Soviet nuclear weapons "parity" of a sort and the celebrated political "detente," both sides have been able to overlook prior objections and to initiate some encouraging steps toward arms control accommodation. These steps include the Nuclear Test Ban Treaty (1963), which we have already discussed; the treaty barring the interjection of nuclear weapons into outer space, signed in 1966; and finally, the Nuclear Non-Proliferation Treaty of 1968.

The reasoning which led to the Non-Proliferation Treaty reveals much about the extent and substance of the recent super power rapprochement. The treaty, signed by 57 nations (excluding West Germany, France, Communist China, and Japan), calls for a halt in the spread of nuclear weapons to nations which do not already possess such weaponry, but does not exclude distribution of fissionable material for "peaceful purposes."

A central point of contention in reaching an agreement was the nature of guarantees to nonnuclear nations from the great powers, a problem circumvented in part by bilateral assurances and a manageable "escape" clause. Great power motives for such an understanding were variously interpreted as a joining of forces versus the imminent threat of China, as a smoke screen to obscure great power actions in Vietnam and Eastern Europe, or merely as an effort to insure nuclear hegemony in a burgeoning nuclear world. Whatever the motives, most international leaders agree that the treaty is a step in the right direction toward the eventual demise of the "balance of terror."

The Role of Political Decision

The root of the difficulty in reaching agreement about disarmament lies in the political preconceptions each side has brought to the analysis of issues of arms control. So long as both camps feel their security is better served by a continuing arms race, disarmament will remain an ephemeral idea. So long as both prefer the great but familiar risks of open conflict to the unknown dangers of living under military wraps in an untried and possibly entrapping control system, there is not enough appeal in the new to justify abandonment of the old. So long as the cold war retains its active growing edge, arms reduction (which would inevitably tend to stabilize relations) is of limited political relevance.

Disarmament, like the arms race, is much more a political than a military and technical question. The arms race is not a cause of the tension between East and West, nor would arms control itself ease conditions. The cold war period has been a political exercise, and its mitigation demanded new political judgments as well. Only when Moscow and Washington conclude that the probability of their being obliged to use military establishments in their own defense has decreased will a climate conducive to additional realistic disarmament discussions exist. Only the future can state with certainty whether the tensions of the age will permit such a reassessment of the political situation. No one now alive knows if mankind has enough time to devise an escape from the military dilemma in which it has placed itself.

REFERENCES

° Aron, Raymond, *On War*. Garden City, N.Y.: Doubleday & Company, Inc., Anchor Books, 1959.

Brodie, Bernard, *Escalation and the Nuclear Option*. Princeton, N.J.: Princeton University Press, 1966.

° ———, *Strategy in the Missile Age*. Princeton, N.J.: Princeton University Press, 1965.

° Garthoff, Raymond L., *Soviet Strategy in the Nuclear Age*. New York: Frederick A. Praeger, Inc., 1962.

Green, Philip, *Deadly Logic: The Theory of Nuclear Deterrence*. Columbus: Ohio State University Press, 1966.

° Indicates paperback edition.

* Halperin, Morton H., *Limited War in the Nuclear Age*. New York: John Wiley & Sons, Inc., 1963.

Heilbrunn, Otto, *Conventional Warfare in the Nuclear Age*. New York: Frederick A. Praeger, Inc., 1965.

* Hoffmann, Stanley, *The State of War: Essays on the Theory and Practice of International Politics*. New York: Frederick A. Praeger, Inc., 1965.

Huntington, S., ed., *Changing Patterns of Military Politics*. New York: The Free Press, 1962.

Kahn, Herman, *On Escalation: Metaphors and Scenarios*. New York: Frederick A. Praeger, Inc., 1965.

————, *On Thermonuclear War*. Princeton, N.J.: Princeton University Press, 1960.

* ————, *Thinking About the Unthinkable*. New York: Horizon Press, 1962.

* Kissinger, Henry A., *Necessity for Choice*. Garden City: Doubleday & Company, Inc., Anchor Books, 1961.

* Knorr, Klaus, *On the Uses of Military Power in the Nuclear Age*. Princeton, N.J.: Princeton University Press, 1966.

* Lefever, Ernest, ed., *Arms and Arms Control*. New York: Frederick A. Praeger, Inc., 1961.

Menges, Constantine G., *Military Aspects of International Relations in the Developing Areas*. Santa Monica, California: Rand Corporation, 1966.

* Morgenstern, Oskar, *Question of National Defense*. New York: Random House, Inc., Vintage Books, 1959.

* Preston, Richard A., *et al.*, *Men in Arms: A History of Warfare and its Inter-relatonships with Western Society*. New York: Frederick A. Praeger, Inc., 1962.

* Schelling, Thomas C., *Arms and Influence*. New Haven: Yale University Press, 1966.

Von Clausewitz, Karl, *War, Politics, and Power*. Chicago: Henry Regnery Co., 1962.

* Waltz, Kenneth N., *Man, the State and War*. New York: Columbia University Press, 1959.

Wright, Quincy A., *Study of War* (2 volumes) (2nd ed.). Chicago: Chicago University Press, 1965.

* Indicates paperback edition.

TEN

Ideology and Prestige

One of the features of contemporary world politics that distinguishes it from the "classic" pattern of an earlier era is the manipulation of mass beliefs and popular ideas by decision-makers. The emergence of mass movements of vast size and irresistible force has diluted the once exclusive control of foreign policy exercised by highly skilled elites. Careful strategic calculations are explained in simplistic formulations of international reality, their relevance in no way mitigating the militancy with which they are defended. Mass man as well as his ways of thinking are manipuated by the national and international political process.

IDEOLOGY AND WORLD POLITICS

In a manner unknown to history since the great shocks of the Renaissance, the Reformation, and the Industrial Revolution washed away the underpinnings of the unified society of the Middle Ages, men have turned to all-encompassing belief systems to explain reality. In contrast to the rational man who was the ideal of the eighteenth century and the optimistic man who characterized the nineteenth, the present century has at its center the "true believer." Individuals adrift in a universe that grows more difficult to comprehend and cope with every day increasingly find the relief and comfort they seek in systematic, comprehensive systems of belief.

This tendency, running through the entire fabric of social life, is sharply reinforced in mattters concerning international relations. The world has grown uncomfortably smaller, and national groups everywhere have been wrenched from a cultural isolation that had endured in some cases for centuries. However, the great increase in the number of international problems demanding solution has been accompanied by a marked decrease in the probability of their solution. Faced with an agonizing dilemma of impossible choices, entire societies have fled from the reality of coexistence (in its noncommunist and literal sense) to the fantasy of ideological formulations of world mission. Consciously taking refuge in an ideological Utopia, states have given the conduct of international political relations a measure of tension, danger, and potential explosiveness that has no parallel in history. The secular rationalism of contemporary ideologies has moved superstition from the realm of religion to the arena of politics.

The Nature of Ideology

An ideology may be defined as a self-contained and self-justifying belief system that incorporates an over-all world-view and provides a basis for explaining all of reality. Beginning with certain postulates about the nature of man and his place in the world, it develops from this a theory of human history, a moral code, a sense of mission, and a program for action. All ideologies purport to embody absolute truth, reinforced with certain supernatural (or superhuman) justification. Adherence to the system is thus both a rational and moral act, and disagreement is not only error but sin.

Ideologies are not new in international politics. Every system of government and every national group has at some time found it expedient to ground its international conduct on what it conceived as eternal verities. But the mass movement, defined here as an ideology with implications of social action which gathers sufficient adherents to become a real force, is a contemporary political phenomenon. Ideological formulations of international issues color the bulk of today's confrontations of states.

An ideolgical approach to world political problems displays certain marked characteristics.

1. Ideology leads inescapably to the formulation of problems in moral terms. An international dispute thus becomes a clash between good and evil, with the stakes never less than absolute vindication or total defeat.
2. Ideological controversy (which is inevitable in any contact between states embodying total belief systems) is not susceptible to compromise or accommodation. No ideology permits bargaining with evil.
3. Ideologically-oriented policy can never "succeed" in the sense that strategic calculations can be crowned with success. States cannot kill ideas, only people; wiping out a population in no way destroys their unpopular beliefs.

Ideology and Foreign Policy

Ideologies have served historically to fill the needs of men, usually by attempting to bridge the gap between the prevailing limits of reason and the psychological needs of man within a society. Although often beginning modestly, they tend to grow all-encompassing and soon claim for themselves universal truth. Ideologies also show a propensity for becoming outmoded, going through stages of Messianism, corruption, misuse, and eventually—as circumstances change—meaninglessness. They often lead to the generation of their antithesis. Ideological conflict, if disaster is to be avoided, requires that militancy be replaced by toleration, and hostility by mutual respect.

The role of ideology in international politics, or the degree to which ideology affects the formulation of a state's foreign policy and the resulting implications for international politics, have become increasingly important questions. This issue has been magnified by the challenge of present-day ideological formulations of world politics. One important question concerns whether governments adhere strictly to a foreign policy formulated according to dogmatic ideological tenets, or whether they follow the traditional method of realistic appraisal of concrete situations within the context of their individual national interests and the relevant information available concerning those situations.

Another question involves the overlap of theory and reality. Are not both ideology and realistic appraisal present, although in varying degrees, in the formulation of foreign policy by almost all states? Every state is equipped with a priority system for the determination of foreign policy goals and tactics. There are certain levels of action in which either ideology or realism is predominant, and between these two extremes some sort of balance is achieved. There is, however, no fixed relationship that can be postulated; rather, ideology and realistic appraisal meet in each distinct situation of foreign policy, with different degrees of emphasis. In this parameter, ideology plays the smallest role in the most restricted choice situations, but becomes increasingly effective when there is greater freedom of choice of alternative action possibilities. In attempting to discover which tendency—ideology or realistic appraisal—operates more strongly, it must be remembered that a state can remain consistent with its ideological tenets although its actions appear strikingly at variance with its stated purposes.

What evidence is there for continuity of purpose; how may we determine to what extent ideology conditions foreign policy decisions? One must infer a state's intent from the content of a whole series of actions, and allow for a possible discrepancy between what is said and what is done. We cannot draw accurate conclusions from a series of statements, since verbal consistency does not necessarily imply consistency in action. There must be a connection, however, between ideology and action. The nature of the state dictates that its actions implement its real purposes, but not necessarily a verbalized ideology. The possible relevance of verbalizations cannot be completely discounted, but their importance is only a function of their congruence with action.

The conflict is therefore between the systematic world-view imposed by an ideological approach to action and the uneven, incomplete, and paradoxical fashion in which the real world impinges upon a state. Ideology and national interest both have their roots in a system of values, but they differ in their compulsions to action. Ideological formulations make generous use of concepts of inevitability or impossibility, and lead to one-dimensional foreign policy thinking. A pragmatic national interest is fixed only in its (possibly Utopian) view of the future, and is infinitely flexible in its intermediate goals and objectives and in the tactics adopted for their achievement.

Ideology may, of course, become the source for postulations of national interest and long-range goals. If these aspirations are deeply rooted in the social dynamic of a people, and if the government is adept at tactics, a successful foreign policy is possible. But if ideology intrudes into situational analysis and the range of state action is cast in terms of imperatives of belief, statecraft in the classic sense is left helpless.

Ideology: Myth and Reality

Man relates himself to the facts of life by creating myths, which shield him from and make comprehensible to him the realities of social life. Political society is invariably sanctioned by myth. Even such theorists as Hobbes and Locke, who appeal to reason for a basis of political society, posit such notions as "rational man" and "natural right."

Man realizes that life without purpose adds up to nothing—it cannot be measured—so his intervention into political society provides the measure of his failures and achievements. Such political action expresses the human strategy, which subordinates reality to higher human priorities and goals. It also represents the human project, designed to give purpose and meaning to life. Thus man refuses to accept reality; determined to impose a new reality upon the earth, he is suspended between perpetual aspirations and perpetual frustrations.

International political life in the twentieth century reveals a discordant pluralism totally unsupported by a transcendent myth. Successful political action in such a world demands a convincing ideology, but the issue is not whether ideology is predicated upon myth, nor whether myth and reality are identical. An object is real in a given context only when it functions in that context. The myth of Pegasus had an operational reality in the Golden Age, but not in the modern concept of objective reality. Beauty exists in the public context of nature; art and heroes exist in the public context of history. In other words, contemporaneity begets reality; what exists in the present situation is real.

Myth is creative of reality when it becomes the substance of consensus in a given society. It is delusive when it confounds appearance with reality. Myths remain relevant until environmental change demolishes their institutional structures. Stripped of its supporting myth, the structure is vulnerable to revolutionary pressure; a new myth will eventually appear on the horizon. However, potent as myths are in creating reality, they cannot form the exclusive or quasi-exclusive basis of behavior in international politics.

IDEOLOGICAL FORMULATIONS IN WORLD POLITICS

The post-World War II era marked a challenge to the traditional criteria and concepts of the classic international system. New formulations arose to compete with the time-honored precepts of statecraft. Their advocates sought, with varying success, to apply them in a nontraditional world. We may view these as ideologies, each seeking an appropriately changed situation in which to be applied.

By 1950, three such ideologies had found more or less precise expression, and their subsequent interplay has given the postwar world its definitive coloration and shape. Since any ideology other than simple nihilism must incorporate a utopian vision of perfect order, these doctrines may be initially compared in terms of the ideal each considered itself to be serving.

The first was, of course, the world-view of communism. Its utopian vision was of a classless and therefore stateless society in which all men would live in relatively unfettered brotherhood. Its operational emphasis was (and remains) protection of existing communist beachheads in the world and, at a somewhat lower priority level, extension of communist influence by persuasion, subversion, and war. Purporting to be "scientific," its perfect world order was postulated as attainable, feasible, and inevitable.

The second great utopia was projected by the United States. American doctrine envisaged a world organized under law into a peaceful and harmonious society of states, in which individual and group obligation to the community of mankind placed limits on the freedom of states—a translation into international political terms of the familiar domestic political philosophy of Americans. Committed ideologically to free will and personal responsibility for action, the United States could not predict the realization of its dream, only its possibility.

The final ideology was the revolutionism of the anticolonial world, eventually given many specific forms but first verbalized clearly by independent India. Its utopia was a world almost entirely nonpolitical, in which distinctions among states were obliterated in favor of global cooperative efforts to elevate the material misery of the human race. In practice, this meant secession from the familiar problems of world affairs and continued emphasis on issues of underdevelopment, race, and cultural diversity in the name of a higher morality.

From each of these utopian postures were derived formulations of the minimum requirements necessary for a believing state compelled to exist in a nonideal world. To communists these included prevention of any hostile coalition strong enough to menace existing communist systems, and preservation of sufficient instability and tension in the noncommunist world to permit continued expansion of communist power. For Americans the requirements included adequate stability in the world to give existing mechanisms of international organization a chance to survive and grow, while at the same time preserving the uniquely favorable position enjoyed by the United States. Anticolonialist requirements were somewhat more numerous, beginning with the simple idea of early liquidation of colonialism and extending to establishment of inhibitions and limitations on all major states by international mechanisms. The anticolonialists wished "a plague on both your houses" to the cold war enemies, but generalized the curse to include all aspirants to high status and broad spheres of power in the international arena.

Out of the clash of these requirements has come the subject matter of international relations since 1945. The cold war itself, especially in its acute phase, brought the minimum demands of the United States and the

Soviet Union into close and often irreconcilable juxtaposition. Only in the latter years of the struggle (since approximately 1955) did the hostility between Moscow and Washington become restrained as the third world demanded and received a hearing from both sides.

The Soviet Approach to the World: A Form of Communism

How does the Soviet Union approach the world? What are its operative assumptions? How does it construct its own mission? Through what sort of intellectual filter do Soviet decision-makers see the outside world?

The Soviet Union, thanks to its official ideology and one-sided propaganda attack on domestic consensus, has a unified verbal answer to these and all related questions. Marxism and its later derivations profess to unlock the riddle of history, and to enable true believers to understand the basic nature of world relations. The verbalized Soviet approach to the world has since 1917 been that of orthodox (as of any given moment) communist theory.

The Soviet Union sees itself ideologically as a revolutionary power committed to the destruction of existing institutions and patterns and their replacement by an entirely new order. Such an approach necessitates the assumption that all existing international arrangements are inherently temporary (except those already under Soviet control) and subject to change by Soviet initiatives. Any understanding or agreement with non-communist powers is by definition tentative and designed only to serve a long-range strategic purpose. Conflict is to be protracted indefinitely until victory crowns the entire effort and utopia becomes a fact.

A distinct evolution is apparent in the Soviet atttitude. Beginning from a position of a great psychic and physical insecurity, Kremlin leadership felt obliged to strike a continuously militant pose and to fight verbally battles they were incapable of prosecuting in action. As the processes of history have subtly modified the nature and expanded the dimension of the world role played by Moscow, and as the Kremlin itself has gained in self-confidence and prestige, the necessity for extreme positions and flamboyant language has gradually disappeared. Moscow's interest in preaching the message of revolution is reduced exactly to the extent to which it is acquiring a stake in the existing order. Far from being a revolutionary and radical force in world affairs, contemporary Soviet policy is more like the nineteenth-century ideal of a great power functioning within the European concert; the *arriviste* is being won over by the Establishment. It is a sardonic coincidence that this in-group is losing its status and its power to control events just as it is expanding its ranks to include the Soviet Union.

The United States Approach to the World: A Form of Democracy

The American approach to the world is the result of a peculiar amalgam of vigorous tradition with accidental historical circumstance. There are three important identifiable ingredients among the basic assumptions about international politics upon which the United States rests its strategic concept: (1) the historic American theory of international relations; (2) the new sense of national importance and mission that came with victory in World War II and the role of leadership that the nation was forced to play in its aftermath; and (3), hopefully to be thought of as a dimension of continuous expansion, a greater degree of realistic understanding of the nature of the international system in the twentieth century. Each makes its own contribution to the conceptual framework of American strategy.

American culture portrays international relations as taking place within a universal system and order governed by and amenable to both logic and morality. Individuals who operate the controls of government are rational and moral creatures; the purpose of international relations is advancement of the common interests of mankind, to be achieved through cooperative action by all states and the solution of "problems" as they arise. Peace marked by amicable resolution of differences and a steady stream of formal (i.e., legal) agreements on particular issues is the normal condition of the world. War is abnormal, the result of the unpredictable appearance of individuals or groups who insist upon immoral and illegal behavior. As an abnormal system, war is outside international relations proper; the task of the state caught in a war is to end it as soon as possible, punish those responsible, and "get back to business" with minimum loss of time.

Although never put so baldly as we have summarized it here, this ideal has energized American action for a century and a half. This was the image of utopia—amplified by institutions for both affirmative cooperative behavior and the punishment of evildoers—for which the Wilsonians fought so bitterly and so long. It still affects the conceptual and the operational atmosphere in which American policy is decided, and remains in some form as a recognizable key ingredient in the American self-image. Any more elaborate or sophisticated strategic exegesis must build upon these principles if its advocates wish it to gain public acceptance and support.

The second element in the American world-view is the new sense of historical importance with which the postwar generation has been forced to come to terms. Up through World War II, Americans were permitted by history and their own code to conceive of themselves as virtually non-participating observers of the international political process, dealing with an intrinsically corrupt system at arm's length and trapped into direct involvement only on widely separated occasions. The nation's normal world mission was to act as a moral example; when events conspired to draw the United States into the thick of battle, the national purpose was to set things right, to provide others with a more reliable guide to future action by institutional change, and then to retire gracefully to the lofty observation of the eccentricities of international politics. All of this philosophy was swept away by World War II, the birth of the nuclear age, and the appearance of the cold war.

Once the most reluctant of dragons, America moved within a relatively few months between mid-1917 and early 1949 into complete acceptance of a starring role. Virtues were discovered in living under the inscrutable gaze of history. The phrase "the responsibilities of world leadership" fell increasingly from American lips, and with each hearing became more palatable. Today Americans enjoy their key position as one of the arbiters of man's fate, even though they may occasionally betray a nostalgic yearning for the days of happy irresponsibility; the thought that some portion of the earth for which the United States has assumed primary responsibility, such as Western Europe, might wish to throw off American sponsorship and strike out on its own causes serious tremors in American political and strategic circles. The public is convinced that the United States will eventually play the largest single role in giving the world its definitive shape.

Finally, the gradually increasing realism of American thinking about world affairs should be mentioned. What we called the "American theory" of international relations was, at least until World War II, accepted less as a utopian dream than as a serious description of international politics, an illusion that had survived almost undisturbed all the shocks of the twentieth century up to 1939. The searing experience of World War II, however, began the eye-opening process reinforced by the two decades of the cold war.

Let us indicate briefly the major elements in the new realism. First, the United States is less inclined in the 1960's than it was in the 1940's to seek absolute solutions to problems, or even to formulate issues in simple dichotomies. Second, Americans appreciate the irrelevancy (or at least the frequent inapplicability) of private morality to the behavior of states. Third, there is reduced acceptance of the crisis-relaxation alternation in American policy, and a correspondingly greater search for a significant dimension of positive and affirmative action. Finally, the distinction-blurring concept of "mankind" has been replaced to a great extent by a more sharply focused and clearly rationalized idea of American interest as the controlling criterion of purpose.

These disparate elements combine to produce a reasonably clear and workable world-view for the use of American strategists. The United States now conceives of the international system as unstable but capable of being stabilized, as disorderly but capable of order, and as potentially warlike but capable of being structured on a continuing basis of peace. The image of the world adopted by the United States thus contains its own built-in action imperatives: the United States, by the definition of the problem it faces, is obliged to seek a solution.

The controlling impulse of American strategy is the creation of a peaceful, orderly, and stable world—translation into operational terms of the prevailing national myth. Although popular treatments of the subject extract considerable ideological comfort from the thought that the achievement of United States ends would redound to the benefit of the entire human race, in reality the motivations underlying such a formula are the most practical American strategists can discover. A world such as this would be one in which American security risks are reduced almost to the vanishing point, American economic and status-prestige concerns receive full satisfaction, and the final vindication of American doctrines about man and society is complete.

The Non-Western Approach to the World: Revolutionism [1]

Implicit in the definition of a nation-state is a set of common beliefs and values that holds the group together. Revolutionism has become the basis for such a response in many of the emerging states. It posits revolution as an ideology that incorporates an over-all world-view and provides a basis for change.

The recent entry of dozens of new, small, and non-western states into active participation in world politics is similar to the sudden eruption of the bourgeois into the politics of the post-Feudal period. As did their middle-class predecessors, the new states find the sanctified values of international politics largely irrelevant to their concerns. Consequently, they are revolting against the assumptions that things will remain as they have been.

[1] *Revolutionism* is used as a concept designating revolution as an ideology.

Though revolutionism is diverse in form, and offers no blueprint for world revolution, it stresses a common theme—it is nationalistic, anti-hierarchic, and socialistic. The nationalism of revolutionism ranges from tribal factionalism to supranational Panism. No two revolutionists [2] seek identical nationalistic goals; nationalism is seen by some as a means of recapturing past glories, while others emphasize the immediate and future problems of building modern societies. But in every case, revolutionism seeks to demonstrate that emerging, non-western states will take their rightful place in the world, despite the ancient western claim that they are incapable of doing so. The revolutionist can overcome the inferiority forced on him in a western and white man's world by excluding "them" from his state, creating a new nation, developing a modern society, and acting in concert with other revolutionists at home and abroad. This imposed inferiority has left a deep emotional scar, causing the revolutionist repeatedly to assert his nationalism in order to prove that he is modern, progressive, and viable.

In contrast, revolutionists quickly identified western institutions to be emulated, one of the most obvious being the nation-state. Their central values were the achievement and maintenance of national unity and independence, and they donned the cloak of western nationalism in their independence movements. But western thought and values did not penetrate deeply enough to give the non-western revolutionists grasp of the principles upon which the nation-state rests. They assumed the outward manifestations, the language and apparatus of statehood, but the real bases for unity were ignored.

Application of these standards to their situation, where national consciousness is nonexistent, has been very difficult. The dichotomy between freedom and authority has required an unfortunate consolidation of power at the expense of individual freedom. No matter how often they are cited by the revolutionists, the conditions of western democracy seldom exist in their own societies.

In their colonial past, many of the new states were denied racial equality and national political freedom. Rebellion against this enforced inferiority and the drive for acceptance and racial equality developed into revolutionary urgings. Nonwhite, non-western, and non-Establishment characteristics were proclaimed to be the framework of a unique personality of which its possessors should be proud. What began as an attempt to give the revolutionists a sense of personal worth and self-respect rapidly changed into an emotional reaction to white and western domi-

---

[2] *Revolutionist* refers to an adherent of revolutionism.

nation which could easily be distorted into non-western racism and extremism.

It is here that the concept of antihierarchy is realized. As the basic ingredient of nationalism, antihierarchy serves two primary functions: it provides the unity and support for a successful liberation movement in areas still under great power domination, and it provides the commonly perceived threat which revolutionists invoke to preserve both their domestic and international positions. The new states gained their independence at a time when sovereignty had become compromised by the technological necessities of interdependence, making self-sufficiency no longer possible. As the ideals of the nationalist movement were compromised by the realities of the situation, ambitions remained unfulfilled and the new states were beset by acute problems of development.

Proceeding from the premise equating Establishment-West-White supremacy and capitalism, it is charged that these interests continue in a postindependence attempt to exert de facto political control by economic means. Revolutionists claim that the independence and progress of the new states is threatened by covert foreign economic domination, which is denounced as the direct cause of the immediate failures of the postindependence period.

The revolutionists' universal predicament is mass poverty. A lack of relevant skills and managerial talents, inordinate income differentials, and the desire to overcome a Marxian, colonial self-image are the intertwined problems of these societies. Revolutionists believe that socialism is the only answer to the need for a moral and just social order. Human dignity, social justice, and equality of opportunity are promoted as the highest social values. The revolutionists advocate elimination of class privilege and distinctions, without resorting to class warfare.

The socialism of the revolutionist is a comprehensive program. Although it guarantees improving the lot of both workers and peasants, problems of the latter are emphasized because of the agrarian base. While it believes in democracy and individual freedom, it invokes state power more often than western socialists, because the revolutionist's world is in a less advanced stage of political consolidation. Thus, the revolutionist's socialism is concerned primarily with agriculture, national unity, and international politics.

Virtually all revolutionists face serious problems of control, which are a direct result of the drive for independence and for subsequent economic and political development. Foremost among these problems is the need for strong public support of continued economic activities which will aid in capital formation and accumulation without creating new political, economic, and social imbalances in already precarious and unstable situations.

The socialist program provides a control function similar to that of preindependence nationalism. It stresses the basic unity of the state's population, and attempts to imbue the entire population with a desire to work and cooperate in programs of economic development. Such popular support and unity is necessary for the establishment of socialized, independent, and industrialized states. Unless the people are intimately involved, development and stability will not be achieved. Despite universal appreciation of this fact, the means of gaining support and involvement may vary radically.

The revolutionists' self-image is collectivist and egalitarian; they assert that the individual can find fulfillment only in a society based upon such principles. Such a society is seen as having a collective mind which conditions the behavior of every individual and gives the society as a whole the right to force individual deference to the collectivity. This strong assertion of egalitarianism, when united with the assertion of classlessness, defines political rights which do not flow from wealth, status, or power, but must be equal for all members of society.

Revolutionism views the international political system differently from both American democracy and Soviet Communism. Throughout their modern history, many of the new states have been the body upon which the rival great powers trampled. Their attitudes toward international politics stem from a search for a uniquely independent identity and role in the world. In attempting to strengthen their individuality, they are almost inevitably cast into a role between the major powers, but subservient to neither.

The disparate strands of their foreign policies form important intellectual and operational assumptions. These a priori foundations of decision and action, which have conditioned their behavior since the late 1950's, may be phrased as follows:

1. Neocolonialism poses the principal threat to their existence.
2. American-Soviet confrontation is merely a struggle for power and domination of smaller states.
3. The bipolar international system does not accommodate their interests and objectives.
4. They are uniquely suited to adjust the unsatisfactory conditions of the international system.

Revolutionists cannot see either Soviet Communism or American democracy as a prime menace to their autonomy. It is, instead, the continuation of international political tensions which may eventually lead to their physical destruction or exposure to a new menace. Thus, they have chosen to steer an independent course between the conflicts of the two great powers in pursuit of their own national interests.

They recognize the possibilities of major war as a direct threat to their continued existence. The climate of international political tensions is not the most auspicious for their security, since both sides in the global struggle are potential sources of infringement on their sovereignty, and a nuclear war would destroy all hopes for development. A basic tenet of revolutionists is that they are best qualified, by virtue of their aloofness from any bloc, to contribute constructively to the lessening of international tensions.

They characterize their policies as expressions of an international conscience, or as elements of rationality which help to temper the predominance of irrationality on the international scene. They claim a special international mission in enunciating the basic world desire for peace, and feel that, through their positions of mediators with no vested interests in any bloc position, they will be heard by all.

From these basic attitudes, the revolutionists have come to place great faith in international organization. They feel that the United Nations should exert a strong influence in settling international disputes, even among great powers. International organizations become vehicles for increasing the political power and influence of traditionally insignificant states, which are attempting literally to force the great powers to pay them heed.   ·

They reject the structure of the present international system through a strategy of non-alignment, with anticolonialism as its corollary. By adopting a posture that is allegedly more relevant than the alternatives extended to them by either great power, they transcend the present ideological split. As translated from perception to practice, nonalignment is designed to serve specific functions. Stripped to their essence, these include:

1. Reconciliation between national sovereignty and the requirements of security.
2. Harmonization between political independence and economic dependence.
3. Maintenance and enhancement of national solidarity.
4. Maximization of foreign policy alternatives and power in international politics.
5. Establishment of an independent role and individuality in world politics.

Since they have attached an absolute quality to their independence, the new states take intense pride in both domestic and international self-reliance. They are loath to commit themselves to policies before examining them in terms of their own national interests and goals. Alignment with either bloc could commit them to future courses of action over which they would have little or no control, and such future conditions could easily lead them into compromising their national interests.

The immediate goal of their foreign policies is national development; i.e., modernization. They realize that this cannot be achieved alone, but also recognize that economic dependence can lead to at least partial domination of their internal and external affairs by foreign powers. To avoid foreign controls and maintain their sovereignty while receiving massive amounts of aid from the great powers has been the basic problem for revolutionary leaders. A partial answer has involved seeking aid from all available sources while making it clear that their political allegiance is not for sale.

Nonalignment plays another role for these states which is derived from domestic political considerations: it acts as a rallying point to mobilize widespread support behind governmental actions vis-à-vis the external world. The states are caught in the middle of domestic factional struggles among groups which are closely identified with the values of the western tradition, ultranationalists whose response to the outside world may border on racism, and quasi-Marxists, neocolonialists, or socialists inclined toward emulation of Soviet or Chinese models.

To preserve an already tenuous and strained national unity, create a national consciousness, and progress toward promised development, the revolutionist leaders must pursue policies which will satisfy everyone. Nonalignment seems to offer the possibility of avoiding the disasters of civil war or domination by the superpowers. An assertive foreign policy and a demonstration of willingness to support, cooperate with, and receive aid from both blocs are attempts to satisfy the domestic factions in the interest of unity. When revolutionists combine these factors with identification of the colonialist common enemy, they feel that they are keeping the peace at home while serving their interests abroad.

Because they are the products of colonial societies, revolutionist leaders are searching for principles and values consistent with their own anticolonialist idealism. While they were still colonial peoples, they had something specific and concrete upon which virtually everything could be blamed. The colonial regime, portrayed as solely exploitative, was held responsible for disease, poverty, oppression, and illiteracy—all the ills of their society.

By concentrating their fire on the colonial regimes, these leaders were able to arouse the popular sentiment and support necessary for the political revolution that would put them in power. They rode into office on waves of passionate anticolonialism, but their promises of a brighter future were yet to be satisfied. The logic of anticolonialism promised that the winning of independence would demolish all barriers to justice, freedom, and progress. When this did not prove to be the case, social cohesion began to break down almost immediately. Unity achieved in the face of the common enemy was threatened, and with it the very existence of the new states and their nationalist regimes.

Faced with failures, frustrations, and instability as the facade of unity began to disintegrate, the leaders had to do something to preserve what they had sought for so long. Because many of them had been bred on Marxist-Leninist doctrines of imperialism, it was not unusual that they should seek a new foe which could serve a unifying purpose similar to that of anticolonialism. The terror they created was *neocolonialism*, a supposed threat to their independence and progress by continued foreign economic domination.

On the surface, anticolonialism is synonymous with anti-westernism, but this is at least a partial misconception. Revolutionists are passionately derogating the West at the same time that they are attempting to imitate western achievements. Anticolonialism provides a convenient screen for their contradictory attempts to achieve what they believe to be the hallmark of modern nationhood.

THE PRESTIGE RACE

An era such as the present, marked by great modifications in the conditions of international political life and a drastic recalculation of the ponderables of state capability, gives considerations of prestige special significance. States normally wish to acquire high prestige. When the coercive component of state capability has a diminished effect in achieving state purposes, the relative role of noncoercive influence cannot help but increase in importance and scope. This is the special province of prestige.

This chapter has considered the ideological formulation in world politics, and the point was made that ideological conflict is no longer a struggle for the achievement of absolute truth, but rather a competition for results, with the prize going to the system that best approximates in reality the utopia promised in its preachments. The antagonists hope that the impression of competence and effectiveness they convey will produce meaningful political results.

What Is Prestige?

The initial problem facing states is the augmentation of prestige. The notion of "prestige" has no specific content, and must be given meaning in more precise terms. To be "well thought of," a state must decide the characteristics with which it wishes to be favorably identified. It may elect to acquire prestige by military strength, by a reputation for astute diplomacy, by a high standard of living, by an advanced cultural and/or technological level, or by conspicuous dedication to certain abstract principles, such as freedom or justice. It may even select several of these to make up what we might call a "prestige package." Then the state devotes itself to clarifying this image.

However, another difficulty arises. Not only must a state decide the terms in which it wishes to be judged, it must also persuade other states to apply the same standards. This is a far more complex task, involving identifying the state's actions with the values of the judging state or states. A related problem develops from the differing ways in which high prestige may be demonstrated. Does the state wish to be respected, feared, admired, loved, emulated, or disliked? All are, given appropriate circumstances, equally valid ways of demonstrating high prestige; which one a state chooses depends in large part upon the policy results it wishes.

The Race for Prestige

The international scene today displays vast competition for prestige. The major powers are involved on a global scale in a massive effort to put their best foot forward. The states of the non-West, seeking a clearer identity, are actively promoting whatever aspects of their own societies they feel might produce an accrual of greater respect. The older states of Europe, although increasingly preoccupied with their own problems and consequently less sensitive to worldwide implications of political prestige, are nevertheless constantly alert to the social, psychological, economic, and cultural aspects of European prestige.

At least two troublesome aspects of the prestige race complicate the course of world politics. For many states, the prestige competition is a two-sided game in which one state may gain in prestige only to the extent that its adversaries are humbled. This approach, founded on the idea that the total amount of prestige is finite and that a larger slice for one state means a diminished portion for another, is particularly important in some formulations of the stakes of American-Soviet confrontation. Many Americans, for example, are convinced that each American victory is also a defeat for the U.S.S.R., and that every Soviet failure in some way augments America's world image.

The second complication of the prestige race is its inconclusiveness. The relationship between high prestige and the capability of a state to accomplish its stipulated objectives has not yet been clarified; the real "influence" component of prestige is unclear. A suspicion remains that a state's search for international prestige flows from internalized motivations, and that a people obsessed with the need for greater world renown is seeking to assuage internal insecurity. If this condition does exist, it makes the prestige race a self-defeating international enterprise. No rewards formulated in the classic framework of world politics can be derived from such a contest.

REFERENCES

* Anderson, Charles W., *Politics and Economic Change in Latin America.* Princeton, N.J.: D. Van Nostrand Co., Inc., 1967.

Apter, David A., ed., *Ideology and Discontent.* New York: The Free Press, 1964.

* Arendt, Hannah, *On Revolution.* New York: The Viking Press, Inc., 1963.

* Brzezinski, Z. K., *Ideology and Power in Soviet Politics* (rev. ed.). New York: Frederick A. Praeger, Inc., 1967.

* Cohen, Carl, *Communism, Fascism and Democracy.* New York: Random House, Inc., 1962.

* Daniels, Robert V., *The Nature of Communism.* New York: Random House, Inc., 1961.

* Drachkovitch, Milorad M., ed., *Marxism in the Modern World.* Stanford, Calif.: Stanford University Press, 1965.

* Ebenstein, William, *Today's Isms: Communism, Fascism, Socialism, Capitalism* (5th ed.). Englewood Cliffs, N.J.: Prentice-Hall, Inc., 1967.

* Fanon, Frantz, *The Wretched of the Earth.* New York: Grove Press, 1965.

* Friedrich, Carl J., and Zbigniew K. Brzezinski, *Totalitarian Dictatorship and Autocracy* (2nd rev. ed.). New York: Frederick A. Praeger, Inc., 1966.

* Fromm, Erich, *May Man Prevail?* Garden City, N.Y.: Doubleday & Company, Inc., 1961.

* Gyorgy, Andrew, and George D. Blackwood, *Ideologies in World Affairs.* Waltham, Mass.: Blaisdell Publishing Co., 1967.

* Hook, Sidney, *Marx and the Marxists.* Princeton, N.J.: D. Van Nostrand Co., Inc., 1955.

* Indicates paperback edition.

* Johnson, Chalmers A., *Revolutionary Change*. Boston: Little, Brown and Company, 1966.

* Leider, Carl, and Karl M. Schmitt, *The Politics of Violence: Revolution in the Modern World*. Englewood Cliffs, N.J.: Prentice-Hall, Inc., 1968.

* Meyer, Alfred, *Communism*. New York: Random House, Inc., 1962.

* Schapiro, J. Salwyn, *Liberalism*. Princeton, N.J.: D. Van Nostrand Co., Inc., 1953.

Seton-Watson, Hugh, *Nationalism and Communism: Essays 1946–1963*. New York: Frederick A. Praeger, Inc., 1964.

* Sigmund, Paul E., ed., *The Ideologies of the Developing Nations*. New York: Frederick A. Praeger, Inc., 1967.

Wallerstein, Emmanuel M., *Social Change: The Colonial Situation*. New York: John Wiley & Sons, Inc., 1966.

* Ward, Barbara, *Nationalism and Ideology*. New York: W. W. Norton & Company, Inc., 1966.

* Indicates paperback edition.

ELEVEN

Man and
the Forces of Nature

Men live today in a technological age. The assault of human intelligence upon the secrets of the natural world has yielded such spectacular discoveries in the past six decades that the twentieth century has seen greater changes in the conditions of human existence than have taken place in all previous recorded human history. Man is transforming the planet on which he lives and beginning to make real progress toward his age-old goal of breaking free of earth and exploring the reaches of outer space.

The technological revolution of this century has had the same direct effect on the politics of states as it has had on every other feature of social interaction. We have already noted the tremendous impact of advanced technology on the theory and practice of warfare, and the extent to which long-standing postulates have undergone systematic reevaluation. This development has been paralleled in almost every other dimension of international politics; the very organizing assumptions of state life have been called into question as a result of the new relation between man and the forces of nature.

In this chapter, we shall examine five of the hundreds of technological developments and resulting conditions that are putting the state system under such strain. This is not to imply that these few are the most important, or that they are unique in their effect. We shall note their general similarities in modifying and perhaps transforming international politics. The tentative conclusions we shall advance at the end of the chapter are applicable to almost any other technological issues.

The five we have selected for brief analysis and evaluation are: (1) nuclear energy; (2) the conquest of space; (3) the population explosion (a result of technology rather than a new factor in itself); (4) mass communications; and (5) the new patterns in economic production, distribution, and consumption.

NUCLEAR ENERGY

Nuclear energy is represented for most people by the mushroom-shaped cloud towering over the fireball of a hydrogen bomb explosion. The revolutionary aspect of this exploitation of the energy of the atomic nucleus is self-evident. Even if the military potential of nuclear energy is laid aside, the fact that this vast storehouse of power has been tapped by human ingenuity remains a disruptive force.

The Energy Revolution

In the simplest terms, the splitting of the atom resulted in the discovery of a new and virtually inexhaustible source of energy. Without energy modern industrial civilization would be impossible. The historic Industrial Revolution was grounded upon successful conversion of coal to the production of large amounts of energy in the form of heat. Prior to that time, energy came from natural or human sources in small amounts and with great technical and economic waste of wind, water, and human energy. Coal as an energy source was much more efficient and made large-scale enterprise feasible. Since the dawn of the coal age, men have discovered other energy sources of wide utility, particularly petroleum and hydroelectric power. Modern industry has been built on these three bases.

Developments in weaponry demonstrated that the potential energy locked in the atomic nucleus could be liberated. Consequently, the total amount of energy available for human use has increased astronomically. Fossil fuels are limited in amount, and reserves have been dwindling, but the raw material of nuclear reaction is in huge supply. Supplies for thermonuclear uses of the hydrogen atom are infinite in relation to human needs. There is now adequate energy for everyone if it can be harnessed and put to work.

The Second Industrial Revolution

The development of atomic energy is immediately relevant to the pattern of world relationships because it makes possible a "second industrial revolution." States that became industrial giants in the days of coal-iron technology had accidentally been endowed with deposits of these raw materials, of which coal was the more important. Great economic power and world political leadership were built on this base, and states without adequate energy sources were condemned to second or even lower rank.

Now, however, the amplitude of nuclear energy has gone far to equalize the conditions of competition. Nonindustrial states have the opportunity to skip the coal-oil stage entirely and to move directly into the most advanced technology. Already industrialized states have an advantage in their relatively large supply of scientists, technicians, and production specialists, but this is neither absolutely controlling nor permanent in its effect. Fissionable materials are relatively common and the total amount necessary for energy production is by no means huge. The new industrial revolution will result in a substantial reordering of the relative production ranks now held by states, and will also culminate in a much narrower spread between the top and the bottom.

Nuclear Energy and World Politics

The military uses of nuclear energy have been a factor of division and have intensified competition and tension in the relations of states. Each nuclear power has sought to confine its advances to itself and to monopolize all its rewards. The attempt to develop nuclear energy for nonmilitary purposes on an exclusively national basis has not been a success. International cooperation in the peaceful uses of nuclear energy has been a natural development for a number of reasons.

First, the theoretical simplicity of the task has not been matched by an equivalent ease in execution. Scientific and technological elaboration of what is already known is an extremely expensive operation. National competition in this area condemns each state to repeat each stage in the process, while cooperation enables all to build on the totality of everyone's findings.

Second, for most effective use, nuclear energy arrangements should be on a larger scale than most smaller states can develop. Cooperation in establishing supranational research and development programs could obviously result in dividends beyond the capacity of individual states to muster.

A third factor is the attitude of the scientific community toward itself. Committed by professional ideology to freedom of knowledge and the exchange of ideas and findings in a common pursuit of truth, scientists have formed a powerful pressure group urging governments into cooperative ventures.

Finally, public imagination has been captured throughout most of the world by the possibilities of a future made lighter by ample energy supplies, and a considerable degree of public approbation greets each new step in its realization.

The two most conspicuous examples of international cooperation in the exploitation of nuclear energy for peaceful purposes have been the International Atomic Energy Agency (IAEA), established in response to American initiatives as a specialized agency of the United Nations, and the European Atomic Community (EURATOM), set up by the six states of the European Community. These two enterprises provide for joint and cooperative exploitation of the peaceful possibilities of nuclear energy. Up to the present their record of accomplishment is not extensive, but the nature of their task calls for a long period of preparatory work before a few visible results can be followed by an outburst of specific applications. Other cooperative efforts of less impressive scope are in the making as well.

Thus the impact of nuclear energy on world politics is ambivalent. When put into military channels it threatens the world with devastation and destruction, whereas in its peaceful aspects it promises enormous good. The sheer magnitude of the prospects for good or ill suggests that, whatever their ultimate impact, the forces locked in the atom's nucleus cannot be confined either within the national boundaries of a single state or even within the limitations of the traditional nation-state system. The relevance of nuclear energy is supranational, and whatever solutions are found to the problems and opportunities it presents must be on a supranational scale.

THE CONQUEST OF SPACE

The nuclear age dates from 1945, but the age of space has been a reality only since 1957 when—in the course of a massive multistate scientific effort under the auspices of the International Geophysical Year—the Soviet Union and the United States launched the first artificial space satellites. Since that time, the attempt to gather more scientific information about the reaches of space and to launch vehicles and men deeper into the universe has become increasingly concentrated. The Soviet Union in 1961, and the United States early in 1962, put human beings into orbit around the earth and brought them back safely. Plans for larger vehicles, longer flights, and eventual manned voyages to the moon and beyond were immediately announced. In view of the rapidity with which the penetration of space has been proceeding, very few nonspecialists are willing to minimize the probabilities that these and even more spectacular steps will be taken as scheduled. So accustomed have individuals become to rapid progress in space exploration that few pause to reflect how recently the entire enterprise began.

The Breakthrough into Space

The birth of the space age was made possible by intensive cooperation among many kinds of scientists and technologists aided by generous appropriations of funds and materiel by governments on both sides of the Iron Curtain. Physicists, biologists, meteorologists, physiologists, chemists, metallurgists, and dozens of other scientific specialists made direct and indispensable contributions. In addition, every type of engineering and technical skill played a direct part. The two critical areas of technological advance, without which a breakthrough would have been impossible, were the development and refinement of the science of rocketry (especially the development of booster thrust) and the sophistication of metallurgy which, coupled with dramatic advances in pyrotechnics, permitted the construction of space vehicles capable of withstanding the strains of launching and friction of reentry into the earth's atmosphere.

Spectacular landmarks in astronautics include the first satellite, Sputnik, launched by the U.S.S.R. in 1957; successful use of satellites as communications devices by the United States in 1960; successful photography of the hitherto unseen side of the moon and the landing of a rocket on the moon's surface, accomplished by the Soviets in 1960; the first manned orbital flight made by Russia's Yuri Gagarin in 1961; the Telstar communication satellite and other orbital breakthroughs in 1962; the Soviet spacecraft Luna IX's first successful semisoft lunar landing with a 220-pound instrument package containing a television transmitter in 1966; and the American Surveyor I's soft landing on the moon, also in 1966.

Great advances have been made since the launching of the first Sputnik. This is evidenced in the successes of the American Apollo 11 mission of astronauts actually landing on the surface of the moon and the Soviet Zond program which places the U.S.S.R. within a step from the same accomplishment.

The extent to which men have already penetrated space, and the justified sense of real accomplishment, should not obscure the fact that, compared with the enormity of the task men have set themselves, no more than the merest scratch has been made on the surface of space. Space is, of course, an infinite notion. Travel until now has been little more than 250,000 miles out into space, a tiny centimeter in relation to the infinite expanses of the universe. The deepest ranging probes have gone only a small way into the solar system, with unmanned vessels having been sent to investigate conditions on Mars and Venus. Beyond lie galaxies and nebulae as yet only dreamed of. Man dare not lose sight of the awful immensity of the universe into which he is venturing.

However, a remarkable technical and scientific harvest has already been gathered in the few short years in which space efforts have been progressing. The instruments for further action are either at hand or on the way to development; the extent of knowledge is adequate to support and justify a constant forward movement along this frontier. Interestingly, the two most active areas of scientific and technological progress are those that focus upon the smallest unit of scientific inquiry—the atomic nucleus—and the largest—the cosmos itself. In these two areas the most fundamental questions are leading to extremely interesting and useful answers.

The Space Race

It is an interesting commentary on the spirit of the times that the great breakthrough into space has been conceived of as a race between the Soviet Union and the United States. Sputnik was a great blow to American pride and self-esteem, since the American public had assumed that the United States' primacy in the advance into space was inevitable and right. A powerful reaction followed the initial U.S.S.R. triumph. The long-range program for gathering scientific data, leading gradually to manned space flight, was transformed into a battleground of the East-West confrontation. The U.S.S.R. obviously enjoyed its sudden (perhaps unexpected) reputation for scientific and technological leadership, and accepted the American challenge. Since 1957, the exploration of space has been a competitive venture.

The Soviet Union has had considerable success in maintaining its lead in spectacular breakthroughs. Its greatest prestige-augmenting accomplishments were unquestionably the successful attempt to hit the moon, the trailblazing manned orbital flights, and the soft lunar landing. Yet there is evidence that the United States is well ahead in over-all sophistication concerning space and its problems, and that the Soviet Union senses its relative deficiencies in these respects and is interested in changing some of the terms of the contest.

Following the early Russian successes, most Americans succumbed to a "let's catch up" philosophy toward the space race. In spite of American successes in communications and manned satellites, this attitude continued into the mid-1960's. When astronaut Edward White took his "walk in space" during the four-day Gemini IV flight in June, 1965, a public controversy arose and NASA was accused of "prematurely" trying to match a similar Russian feat. The public and the news media still thought of the United States as "closing the gap" in the space race with the Russians.

Political and Military Considerations

The stakes in the space race have been both political and military. The political aspects, clustering about the much discussed but undefinable rewards in prestige that accrue to the state holding the lead, have been perhaps the more obvious. There is no doubt that Soviet successes have had a profound impact upon mass opinion in much of the less developed world, and have gone far to destroy the myth of Russian technological backwardness. The widespread dismay and frantic and concerned self-analysis of segments of the American public in the face of Soviet advances have contributed as well to the possibility of a drastic revision of their respective world images.

Yet the political rewards that some pessimists in the West have been prepared to concede to the Soviets as a result of their leadership in the conquest have proved disconcertingly small. There has been some doubt whether prestige in space exploration is a politically negotiable commodity, and about the real extent to which Soviet success has damaged the United States (except possibly in the eyes of Americans themselves). Moscow has obviously enjoyed Washington's discomfiture, but apart from this almost routine behavior, the political consequences of the space race have been either minimal or as yet undiscovered.

The military significance of space achievements has been widely debated by both eastern and western observers. Soviet leadership in booster thrust was evidence for a time of a dangerous "missile gap" in Moscow's favor, although this argument was eventually abandoned by both Russians and Americans. Earlier, there was talk about the possibilities of manned "space stations" for reconnaissance and possibly attack purposes, but their real military advantages were difficult to isolate. Soviet development of fractional-orbiting vessels capable of delivering nuclear warheads from outer space to a target on earth provides a concrete example of the use of outer space for military purposes. But generally speaking, the level of scientific knowledge (and perhaps the imagination of military leadership) is not yet adequate to capitalize on these considerations. Neither doctrine nor technique is able to explain the full military advantages of a command of outer space.

The radical advances in missiles and rockets which exemplified the space race after 1957, plus the Soviet policy of cutting its military manpower and emphasizing weapons of strategic deterrence, brought on a continuing debate in the United States about force levels and budgets. In an era when evaluation of the real contribution of men and weapons to national security was the most difficult in history, the dispute was inevitably inconclusive (or perhaps indeterminable). Neither the "budgeteers" nor the "security" group had enough concrete data to give their arguments the strength needed to win a consensus.

Cooperation in Space

A countertrend to the space race began to manifest itself during 1961 and 1962—a strong urge toward the cooperative exploration of space without political overtones. Proposals for cooperation had been frequent during earlier stages, but the pressure for political and possibly military advantage had prevented their implementation. Proposals to declare space "out of bounds" to the East-West confrontation, and to share both the costs and the findings of further explorations, were accepted in principle, but considerations of timing, prestige, or national security vitiated these preliminary efforts.

The successful accomplishment by the United States of a manned orbital flight early in 1962, however, brought the race to its closest approximation of prestige parity since it began. In his congratulatory message, Premier Khrushchev—in a relatively friendly manner—raised the possibility (originally an American proposal) of the two space leaders developing ways of extensive cooperation in the future penetration of space. American response was affirmative, and negotiations for the formulation of areas and techniques of joint interaction were immediately initiated in a climate of relative goodwill and free exchange.

The apparently sincere acceptance of cooperation in space by the two states which had been competing so grimly was both important in itself and profoundly suggestive. If it were actually institutionalized, one dimension of an exciting but relatively unproductive dispute would be eliminated from the American-Soviet confrontation. Furthermore, cooperation in space would affect the remaining areas of open conflict between the two; it would be difficult to maintain a complete "we or they" approach in a political matter if both sides were working cooperatively on so newsworthy and extensive an enterprise as space exploration.

Under Presidents Kennedy and Johnson, the United States went far during 1963 and 1964 to repudiate the "race" by inviting the Soviets to participate in a cooperative program of space exploration. Khrushchev himself claimed in 1963 that the Soviet Union had never considered itself in a race, and "wished the United States well" in its own effort. The test ban treaty in July, 1963, which, among other things, banned nuclear testing in outer space, and President Kennedy's revolutionary proposal before the United Nations for joint Soviet-American exploration of the moon, were both indications of the different posture being assumed by the United States.

THE POPULATION EXPLOSION

Science and technology, joining forces in the fields of public health and preventive medicine, have brought to the world one of its largest contemporary problems: the so-called population explosion. The number of human beings on earth today is by far the largest in history; one significant study points out that one-third of all the people born in the entire history of the human race are alive today. In certain parts of the world, new lives are not the blessing western peoples find them to be, but are in a real sense a crushing burden.

Only in the recent past have western political leaders become alarmed by the steady acceleration of birth rates in many parts of the world. Now that population has acquired a political dimension, it has become a matter of great concern to many governments. Unfortunately, the degree of awareness of the problem has not been matched by any equivalent growth in facility for dealing with it.

Causes of the Population Explosion

The population of underindustrialized lands has traditionally stabilized at the maximum supportable by local food supplies and prerequisites of living. It has been kept in check by the so-called "Malthusian restraints": war, epidemic, famine, and disease. A predominantly youthful population (because of short life span), relatively low regard for the sanctity of human life, and very high birth and death rates were generally regarded as characteristic in most less developed countries.

In the twentieth century, these lands began to benefit from public health measures, improved sanitation, and modern medicine. The results have been spectacular; death rates have dropped at a sensational rate, primarily in infant mortality and in epidemic diseases breeding in filth, while birth rates have increased. As more infants have survived to become parents, population figures have soared, with the result that population pressures have begun to force the hand of many governments.

There are no absolutes about the problem of population, no magic optimum figure for the human race or any part of it. Population pressure is a relative factor; a society suffers when any increase in its over-all population results in a reduction in the amount of goods and services available for any individual. When an increase in the number of mouths to feed means less food for each mouth, a population problem exists. The crisis in some states is almost frightening. For example, the annual increase in population in Egypt and India is greater than that in productivity. Neither state can, by its own efforts, accumulate the surplus capital necessary for the industrial development that offers hope of surcease from the maddening pressure of human biology. All states with serious population problems stand in dire need of external assistance if they are not to be drowned in a sea of undernourished bodies.

Political, Social, and Economic Effects

The consequences for the states directly affected by the population explosion are simple and devastating. Since no modern government (at least in the West) dares plan wholesale starvation for removing the burden of excess population, all must accept the primary responsibility of keeping their citizens alive. But this does not alleviate or even palliate the situation; birth rates remain high and each year the crisis becomes more intense. State plans for long-range development and social stabilization are repeatedly deferred in favor of frenzied annual attempts to ward off famine. Systematic and sensible social planning in such a climate is obviously impossible.

Within the society itself, the constant specter of starvation haunts everyone. Although for centuries this situation was accepted passively, today powerful ferments are at work in once quiescent societies. There is a movement to demand rapid improvement in the conditions of life. The tenor of political discourse in these societies has grown more extreme as distress augments political self-consciousness. The governments are less willing and able to withstand these pressures, and measures of increasing desperation gain steadily in attractiveness to their beleaguered policy-makers.

At this point, the problem becomes pertinent to international politics. Governments under such pressure at home and with so little room to maneuver before their own peoples are neither forces for stability in world politics nor free to make long-term international commitments. A state containing an exploding population is incipiently revolutionary. The tragedy of this situation is that any such revolution is by its own terms destined to failure. Population pressure cannot be relieved by a change in government. Oversimplified but persuasive "explanations" of the problem, suggesting that the root of national difficulties lies in the machinations of malevolent enemies, may open the door to particularly dangerous international adventures. Several of these have occurred since World War II.

Thus the reproductive habits of individuals in the tropics are of direct relevance to stabilized and industrialized states of the western world. Population pressure is a major contributing element in the militancy of the non-western revolution, and must be faced by the more fortunate peoples as they devise a long-range response to this new challenge. The ultimate destiny of modern civilization may well rest on mankind's success in seeing that all human beings are provided at least a minimally tolerable share of the world's resources.

Avenues of Solution

It is probably presumptuous to discuss any "solution" to the problem of population; the most we can seriously consider are some possible lines of attack. No quick results can be expected, and the tensions produced by population problems will form part of the context of international politics for a long time. Nevertheless, a combined internal and international approach does offer some promise of eventual relaxation of the impersonal threat of overpopulation.

Internally, there is already some evidence that forthright and courageous leadership of an extensive program of education and preventive techniques can help in reducing birth rates. This is a matter in part of development of a simple and efficacious contraceptive, and much research and effort has already gone into this task. However, religious and cultural barriers will remain strong even after the requisite medical findings have been made widely available, so the courage and determination of a government become crucial. The only way to develop a viable social structure may be a broadly-based campaign to modify traditional social customs. Only exceptionally strong leaders are likely to run such a risk.

Internationally, the population problem can be best attacked by development programs inspired and financed by advanced states. If performed on a sufficiently large scale, avoiding digressive elements of competition and prestige accrual, the vicious circle of an increase in population eating up each year's economic growth might be broken. Only some such effort has any chance of real success over the long term; palliative techniques merely defer the day of reckoning. This approach does not demand that every overpopulated state immediately undergo industrialization, but that the economic structure be sufficiently rearranged to free the optimally productive portion of the population from subsistence agriculture. Specialization in a controlled economic system will make it possible for the necessary foodstuffs to be imported from more productive areas.

Population Pressure and the Shape of World Politics

Some ecologists and biologists argue that the pressure of population is the most influential single factor in shaping the future of the human species. In political terms they contend that ideological and nationalistic drives pale in comparison to the frantic search for subsistence by two-thirds of the world population. Unless this challenge is met head-on, they contend, a new wave of barbarism will threaten to sweep the planet.

Regardless of how seriously these warnings may be taken, and after a mere cursory examination of population figures, the observer cannot escape the conclusion that the international political system must adjust to this stark phenomenon. Whether it leads to war and destruction or to a new cooperative climate for solving common problems, the rising tide of humanity is a political problem of the first order. We will hear much more of it in the years ahead.

MASS COMMUNICATION

Mass communication devices and techniques are another entry in the list of technological advances that have gone so far to revolutionize life in the twentieth century. It is now possible for one man to communicate simultaneously with an audience numbered in the tens of millions. Development in 1965 of commercial satellite telecommunications—the Early Bird system—seems to indicate that an even greater role can be played by the communication media in the future. This capability to affect the emotions and increase the knowledge of vast numbers of people within a short time span has had a profound effect on patterns of social life everywhere. Information, entertainment, intellectual stimulation, and political leadership are all part of the content of the mass media. Anything so powerful in its impact directly affects international politics as well.

Mass Media in World Politics

The primary relevance of mass media to international politics has already been noted in our discussion of propaganda. New techniques of conveying messages to an audience have led to great advances in propaganda effectiveness. We identified four different audiences for national propaganda efforts: the state's own people, the people of its allies, the people of neutral or uninvolved states, and the people of its opponents. In reaching each of these audiences, the propagandist makes extensive use of the mass media.

At home, electronic media (radio and television) are used widely, with applications varying according to the richness of the technical installations and the sophistication of the home audience. Printed and visual media—books, magazines, motion pictures, posters—also play a large role. The problem of access is much more complex when a foreign audience is being approached; the audience is in no sense "captive" and must be reached more circumspectly. Radio is especially valuable, since home radio receivers are common everywhere and the technique of beaming shortwave broadcasts is so well developed. Television is useless without receiving sets, which are few outside the western world. Printed media and the cinema obtain audiences in foreign countries only by sufferance, and their effect depends upon the delicacy and deftness of their approach rather than the strength of their messages.

Western manipulators of the mass media of communications tend to aim at the largest possible audience, even if this demands a dilution of their message content. Communist mass communicators, however, tend to emphasize impact upon the individual listener more than pervasiveness of reception, and risk alienating many members of their audience in the interest of securing strong responses from a minority segment.

Image Projection in Foreign Policy

Contemporary concern, especially in the West, with matters of prestige and status in international politics has led to a concern with the "image" a state "projects" in the course of carrying out its world role. Each self-conscious state tends to formulate the most desirable ego-image, and then seeks to project it and gain its wide acceptance abroad. These images vary widely according to the values each society prizes. One state may project strength, another culture, a third moral integrity, a fourth cunning and resourcefulness, and so on. Dissemination of the controlling image and its manipulation for the state's policy purposes are the major tasks of mass media in foreign affairs.

Image projection is an elusive business, even within a homogeneous society with a stable value code and the available resources of the communications industry. In international affairs, the image that one state holds of another is only partially the result of deliberate projection by the government concerned. It is also made up of historic impressions, random and uncontrollable events that come to symbolize the state, "unintentional propaganda," such as the behavior of tourists and government officials, motion pictures, and so on, and the image of that particular state which other governments, for their own purposes, choose to project. Image projection in this case falls far short of its alleged goal.

National concern with image projection has had a clear impact on the formulation and conduct of foreign policy. Many states insist on adhering to their image in performing the routine and special tasks of foreign policy. A state committed to an image of strength may overlook opportunities for successful compromise. A state conceiving itself as superior in culture may be caught in irrelevant posturing with no policy content. The dangers of "imagery" in foreign policy frequently overshadow whatever gain it may promise. Mass media do not make very effective instruments of foreign policy, as excessive reliance on these devices may well produce more difficulties than it solves.

Destructive and Constructive Applications

The methods of mass communication, like almost any technical skill, are neutral and without policy significance. However, they may be put to destructive and dangerous uses or they may serve constructive ends; the decision is left to responsible policy-makers. Examples of both categories abound in the contemporary world.

Destructively (at least potentially), mass media are appropriate for intensifying nationalist hatreds and the tension component of an international confrontation. By mass methods the people of one state may be worked into a condition of intensive hostility toward another people, and great pressure may be generated. Adamant public positions on crisis issues can be developed, while equally powerful drives for adoption of new policies can be unleashed. Perhaps more significant than any of these is the role of mass media in filtering and interpreting the flow of information received by the audience. Whether acting on its own or as a tool of the government, the mass communication machine in any state is the means whereby individual citizens acquire both factual data and authoritative interpretations of the problems their government faces. The state of mass opinion in a modern society at any particular moment is to a major extent the work of the mass communicators in that society.

Constructively, mass communication media are potentially important to the creation of a supranational consensus. In today's rapidly moving world, opinion can focus on a particular issue in time to affect its outcome only if the mass media purvey the information widely and quickly enough. Technical execution of the task is relatively simple, in view of the advanced state of the art today. The difficulty is due partly to the national identification of the communicators and to the confusion of motivations and evaluation displayed by these individual practitioners. A cohesive international community, such as we shall examine in Chapter Thirteen, is conceivable only if individuals are tied into a single and responsive communications network. This is the great opportunity that lies before today's technologists of message transmission.

PRODUCTION, CONSUMPTION, DISTRIBUTION

A final technological problem is constituted by great changes in world production, distribution, and consumption of economic goods. Each of these three areas has been affected directly by the technological revolution we have been analyzing throughout this chapter. So vast are the economic implications of modern technology that we can do no more than suggest a few of the leading considerations.

New Production Techniques

Almost every aspect of industrial technology has affected production in a remarkable way. Best known of the new techniques is "automation" —the application of electronic controls and simplified patterns to the production of higher quality goods by only a fraction of the manpower formerly needed. Even nonautomated industry has been so revolutionized by new techniques that almost any factory built before 1945 is obsolete today. This has been dramatically demonstrated by the industrial success of the war-devastated states of Europe since 1945. Forced to rebuild industrial plants from the ground up, they have been able to incorporate new arrangements and techniques, with a consequent impressive gain in productivity.

The principal result of new production techniques has been a great increase in the capacity of the world economy to produce goods of all sorts. More goods are available for consumption than ever before, and the trend is toward a continuation of the upward spiral of productivity.

This phenomenon is independent of any considerations of profit margins, markets, or employment; it is simply a macroeconomic conclusion that the world, viewed as a unit of production, is increasing its gross product at a significant rate. The social and political consequences are functions of decisions made in other contexts, and cannot be inferred from the mere fact of an upward trend in production. It is up to the statesmen of the future to decide how this new abundance can best be put to the improvement of the lot of mankind.

Rising Consumer Expectations

Paralleling the revolution in production technique is an analogous upward curve in the expectations of consumers. The so-called "revolution of rising expectations" is usually thought of as characteristic of less developed but newly-awakened preindustrial societies, and indeed it is ubiquitous in them. But consumption levels even in industrialized states have risen since 1945, and will probably continue to do so. Regardless of the standard of living enjoyed by an individual, he constantly receives stimuli urging him to elevate his expectations still further. Although the United States, with its consumption economy of "affluence," has long set the trend for higher standards of living, Western Europe, the Soviet Union, and the semi-industrialized societies in the Middle East, Latin America, North Africa, and Southeast Asia have recently followed suit.

Worldwide interest in consumption of economic goods has placed many governments in a dilemma. Most are committed to collectively phrased nationalist goals whose attainment will call for a significant portion of national production to be committed to the so-called "public sector" of the economy; a heavy burden of armament and the capital formation prerequisite to industrial development require that individual consumption be limited. However, the increasingly vocal demand of the mass public for more of the better things of life inhibits the vigor with which the government can prosecute the themes of sacrifice and dedication so necessary to public programs. No government has yet found a satisfactory escape from this quandary.

The Problem of Distribution

The nation-state system divides the world into a collection of commonly accepted independent and self-sustaining economies. Some of these are productive of surpluses, while others can do no more than budget deprivation. At the subsistence level, for example, today's food production potential is adequate to feed the entire population of the world; in other words, hunger exists only because of failures in distribution.

How, within the present structure of the world economy, can distribution be rationalized so that increased productivity can be reflected in increased consumption and a richer and better life for everyone? Some of the world's most serious thought has been addressed to this question in the past decade and a half. In the next chapter we shall look at these economic issues more directly; here we need only reflect on the strange turns of fate that make some economies suffer from an excess of productivity and others from an excess of consumer demand, while a combination of social, economic, and political inhibitions impede the socially and politically useful distribution of needed goods.

Political Significance

The political ramifications of these general observations are self-evident. The basic economic issues of production and consumption have been sharpened by the technological breakthrough of the contemporary era. Politically, the world emphasizes division and separateness; economically, the maximum social advantage is attainable only in a system emphasizing unity and joint action. The economic problems of the contemporary world are insoluble on a national-state level, except for a few fortunate states of great expanse and rich resource endowment. Perpetuation of the national attack on global economic issues can do no more than buy time, and may possibly eventually worsen them or intensify their deficiencies. Here, as in other areas, no automatic or guaranteed response to the challenge of technology exists. Statesmen will discover new and possibly more rewarding approaches only insofar as they are able to devise new structures for action that leave room for a broader basis of calculation.

THE LESSON OF TECHNOLOGY

The technological breakthroughs of World War II continued to expand when the fighting ended. Symbolized by the nightmare of nuclear warfare, the new technology had countless forms and almost totally revolutionary effects. Factors of time, cost, risk, consensual permissibility, and effective leadership were twisted out of their familiar shapes by the only half-appreciated and imperfectly understood effects of the technological revolution.

The era that opened with the mushroom cloud over Hiroshima was a dramatically new political age. We see this even more clearly today than did the statesmen of those days. The prevailing interpretations of the new dimensions of world politics in 1945 were familiar and orthodox, rooted in the same calculus of possibility and probability that had governed the decisions of statesmen for 300 years. But the world had changed for all time between 1939 and 1945; the basic political problem of the reconciliation of liberty and authority had totally new terms of reference. Only in such a world could the cold war be born, grow to maturity, and ultimately enter its decline. Modern political power is inseparably wedded to modern technology, and the capacity of a state to exert pressure to accomplish its objectives depends in large measure on the extent to which its decision-makers have mastered contemporary techniques.

The effect of the technological revolution has been to bind the inhabitants of the planet more intimately, with all sharing both discomfort and opportunity and all destined for a substantially common fate, ranging from the threat of nuclear holocaust to the possibilities of an undreamed of higher worldwide standard of living. Statesmen of the twentieth century would do well to recall Donne's preachment, "No man is an island, entire unto itself," for neither is any nation.

Men are prisoners of their own habits. The nation-state system—the international political order whose dynamic we have been examining throughout this book—is not as old as other human social systems, but its history is rich and its appeal powerful. Statesmen and other politically alert peoples have not yet fully grasped or adjusted to the meaning of technology for international politics. The fundamentally atomistic principle of "every state for itself" is still the sanctioned basis of state interaction, in spite of evidence that the kinds of problems posed by the new technology do not yield solutions on such a basis. The current stasis of world politics reflects policy-makers' and political leaders' lack of success in their attempt to force the new wine of technology into the old bottles of national interest and power politics.

So the new generation of problems spawned by man's partial exploitation of the forces of nature conspire to force hard choices on political leadership. These issues may eventually succumb to traditional forms and patterns of action. As of today, however, the available evidence strongly suggests that the opposite will be true, and that effective attack on major issues will require new organizational patterns for action and response. Technology will almost certainly require major modifications in assumptions and structures.

REFERENCES

Aron, Raymond, *Progress and Disillusion: The Dialectics of Society.* New York: Frederick A. Praeger, Inc., 1968.

* Bloomfield, Lincoln P., ed., *Outer Space: Prospects for Man and Society.* Englewood Cliffs, N.J.: Prentice-Hall, Inc., Spectrum Books, 1962.

* Ellul, Jacques, *The Technological Society.* New York: Alfred A. Knopf, Inc., 1964.

Galbraith, John K., *The New Industrial State.* Boston: Houghton Mifflin Company, 1967.

Goldsen, J. M., ed., *Outer Space in World Politics.* New York: Frederick A. Praeger, Inc., 1963.

* Haskins, Caryl P., *The Scientific Revolution and World Politics.* New York: Harper & Row, Publishers, 1964.

* Herz, John H., *International Politics in the Atomic Age.* New York: Columbia University Press, 1959.

* Huxley, Julian, *Man in the Modern World.* New York: New American Library of World Literature, 1961.

Mudd, Stuart, ed., *The Population Crisis and the Use of World Resources.* The Hague: W. Junk, 1964.

Organski, Katherine, and A. F. K. Organski, *Population and World Power.* New York: Alfred A. Knopf, Inc., 1961.

Russell, John E., *World Population and World Food Supplies.* New York: The Macmillan Company, 1954.

Schramm, Wilbur, ed., *Mass Communication* (2nd ed.). Urbana, Ill.: University of Illinois Press, 1960.

* Toynbee, Arnold, *Industrial Revolution.* Boston: Beacon Press, 1956.

* Indicates paperback edition.

TWELVE

Trade, Aid, and Development

For over 300 years the state has been a viable action unit for the conduct of political relations among peoples. The logic of statehood and the assumptions of the state system were laid down in the western world in the era before the Industrial Revolution. When this great transformation in the method of production launched the massive reorientation in the conditions of human life that still exists today, the incompatibility of the state form with rational economic life for individuals became apparent.

Granted the expectations of individuals everywhere, no state is economically self-sufficient. All are in some measure dependent upon outside sources for some share of their economic goods. Resources are not distributed among states in any recognizable proportion to demand; raw materials inadequately supplied in one state may be in surplus in a neighboring state. States differ in their productive skills and plants, so that many commodities are obtainable advantageously or even exclusively only from certain favored states. Since all people today have economic goals, these differences in physical, political, and human economic circumstances lead to different and often conflicting economic policies by governments.

ECONOMIC FORCES IN INTERNATIONAL POLITICS

Economics has been one of the fundamental determinants in the evolution of international politics. The breakdown of feudalism, the emergence of the nation-state, the rise of colonialism, and the new force of regionalism were all related in some way to the fluctuating nature of economic systems and the major evolutionary trends of world economic patterns.

Economic Interdependence versus Political Independence

International prosperity is a function of production for use and exchange, the exchange of monetary units of different countries, and the conditions for exchanging goods or services between states. Due to the state system under which areas are separately organized for political purposes, each state must perform many economic functions that place it in opposition to other states. The free movement of people and goods necessary to economic wealth is thus checked, and the problem of supply and demand as well as the disparity between human needs and human resources assumes international dimensions.

Despite the unequal endowment of economic potential and productive capacity among states, it is nevertheless true that sheer subsistence is possible for virtually all states. However, in societies in which the population explosion (Chapter Eleven) is taking place, serious pressures are already developing. Greater numbers of people often mean a reduction in per capita food supply when it is already dangerously low. Such a society is thrown upon the mercies of the world economy, its survival contingent upon its adjustment to the vagaries of international economic relations. Since such unhappy states are often also the sites of generous raw material endowments, at least some of the ingredients for a mutually profitable economic relationship with industrialized states are already present.

The issue becomes even sharper when the crucial factor is not simple survival, but the ubiquitous notion of a rising standard of living. The "standard of living" has become a societal value judgment incorporating individual and group economic expectation. In addition, it is an intricate blend of necessities, comforts, and luxuries that reflects a large portion of the ethos of the society. When a people is determined to raise its standard of living, a powerful dynamism is added to its foreign policy, and the conflict between economic interdependence and political independence becomes sharper than ever.

Modern Economic Trends in World Politics

From the point of view of the industrialized states, recent economic trends have created a situation of major relevance to the course of world politics. Although communist and other Marxist analysts have claimed that economic factors explain the entirety of western foreign policy in the postwar world, we need not be overly concerned about these strictures. It is undeniable, however, that some of the conditions we shall point out have predisposed several western governments to follow certain lines of policy. Denial of a strict economic determinism does not imply that economic forces are completely without influence in international politics.

The modern economic problem begins with the fact that large-scale mass production is the most efficient procedure for most commodities. The steady growth of productive units creates a constant need for reinvestment, growth capital, and a growing margin of fixed overhead costs. With so much of its net worth tied up in plant, and with overhead cutting deeply into profit, a typical firm feels a great need to maintain continuous operation. Adding to this pressure is the role in western states of organized labor, which has become a politico-economic force determined to keep production moving and thus ensure its employment. Full employment is both a social and an economic desideratum in western society.

But constant operation and steady growth require a guaranteed supply of raw materials and an expanding market. Capitalism demands a cash profit, and markets must be found for production if the firm, the industry, and the economy are not to smother in a flood of unsold goods. Here still another fixed cost factor appears: the necessity of expanding the distribution, advertising, and sales aspect of the enterprise to satisfy the demands of the balance sheet.

A few nations, including the United States, are fortunate in possessing a large and prosperous domestic market to furnish the consuming base of their economy. However, expansion and growth lead most states to the search for markets abroad, and here the dilemma runs full circle. Competition with other states, frequently within the domestic market of a second economy, has obvious political implications. It is almost inevitable for an industry pressed for new markets to beg help from its government. It is equally natural for an economy "menaced" by foreign competition to seek its own protection through tariffs and other restrictive measures.

The problem is intensified for a state and an economy that has expanded production and sales under favorable circumstances and then faces a possibility of losing its advantage. This is sometimes thought to be the situation of the United States vis-à-vis a newly prosperous and rapidly integrating Europe. Committed to growth and expansion, but in danger of losing markets, such an economy cannot escape from its overhead or from its social responsibilities to its labor force. Classical economics does offer a solution: such an economy must rationalize itself so as to be better able to compete for markets. However, the highly structured and therefore relatively inflexible nature of modern industrial societies would require such massive social and political costs for major overhaul of a productive plant that few states dare to make the attempt. It is usually thought to be easier and safer to attempt political palliatives of protection and subsidy. This in turn invites retaliation, and the vicious circle is renewed.

The Economic Revolution in Europe

The one industrialized area which has been able to bring about a full-scale revolution in its economic habits is Western Europe. The end of World War II found the once dominant economies of Europe prostrate. Industrial plants were destroyed by the war, capital was dissipated by Nazi occupation and looting, labor forces were dispersed and demoralized, and the economic situation with regard to the Soviet Union and the United States was desperate.

What was worse, the atomic age and the new technological revolution were upon these economies. As individual states, they lacked the financial and technical capacity to conduct the basic research necessary for exploitation of the new potentialities. The new possibilities of production, furthermore, made no sense in view of the narrow national markets in Europe. The economies of such once viable states as France or Italy, to say nothing of smaller ones like Belgium or Denmark, had been made obsolete by the new technology. Even under the best of circumstances, Europe was out of date.

If the impact of the atomic revolution were at all comparable to that of the coal-iron revolution of the eighteenth century, any unfortunate state left out of this development would decay. Many European advocates of economic integration argue that, should their effort fail, Europe will bear the same economic relation to the United States or the Soviet Union as prewar Asia, Africa, or Eastern Europe did to the productive centers of Germany, the Low Countries, or France. It was realized shortly after the end of the war that Europe needed a broader and more efficient economic base adequate to the new demands and new opportunities of a nuclear era.

The consequence was the politico-economic trend of European integration. The goal of this ambitious project, already far advanced in the few years since its launching, is the creation of a new entity in world political and economic relations to be called simply "Europe." Purely political and military efforts, such as the European Defense Community (EDC) and the European Political Community (EPC), have thus far failed; military cooperation with the United States via the North Atlantic Treaty Organization, while useful in security matters, has produced no real steps toward unity. Only in the economic realm has Europe made real inroads into sovereignty.

The first moves were on a continentwide basis, with the Organization for European Economic Cooperation (OEEC) uniting 15 states on the principle of "self-help and mutual aid" for implementation of the American Marshall Plan in 1948. At almost the same time, the Council of Europe (1949) became the first overt expression of the "European movement." Both of these ambitious projects, although contributing to the nascent sense of common interest and destiny, demonstrated that it was difficult to move toward European unity without an effective delegation of sovereignty.

It was not until a smaller core of six states (France, West Germany, Italy, Belgium, the Netherlands, and Luxembourg) resolved to pool their sovereignty in certain specified economic fields that real steps began to be taken. The Schuman Plan led in 1951 to the creation of the European Coal and Steel Community, a merger of the steelmaking capacity of the six states into a single unit independent of national boundaries. The success of this bold move stimulated decisions in 1957 to establish the European Atomic Community (EURATOM) to pool atomic research and development, and the European Common Market—the farthest reaching step of all—which by 1972 was to eliminate all trade barriers among the six states and create a single market of almost 200 million people.

The Common Market crowned the revolution in Europe. So powerful has been its attraction and so gripping its prospects that the other states of Europe—notably Great Britain—continue to seek admission. Even pessimists are virtually convinced that the European breakthrough is an accomplished fact, and the birth of a new economic entity is imminent. The conceptual step to workable political integration will be short, however difficult its practical accomplishment may be. The economic lessons of the European experience have relevance to all states, and are being closely studied everywhere; even the Soviets have paid the European Community the compliment of imitation.

NEW PATTERNS OF INTERNATIONAL TRADE

The requirements of international economic life raise the question of international trade—the exchange of commodities among sovereign states (or the people thereof) in response to mutual needs. As with other aspects of foreign economic relations, all trade policy represents some compromise between the interests of individual citizens bent on private gain and the collective concern of the government for the over-all economic welfare of the society. Individuals are normally motivated by considerations of economic interest, whereas the state's approach is as "political" as it is in defense policy, propaganda, or direct diplomatic maneuvering. Thus the movement of goods and services in international trade at any moment in history follows patterns dictated by the states' judgment of political expediency.

Doctrines of International Trade

There are two general theories of international trade that reflect the conflicting points of view of individual traders and the collective force of the state. One, called in its earlier manifestation "mercantilism," emphasizes the right and duty of the state to control the nature, amount, and flow of trade in the national interest. It therefore demands extensive government regulation of trade and submission of individuals to general policies laid down by the state. The second theory, rooted in classical economics, calls for absolute freedom in movement of goods across national frontiers in response to economic laws, with no reference to government attitudes. "Free trade" thus maximizes the role of profit and individual enterprise, and contends that each state and the world economy at large profit best when the volume of international trade is at its maximum.

Mercantilism was founded on an assumption that wealth consisted of "treasure"—precious metals and stones—and argued that state policy should be directed at creating a "favorable balance of trade" which resulted in a net increase in the supply of wealth. International economic life was a matter of state competition, for a limited supply of treasure and economic conflict among nations was a postulate of the theory. Trade, in this context, was a zero-sum game in which one side gained only to the extent that another lost.

Free trade theories reject the doctrine of conflict and argue that trade, if permitted to follow its natural bent, results ultimately in maximum profit for all participants. Doctrines of "comparative advantage" call for international division of labor, with each unit specializing in the production of commodities which it can sell most competitively on the world market. Ingenious adjustment mechanisms deduced from such premises suggest that laissez faire is even more applicable to international economic relations than to domestic supply and demand.

Mercantilism flourished in the preindustrial era of the state system, reaching its maximum application during the seventeenth and early eighteenth centuries. The rise of mass production and the necessity for early industrial powers to seek markets led to the development of classical economics, abandonment of mercantilism as a government policy, and energetic advocacy of the principles of free trade by Great Britain. This doctrine, fulfilling the requirements of the early industrial leaders, became authoritative during the nineteenth century. British wealth and preeminence were pointed to as proof of the theory's validity.

The twentieth century, however, has seen the complex structure of multilateral trading arrangements crumble under the dual impact of economic depressions and the rise of integrative nationalism. Although all governments agree that free trade is theoretically impeccable, neo-mercantilism has become the practical controlling principle of trade. Almost all states have found ample pretexts since 1914 to depart from free trade principles in the national interest, and trade has struggled for many years within a complex framework of politically inspired restrictions. The economic theory of mercantilism is dead, but its policy and practice remain very much alive.

Trade since 1945 [1]

The economic catastrophe of World War II and radical changes in the structure of the international political system since 1945 have had a great effect on the theory and practice of international trade. First, critical economic conditions forced the government of many countries to deal with international economics on the basis of "every man for himself"; all government resources were directed to halting an economic collapse, and trade suffered seriously. Second, the early cold war period split the world into political blocs that soon knit together economically and diverted trade from many of its historic channels. Third, it became apparent that economic health could not be restored to the world on a state-by-state basis; some form of multilateral economic action was crucial. This applied to both the war-shattered older industrial economies and the newly-emerging underdeveloped states. The interaction of these factors has led

[1] See tables.

to what may be called controlled multilateralism, a curious paradox in which governments, acting on behalf of collective national economies, attempt slowly and steadily to win acceptance of the principle of multilateral and liberated trade.

World Trade: 1968 (in Millions of U. S. Dollars)*

	Exports		Imports	
Industrial countries—Austria, Belgium-Luxembourg, Canada, Denmark, France, Germany, Italy, Japan, Netherlands, Norway, Sweden, Switzerland, United Kingdom, United States	155,800		160,600	
Other developed areas:				
Other Europe—Finland, Iceland, Greece, Ireland, Portugal, Spain, Turkey, Yugoslavia	7,070		11,400	
Australia, New Zealand, and South Africa	6,700		8,160	
Total		13,770		19,560
Less developed areas:				
Latin America	11,500		11,200	
Other Western hemisphere—Barbados, Guadeloupe, Guyana, Jamaica, Martinique, Netherlands Antilles, Surinam, Trinidad, other	1,900		2,900	
Middle East	9,200		6,700	
Other Asia—Brunei, Burma, Cambodia, Ceylon, China (Republic of), Hong Kong, India, Indonesia, Korea, Laos, Malaysia, Pakistan, Philippines, Singapore, Thailand, Vietnam, other	11,000		15,600	
Other Africa	9,000		7,800	
Total		43,000		44,900
World Total		212,600		225,100

* Figures are rounded.
Source: *International Financial Statistics, 1968* (International Monetary Fund, May, 1969), 32-35.

World Trade: 1967 (in Millions of U. S. Dollars)
Comparison of Soviet Areas, United States and Canada

	Exports	Imports
Soviet areas	7,839	8,293
United States and Canada	35,568	43,603

Source: *Direction of Trade*, Annual 1963-1967 (Washington, D.C.: International Monetary Fund, 1968).

In the contemporary world, therefore, neomercantilism and free trade exist simultaneously. States seek to expand their trading opportunities and increase their volume, yet all exercise extensive controls in order to advance their political purposes. Only in Western Europe, where the decision has been to liberate all intracommunity trade from controls, have national interests been subordinated to some broader notion. Elsewhere this perplexing amalgam of freedom and control is dominant as governments are caught by the contradiction between economic imperatives and traditional political values.

Contemporary Trends in the Conduct of Trade

Blurred contemporary doctrines of trade are clearly demonstrated by varying trends in the conduct of trade. At least four practices are in evidence today: (1) general lowering or elimination of tariffs; (2) the preference system; (3) international control of buying, storing, and selling of specific products; and (4) the quota system.

LOWERING OR ELIMINATION OF TARIFFS. This is a reflection of the trend toward a policy of free trade. Various multilateral as well as bilateral and regional efforts have attempted to meet new conditions. A leading example of multilateral effort is the General Agreement on Tariffs and Trade (GATT), which came into effect in 1948. By the terms of this agreement, over 70 trading states meet periodically to negotiate both general and specific tariff reductions. The United States has been committed to tariff reduction by bilateral negotiation since 1934, and in recent years has made increasing efforts to gain the capacity to act quickly and extensively in this direction. The Trade Expansion Act of 1962 authorized President Kennedy to negotiate multilateral trade agreements. The negotiations, known as the Kennedy Round, began in 1964 and were concluded in 1967, the agreements going into effect the following year. Centered around expansion of trade and mutual multilateral reduction of tariffs, and hence increase in the volume of world trade, these efforts have so far been relatively successful.

The concept of the common market, as developed in Europe and attempted in Africa, the Middle East, and Latin America, is another example of this trend. These markets eliminate the tariffs between member states and present a unified tariff wall to the rest of the world. The success of this policy, which will create a larger consumer market for member states and yet protect their internal market from outside competition, can be seen in the remarkable industrial growth of the member countries of the European Common Market. In 1968, final industrial tariffs were abolished in favor of a uniform tariff for all six members on imports from the outside world.

THE PREFERENCE SYSTEM. This is best illustrated in the Commonwealth of Nations and the European Community. This procedure was developed to encourage trade between former colonial powers, principally Great Britain and France, and their former colonial areas. A similar pattern of preference exists between the United States and the Philippines, allowing goods from the privileged area to escape tariffs which must be paid for other goods. The advantage for the mother country is the retention of the former colony as a consumer market and a source for raw materials, while the former colony is able to maintain close relations with an industrial power. The preference system is clearly a reversion to a sophisticated mercantilism.

INTERNATIONAL CONTROL OF BUYING, STORING, AND SELLING OF SPECIFIC PRODUCTS. This is carried on by international trusts. Committees or international cartels were formed in the past to control the export and trade of wheat and coffee. At present, many products, such as oil, tin, rubber, and copper, are controlled by international trusts or consortia made up of states that export these products. The groupings were formed to regulate production and marketing of these commodities in the interest of guaranteeing a regular return to member states. This policy is designed to escape the boom and bust cycle of single-commodity economics.

THE QUOTA POLICY. This has been developed to stabilize underdeveloped states which are producers of a single prime commodity. Large consumer states permit producers a certain share of the market, usually at a prescribed price; the producing states can then count on a guaranteed sale and thus plan production. The United States has had extensive quota systems for sugar, tin, and copper—all important to particular producing states in Latin America.

The Less Developed Areas in World Trade

The new states which have emerged upon the world political scene have become participants in international trade relations. Freed from their colonial status, and with considerable control over their economic destinies, they exert a new influence on world economic relations.

Although endowed with relatively low cost labor and varying degrees of raw material resources, they lack capital and technological know-how to become industrial and exporting units. However, thanks to strong leadership, the strange workings of the great power competitors, and the preoccupations of industrialized states with their former colonies, the process of production for export is slowly emerging in all areas of the less developed world. The total exports are not yet impressive, and the trend will depend to a large extent on the policies of the industrial states.

The new states contribute less than 25 per cent of the world's exports, and two-thirds of that amount is still in raw materials and foodstuffs. These are inevitably low profit trade items, and domestic conversion of raw materials into at least semi-industrial goods will obviously return a higher profit. Also interesting is the extent to which less developed states are now trading with each other. Over one-fourth of the imports of less developed states comes from other less developed countries, thus displaying the classical principle of comparative advantage.

On December 30, 1964, a General Assembly resolution established the United Nations Conference on Trade and Development (UNCTAD). While every UN member is a member of UNCTAD, membership is also open to states outside the UN. The basic objective of UNCTAD is to create an international organization which will improve the trade position of the less developed states vis-à-vis the developed ones by obtaining tariff reduction from the latter on the exports of the former. It is assumed that this improved trade position will help the less developed states to accelerate their economic growth.

So far, UNCTAD has met with little success. This is due in part to the opposition of its industrial members, who are also participants, and in part to both the economic and political weaknesses of the less developed states, and their inability to achieve the proposals contained in the Charter of Algiers presented by them to UNCTAD in December, 1967.

ECONOMIC DEVELOPMENT AND POLITICAL MODERNIZATION

Similar to the tensions of international politics in the nuclear era, which come largely from the inevitably frustrating effort to fit the contemporary environment into traditional political categories, the tensions of national politics in the less developed states represent their equally frustrating effort to fit the modern concept of a nation-state into their traditional institutions.

Problems of Development

While the industrial states constitute about 28.4 per cent of world population, they enjoy about 83 per cent of its annual GNP. The United States has 9 per cent of the world population and 43 per cent of its GNP.

In many less developed states, the average annual per capita income is $184, compared to $3,775 in the United States. Experts set the minimum requirement for existence at 2,000 calories a day; the average American consumes 3,140 calories, the average Indian, 1,980. The industrial states generally have one physician per 1,000 inhabitants; in Nigeria, there is one per 31,740. Four persons out of five can read or write in an average industrial state; in the average less developed state, it is one out of five. In discussing the problems of development we shall examine three main issues: the dichotomy between economic reality and the idealistic aspirations of the less developed areas, the prerequisite factors for economic growth, and the type of economic system most suitable for development.

THE DICHOTOMY BETWEEN ECONOMIC REALITY AND IDEALISTIC ASPIRATIONS. This is significant: non-western states aspire to goals which at this time seem almost unattainable. The populations of most of these states are growing far more rapidly than food supplies. There is poverty, hunger, disease, illiteracy, low productivity, and mass unemployment. These states are predominantly agricultural; current systems of land ownership are not conducive to industrialization or, for that matter, any type of economic stability.

The middle class in these states is very small, without enough influence to stabilize the economy. The poor peasant and the wealthy landowner contribute little to the building of an industrial economy, since it is not in the immediate interest of the wealthy few to invest their money in long-range projects, and the peasant has no money to invest. These conditions make it difficult for the very poor states even to begin their own industrialization. States that enjoy a slightly higher level of wealth can begin to industrialize, but their problem involves keeping the process of development moving forward.

THE PREREQUISITE FACTORS FOR ECONOMIC GROWTH. These are numerous, the principal ones being natural resources, human resources, including labor, management, technicians, and educators, and capital.

The abundance or lack of natural resources often determines the nature of a state's economy—whether it has the ability to produce a variety of goods, or whether it must specialize in and try to export one product in order to import other commodities. Many of the less developed states are deficient in natural resources, which makes self-sufficiency impossible but does not put economic progress out of reach.

Human resources are a prime prerequisite for development. One of the major problems in developing technicians and managerial personnel is that those educated sufficiently for these positions no longer wish to engage in this type of work. The social status of such occupations does not offer the prestige rewards of such professions as medicine or law, and talented people are therefore reluctant to enter these fields. There is thus a shortage of leadership and often a distrust of innovation due to the non-mechanical orientation of these peoples.

The villager, the substance of the non-West, exists on a bare level of subsistence. The industrial worker is the victim of inadequate programs of social welfare and social security benefits. The labor force is not sufficiently stabilized; social patterns conducive to high productivity barely exist. Wages are low and inadequate, and purchasing power severely limits production. Meanwhile, rapid population growth poses a severe impediment for development.

Capital constitutes another major prerequisite for development. There are many types of capital, differing according to the stage of industrialization a state is experiencing; examples include tools, machinery, savings, and investments. One of the problems of the less developed states is their inability to accumulate investment capital. Only those few states that are rich in oil deposits manage to escape a capital shortage.

The problem with respect to capital formation is often not scarcity of capital, but effective use of capital for productive purposes. Many of the less developed states use capital for unproductive "conspicuous consumption," such as jewelry, places of religious worship, oversized armies, and improvement of homes. Furthermore, owing to the absence of fluid capital for entrepreneurs, inadequate transportation and banking facilities, or the lack of skilled labor, it is difficult to find investment opportunities in industries that will yield profits. The problem becomes one of accumulating enough foreign currency to pay for the import of capital goods with which to begin industrialization. Time, money, and technical knowledge are all necessary.

In some less developed areas, a real difficulty involves planning new types of industry. Should industries be capital or labor intensive; that is, should they encourage the country to take advantage of its abundant labor resources, or concentrate on using machinery? This issue is complicated by the question of technical training and maintenance. Establishing an urban industry demands the recruitment of unskilled labor from the rural areas, but there is a real risk involved in selling land and moving to the city in search of employment. Unless the migration is planned by the government, the problem of adequate housing, hospital facilities, schools, and so on, may become insoluble.

THE TYPE OF ECONOMIC SYSTEM SUITABLE FOR DEVELOPMENT. This is no less significant than capital. Socialism has a vast appeal to many less developed states. Private enterprise does not seem suitable or desirable to a state that has been exploited by that system for centuries. Government regulation, supervision, and coordination are a necessity. This conclusion, so repellent to free enterprise theorists, does not imply totalitarianism, but less developed states lack the time to allow pure freedom of economic choice to work its effect.

Approaches to Nation-Building

Prior to and immediately following World War II, popular notions of underdevelopment were dominated by a stereotyped image of non-western states. A state was considered underdeveloped if it failed to fit a model structured by western notions of politics and community—if the state lacked the democratic, competitive, political parties and a high standard of living, it was, by definition, underdeveloped. Few scholars gave serious thought to the dynamic nature of the modernization process, and it was generally assumed that a people emerging from colonialism would express their independence in a systematic effort toward construction of a modern nation-state.

After the initial enthusiasm for independence and the concomitant expectation of non-western states evolving along democratic lines had begun to fade, a serious effort was made to reexamine the prior assumptions. International communist conspiracy, premature independence, and politico-economic backwardness were all held responsible for the post-independence turmoil and the failure of democratic institutions to take root in the newly-emerging non-western states. Consequently, the solutions offered arose from a narrow understanding of the non-western phenomenon. Extension of economic and military assistance to the existing regimes was generally considered to be the panacea for restoring the political and economic health of non-West states. As the U.S.-U.S.S.R. cold war rivalry intensified, international development and alternative approaches to the problems of modernization (communist vs. democratic) acquired considerable status as foreign policy issues. The resulting concern with modernization problems as issues in themselves forced the social sciences to devise new categories and techniques for analysis of the phenomenon of rapid social and political change.

Social scientists integrated the sociological, economic, and political theories and methodologies focusing on the emerging states. This combined effort toward a deeper understanding of non-western political development, as contrasted with the exclusively technical problems of economic development, provided one of the most significant advances in social sciences research on emerging states. Resting on the assumption that a significant relationship exists among social, economic, and political development, this approach has been praised for providing the policy-maker with a more realistic method of assessing the long-range problems of development.

Because of the difficulties encountered by the non-West in building modern, politically viable entities out of their transnational societies, the primacy of political development was recognized as the key to the over-all process of modernization. It is now generally assumed that political development is a precondition to fully successful economic development. Accordingly, social scientists use such concepts as "legitimacy," "stability," "articulation," "aggregation," and "integration" in place of "constitutions," "elections," "interest groups," and "legislatures"; this shift in terms is indicative of the concurrent move toward functional and behavioral theory.

Assorted models of underdeveloped countries are being constructed by anthropologists, psychologists, economists, and sociologists with a view toward contributing to a deeper understanding of political development. Scholars in these disciplines assert certain (not necessarily valid) causal relationships. The economist, for example, measures a country's degree of "progress" in terms of gross national product, per capita income, and other objectively quantifiable criteria, while the political scientist has no quantifiable criteria with which to assess the degree of political "progress." The most fundamental difficulty concerns the criteria of development; there is no agreement regarding what constitutes a "developed" polity.

Obstacles to Theorizing on Nation-Building

On the surface, the task of constructing relevant theories about modernization appears reasonably simple. The emerging non-western states seem to react to the intrusion of traditional European values, and serve the same particularistic, value-maximizing function that was the raison d'être of all European nationalist movements. The immediate goal of the nationalist movements of nineteenth-century Europe was to replace alien dynasties with republican, locally-oriented governments. The emerging bourgeoisie simultaneously pursued an internally pluralistic goal—the breakdown of rural-based control over the economy and polity. The bourgeoisie hoped to rationalize these dimensions of life according to middle-class standards.

In the recent non-western experience, the democratization of society by means of increased commercial participation and secular education was accomplished by an elite hostile to traditional values. Thus, the emergence of the new states of the non-West lies well within the generic framework of most modern revolutions. In the sense that the non-western political elites are attempting to consolidate their economies, educate the masses in national consciousness, and suppress irredentism, they are responding to the same revolution in thought that accelerated the development of modern western civilization. Arbitrary boundaries, ethnic diversities, and fresh memories of colonialism make the modernization effort excessively parochial in approach, but essentially the non-western state serves as a vehicle for the values of a new political elite.

By the mid-twentieth century, however, the western states have become administratively dominant; they assist or protect *continuing* value satisfaction. With the decline of the old particularistic values, as a result of manifest abundance and increases in education, communication, and cultural exchanges, the western states have shed much of their original value-maximizing function. They now assert materialistic values, which are more readily harmonized among states. The particularist, value-maximizing role of the non-western state differentiates it from the western state, and it is the performance of this function in the non-West that perpetuates autarchic nationalism.

The phenomenon of the emerging non-West can be largely understood because of its similarity with past events in the West. That it has occasioned few seminal, unified theories or new generalizations about specific aspects of state behavior might indicate that patterns of state action in the non-West can be understood in terms of the same concepts as historical patterns of state action in the West. However, the absence of new theories might also mean that the nature of the non-West is so radically different that no one has yet understood it.

The truth is probably that, while the non-West seems to be similar to the West's international political experience, it is different enough to prompt new research in the general field of comparative politics, especially the methodological dimension. Unified theories of international politics or partial generalizations have not been affected by the emergence of the non-West, but analyses and comparisons of country development have gained new prominence in the literature of international politics.

Although many novel features of the new countries seem to have had little bearing on the theory of international politics, this is not to say that these novelties will never affect theory construction. However, the peculiarities of the non-West, such as the following, make difficult the prediction of states' behavior: the new states often lack the traditional broad-based nationalist underpinning of the older European and American states; they do not have the working institutions of the western states; they retain many of their traditional values. Many of the traditional "constants" upon which past predictions of international state behavior from domestic sources have been based are absent. Scholars have based their concepts of modernization on linkages thought to have existed in the past. The expectations as well as the fears of serious students and statesmen during the pre- and immediate postindependence phases of the majority of new states were based on a connection among democratic theory, stability, and modernization.

This equation, articulated in many variations, generally states that stability plus democratization (broadening the base, interest aggregation, and so on) equals the minimum necessary preconditions for political modernization. An equation of this sort has apparently served as a model for many scholars, the assumption being that examination of a national actor against the model would reveal the stage of development and point the direction in which further study could proceed.

While this was logical methodology, it has not proved useful in understanding the political phenomena of the non-West, perhaps because these three concepts are normative in nature and lack precision. They are also western concepts evolved from the political evolution intimately connected with western nation-states. Since their value to the West is hard to define, their superimposition on a framework for non-western studies was doomed to failure from the start. As focal points for analysis as well as decision, these criteria have not served the cause of comprehension.

It is difficult to generalize about the non-West because of this lack of criteria; modernization has as many meanings as there are national actors in the non-West. In one-party states, it may mean broadening the party base; in others, it might take on a revisionist form by striking alliances with hitherto traditional powers. Additionally, modernization may mean acquisition of a transistor radio or a western suit. There are no commonly agreed criteria as to the meaning or implications of being modern.

Modernization: Problems and Prospects

Environmental changes in the non-West have outstripped the institutional structures of the traditional era. Such western concepts as the nation-state, the secular city, economic motivation, and a progressive as opposed to a static vision of reality have shaken the foundations of the non-West. The promise of higher stages of material and spiritual perfection is competing with the negative condition of underdeveloped existence.

The collision of venerated values, alien concepts, and the realities of the present international environment underline the problem of non-West modernization. The crisis presently facing each of the new states involves coexisting with itself and acclimation to its new political milieu. The non-West is suspended between two developmental stages; a past of tradition struggling against extinction and a future of nationhood fighting for survival.

The non-West is trying to cover a century in a decade; it is attempting to telescope the achievements of the Enlightenment and the Industrial Revolution into one generation. While the changes are gradual in their genesis, they are dramatic in their issues. The new non-western world is in marked institutional discontinuity with the old. The family, the king, the tribe, and religion have all outlived their usefulness as organizing principles. The non-western people have discovered themselves in unfamiliar ways: their horizons are widened, their mental environment transformed. They must find ways to retain their self-responsibility; they are searching for self-sufficiency to maintain their national dignity. They are forced to choose between baptizing change into the spirit of their system, or renouncing the relevance of their value system to life. Since they cannot do the latter, they must choose the former.

The non-West is thus in a state of ferment, giving rise to confusion and, at times, anarchy. Scarcely any nation in the western sense exists within the boundaries of any present non-West state. These states reflect the aftereffects of division of the world by colonial powers, rather than spontaneous political growth. Government is minimal in organization and effect, and the visible symbols of national identity are either few or irrelevant to modern conditions. The state does not respond as a unit since there is inadequate agreement on common norms. Their laws and organizations are not effective because they do not express a given ideological or normative inner order. Most of the non-western states lack a philosophy of society—basic concepts and assumptions agreed upon by people and their leaders for organizing their experience and ordering their relations to nature and community.

This is a period of accelerated historical transition in the non-West, in contrast to the previous 500 years, when it acted as a passive recipient of historical forces. The pressure of new ideas is explosive, and the passing of the old order is fraught with upheavals and disturbances which are manifestations of unendurable stress. Conflict between conservative and revolutionary forces makes smooth transition difficult. While receptiveness to new ideas is strong, reluctance to let go of older ones is still greater. The search for adjustment creates both individual and national crises, for it demands a separation from the familiar in order to espouse something untested. The temptation to maintain traditionalist attitudes until the crumbling process approaches completion and new and more appropriate theories gain spontaneous acceptance cannot be denied.

Resistance to change and deliberate hesitation must be appreciated by outsiders as subconscious devices for self-preservation, which should not be completely discarded before the new values and old aspirations have been more convincingly attuned to one another. Such a process is inevitably slow, and in the beginning it cannot escape inconsistency and superficiality. The personal attitudes that govern group behavior are less easily revised than the institutions which purport to do so in the official and sanctioned ideologies.

The non-western states, currently incapable of meeting their problems with their own resources, are urgently seeking a metaphysic to justify their existence and encourage their progress. These states are still overwhelmingly rural, the majority of their populations are illiterate and their per capita income is very low. Social and geographical mobility outside the urban sectors is severely restricted. The central structures of government are modern in form but not in substance. The non-western societies also display a lack of political integration, partly because they are characterized by ethnic, religious, racial, and cultural pluralism, and partly because of the limited and uneven operation of the processes of modernization. Furthermore, a general characteristic of non-western states is the wide gap in modernization between the masses and the elite.

The processes of change have produced a variety of political consequences in the non-West, principally the widening of the traditional gap between urban and rural areas with respect to the political center of gravity. National politics has become concentrated almost exclusively in the capital cities, and the peasantry is left outside political action.

The disparity between rural and urban standards of living has also grown; as a result, the tribal structure of society is dissolving. Peasants are moving to the cities, a trend which has a double effect. The new population, accustomed to mere subsistence in the village, cannot secure even these minimum requirements in the city. In addition, the new urban proletariat constitutes a heavy burden and a potentially explosive force close to the seat of government. Many of the street mobs of recent vintage have been largely made up of such uprooted peasants.

The pace of non-western governments in coping with the processes of industrialization is lagging behind the problems that arise. Hence, the economies of these societies have not developed social or political integration, an appreciable middle class, or a stabilized labor organization. The disparity in distribution of benefits remains great; shared equally among groups, they are differentiated along communal, racial, religious, tribal, or similar lines. This results in a lack of positive correlation between economic development and greater social and political integration. Finally, the processes of modernization have ushered in secularization, which stands in direct confrontation to religious traditions. Religion remains a vital force among the masses, while the more secularized elite seek to capitalize on religious tensions.

REFERENCES

* Almond, Gabriel A., and G. B. Powell, Jr., *Comparative Politics: A Developmental Approach.* Boston: Little, Brown and Company, 1966.

Almond, Gabriel A., and James S. Coleman, eds., *Politics of Developing Areas.* Princeton, N.J.: Princeton University Press, 1960.

* Anderson, Charles W., *et al., Issues of Political Development.* Englewood Cliffs, N.J.: Prentice-Hall, Inc., 1967.

* Apter, David, *The Politics of Modernization.* Chicago: University of Chicago Press, 1965.

Aron, Raymond, *The Industrial Society: Three Essays on Ideology and Development.* New York: Frederick A. Praeger, Inc., 1967.

Aubrey, Henry G., *The Dollar in World Affairs: An Essay in International Financial Policy.* New York: Harper & Row, Publishers, 1964.

* Black, Cyril, *Dynamics of Modernization: A Study in Comparative Politics.* New York: Harper & Row, Publishers, 1966.

* Black, Eugene R., *The Diplomacy of Economic Development.* New York: Atheneum, 1963.

* Heilbroner, Robert, *The Great Ascent.* New York: Harper & Row, Publishers, 1963.

Johnson, Harry G., *Economic Policies Toward Less Developed Countries.* Washington, D.C.: The Brookings Institution, 1967.

* ———, *The World Economy at the Crossroads.* London: Oxford University Press, 1965.

Kautsky, John H., ed., *Political Change in Underdeveloped Countries: Nationalism and Communism.* New York: John Wiley & Sons, Inc., 1962.

Meier, Gerald M., *International Trade and Development.* New York: Harper & Row, Publishers, 1963.

* Myrdal, Gunnar, *Asian Drama: An Inquiry into the Poverty of Nations* (3 vols.). New York: Pantheon Books, Inc., 1968.

Organski, A. F. K., *The Stages of Political Development.* New York: Alfred A. Knopf, Inc., 1965.

* Pentony, De Vere, *Underdeveloped Lands: A Dilemma of the International Economy.* San Francisco: Howard Chandler, 1960.

* Pincus, John, *Aid, Trade, and Development: The Rich and Poor Countries.* New York: McGraw-Hill Book Company, 1967.

* Indicates paperback edition.

* Shils, Edward A., *Political Development in the New States.* New York: Humanities Press, Inc., 1962.

Triffin, Robert, *The World Money Maze: National Currencies in International Payments.* New Haven: Yale University Press, 1966.

* Indicates paperback edition.

THIRTEEN

The State Form
in Transition

We know that the nation-state is a human device for satisfying the needs and enhancing the welfare of a society. Its organization provides the response to prevailing needs through the performance of specific functions. The state form thus has neither finality nor a perfected form; its changes are a record of man's experience and of his changing needs.

In purely functional response to the chaos resulting from the collapse of the Roman administration in the fifth century A.D., western man developed the institutions of feudalism. The new conditions in Europe during the breakdown of the medieval synthesis saw feudalism gradually replaced by another organizational concept, the national state. Today, the impact of new technological conditions on the state system has launched man on a new process of organization in response to the new needs and conditions of national and international politics.

Should we then assume that the nation-state has become obsolete? If it has, what has replaced it and why? What trends has the new organizational transition assumed? To what degree will this prove beneficial or detrimental to the future development of humanity?

OBSOLESCENCE OF THE NATION-STATE

The question of the obsolescence of the nation-state might best be examined in respect to present changes in its original objects and functions. The state is by no means the same organization it was in the sixteenth century. New missions have been given to it, and many historic functions have gone through a metamorphosis.

The Broadening of the Original Objects of the State

The basic objects that stimulated the emergence of the nation-state have been modified beyond their original scope. In this century, and particularly since the end of World War II, the evolution of the nation-state has been affected by two major trends which may be working at cross-purposes. New dimensions of economic, military, social, political, and scientific realities are forcing states to establish tighter control over all facets of national life and evolve greater purposes with regard to their over-all development. The laissez-faire "night watchman" state of the nineteenth century has given way to the interventionist "welfare" state, which concerns itself with problems of social and economic development formerly considered outside the purview of state action. As the scope of state action in the twentieth century broadened, the nation-state found itself increasingly unable to ensure its welfare and security through independent actions in the world arena. Nowhere is this more true than in economics, where the national state as a totally independent economic unit has become almost nonexistent; the international system is reaching a point where it is more advantageous to disregard the state as the basic economic unit and concentrate upon supranational units of several types. These organizations have already proved of immense value to small as well as great nations. The question growing from this development is: Will economic federation pave the road to political federation, or will it instead further divide the world into economic subregions?

The same phenomenon holds true in the military domain. The nation-state's independent ability to provide military security for its inhabitants is no longer a reality; any territorial state can be totally destroyed, and military strength only conceals this impotence. Alterations in the theory and practice of war during this century have done much to vitiate the notion of unilateral defense and revive the concept of collective security. The search for measures of collective defense has figured importantly in the devaluation of the centrality of the national state. No longer can a nation concentrate on protecting itself; it must participate in protecting the entire world if it is to have any real security.

Significant changes can be foreseen in the social and cultural field. While nations continue to develop their respective cultures and civilizations, and take pride in their traditions, the clear trend is toward an increasing emphasis on the artistic, intellectual, and ethical aspects of mankind as a whole. While the nation-state is still very much alive as a unit of social association, individuals are beginning to regard themselves as members of some larger group: the West (or the non-West), Europe, Africa, Latin America, and so on. Intellectuals in particular often transcend their respective national loyalties. They as well as the masses seem to crave association with others of the same social strata, regardless of national identification. Today's social forces, both conservative and revolutionary, are combining to push the nation-state out of the spotlight.

In the purely political area, assumptions upon which the state was originally formed have changed considerably. The logic of the technological revolution is progressively restricting the area of choice open to states.

Science has been most injurious to the cause of the nation-state. The new Industrial Revolution, which has altered the world economy, the concept of war, and the ability of peoples to communicate, has been a unifying as well as a divisive force. It can cause the total annihilation of mankind (or at least civilization as man is familiar with it), or it can unite the species in a new ascending spiral of progress. Space and its mysteries, for example, provide one of the major hopes for world unification.

The Expansion of State Functions

Traditionally, the minimum functions of the nation-state in world politics—to provide security and protection to its people—were fulfilled because the source of authority possessing the power of protection could be delineated against the interests and aspirations of other states. In other words, security could be approximated because power could be graded, calculated, and compared. However, radical developments in military technology outran the ability of the nation-state to keep abreast of the new economic, political, and social relations engendered by this revolution. Today, no nation is self-sufficient, militarily secure, or immune from political and ideological penetration.

In light of the revolution in communications and technology, the thesis that the objective national interest of the nation-state (the basic content of which is satisfaction of needs and wants through maximum use of power) is static, unchanging, and permanent, loses much of its effectiveness. To equate national interests with national security, and to assume that power is both the ends and the means of state action, is to take an untenable position. The impact of technology in the nuclear age has made it impossible to measure "power" in the old way and make effective use of it for traditional ends. The familiar struggle for power to attain maximum security can have only one consequence in the modern world—constant turmoil, mutual frustration, and possible chaos and annihilation.

We can conclude from the above that the function of the nation-state has been altered to provision of stability and protection by means other than the unadulterated calculus of power. The nature of the contemporary world prevents any dominant national actor from making a decision that fails to take into consideration the interests of other national actors. The classical goals of power and prestige are no longer the cardinal feature of national interest for sophisticated societies. The emphasis is now on discovery of means to regulate and limit these goals for meaningful purposes and common ends. National goals and interests must take into account various other needs at the individual, national, supranational, and international levels.

The impact of technology in the nuclear age has placed a variety of restrictions and limitations on state action. Although the ends of national interest remain the same—to provide security, prosperity, and peace—the means of attainment have undergone a profound change. War, as an ultimate use of a nation's actual or potential power, can no longer be rationally or safely employed to satisfy a state's needs or grievances, or to achieve the fulfillment of aspirations. Yet the "balance of terror" which has prevailed between the superpowers in the late 1950's and 1960's has not necessarily been conducive to the disappearance of the nation-state. Although the great nuclear nations find the use of power less relevant, the smaller states have paradoxically reserved a measure of their freedom of action under the nuclear umbrella provided by the superpowers.

At the same time, the new technology has created problems that defy the human imagination. Concurrent with the possibility of a millennium as a result of the wonders of technology, complete and utter destruction of civilization is also frighteningly conceivable. This factor, along with the paralysis of world politics, has increased world tensions to unprecedented heights.

While the two dominant powers, armed with nuclear weapons and divided by conflicting ideologies, struggle for a world in which their respective ideologies can prevail, the North-South conflict between former colonial powers (and the culture they represent) and the emerging nations has expanded the scope of the world conflict. Rampant nationalism, embedded in the revolution of rising expectations, is demanding its share of the fruits of technology and industrialization, thus further complicating an already tense situation.

What conclusions can be reached concerning the place of the nation-state in today's transformed context of international politics? First, the nation-state obviously can no longer fulfill its former objects of providing security, protection, and welfare independently. Nonetheless, the nation-state remains the basic unit in the international system, and powerful forces work toward its maintenance. The fact that the state is intimately involved in so many facets of national life creates a self-perpetuating national administrative infrastructure which will prove difficult to dismantle. Perhaps the only accurate conclusion which can be drawn at this juncture in history is that the concept of the sovereignty of the nation-state continues to survive, but its content has changed. The more virulent form of sovereignty and nationalism which prevailed in the nineteenth century has largely disappeared from the developed nations of the world, and the nation-states have found that cooperation is not only compatible with sovereignty, but is indispensable for their continued survival. Meanwhile, the evolution of the nation-state goes on rapidly, and new forms of organization continue to test its validity.

At the same time, the new and emerging states, freed from colonial rule, are paradoxically intensifying their efforts to create the myth of the state which the West is discarding. While both East and West are striving to close their ranks for greater military, political, economic, and social collaboration in the form of supranational organization, the emerging states exploit the East-West conflict. However, despite existing conflicts and tensions, the propensity of national actors to broaden their national interests cannot be minimized. In this age of acceleration and nuclear technology, the challenge of universal survival or universal destruction has brought mankind close together in the attempt to find solutions to the problems that divide the world. Human needs have thus become universalized, and nation-states have been forced to work collectively.

APPROACHES TO ORGANIZATION

The dynamic nature of change in the present milieu of international politics is intensifying the search of men and governments for new concepts of organization. The combined consequences of the technological revolutions make organizational modernization in the present international system imperative. As individual governments have broadened their areas of effective control, corresponding areas of international activity must be subjected to regulation and standardization. The rapid pace of international activity on all levels cannot be satisfied with traditional slow devices of international politics.

The new organizations need secretariats to issue directives, gather and disseminate information, conduct research, and foster public relations. Diplomatic practice has been superseded to a great extent by more complex structures. Diplomats have lost their freedom of action, as demonstrated by the increasingly ritualistic role they play, the rise of "summitry," and chronic back seat driving of their home governments.

The recent proliferation of new states illustrates further the utility of the new organizations. Such formal processes as adherence to the provisions of several international conventions provide established practices from which novice states can learn, patterns upon which they can build, and standards of mature conduct to which they can aspire. Knowing that a worldwide organization is evaluating every move is a profoundly sobering influence on any new state.

The Search for a New Order

A man's right and ability to defend his person, property, and family has been, throughout history, the ultimate exercise and proof of man's freedom. The distinction between self-defense and aggression for defensive purposes has always been unclear. Being a social animal, man has naturally extended this principle to the various forms of communal organization which have characterized his heritage. Following the emergence of the nation-state as the primary unit of organized society, exercise of self-defense was collectivized as modern war. In this form, however, the freedom which the individual intended to preserve was cruelly wrested from him. The state, artificially created to bring him security, clearly outgrew its usefulness. Although the individual could find a relative degree of security from his immediate neighbors within the state, the dangerous dynamics of intergroup existence still had to be controlled. For this purpose, supranational organizations, in myriad forms and for multifarious interests, have been created.

From a theoretical viewpoint, the development of new organizational forms has been embodied in the efforts toward international organization, which have been conducted from two major positions—the federalist and the functionalist. The federalists seek a world government, basing their hope for world order on the premise that all nations must ultimately convert voluntarily from long-held sovereignties to allegiance to some form of universal parliament or council. The functionalists, on the other hand, postulate that the future can be assured only by gradual expansion of cooperation on broader levels in response to specific needs. Functionalist theory holds that cooperation in technical, economic, and generally nontechnical areas will produce a "spillover" effect eventually undermining and transforming the political form of the nation-state.

International organization involving voluntary submission by sovereign states of action-competence to an outside and common authority is relatively new on the world political scene, but its logic and force ensure its long life. Furthermore, it appears likely that the trend toward wider forms of international organization will continue until, minimally, the warmaking capacity of the nation-state is eliminated and men can turn to the solution of other abiding problems.

Prior to the League of Nations, the general historical practice had been to formulate international agreements for the purpose of either defensive or offensive concerted action against a particular power or alliance. The League opened a new era of international organization, because no previous international agreement had sought to encompass the whole of the international system, nor had any international compact undertaken to embrace as broad a range of interests. When the United Nations replaced the League after World War II, it was not thought at all remarkable that this second try at general international organization should take on an even broader scope of responsibility.

Contending Approaches

The real novelty of modern international organizational forms can be best observed on the subordinate levels. Such present-day organizations as the International Labor Organization, the World Health Organization, or the International Monetary Fund on the government level, and the World Federation of Trade Unions, the Inter-Parliamentary Union, or the International Organization of Journalists in the private sector, are representative of the character of the new form of international organization. None of these action areas were conceived of in the early days of the state system; all are reflective of current trends and requirements. Functionalism, breadth of scope, and specialization are the major characteristics that differentiate contemporary organizations from such earlier international arrangements as the Concert of Europe, the Holy Alliance, and other eighteenth- and nineteenth-century European associations.

The evolution of organizational forms has touched off a growing controversy over the relative advantages of regional as opposed to universal systems. Supporters of regionalism contend that the universalist ideal is far too ambitious and perilous because it assumes allegiance to a community which does not, in fact, exist. Universalists claim that the regional approach is no more than an extension of the old and dangerous balance of power, doomed by nature to a repetition of its failure. Recognizing the revolutionary changes and needs of modern society, universalists maintain that only through equally revolutionary political breakthroughs can men hope to find peace. Regional organizations, however, have continued to coexist with such universal bodies as the United Nations.

The functionalists gained their greatest impetus from the astounding success of the European Common Market; developments in Western Europe have also strengthened the idea of regionalism. Most contemporary supranational organization has utilized a combination of the regional-functional approach.

NEW ORGANIZATIONAL FORMS

Enumeration of the various military, economic, social, and political organizations which have proliferated in the last decade alone would be superfluous. We have selected three of the new organizational forms for detailed discussion: the European Community, the non-western Common Markets, and the United Nations. These three have developed more elaborate institutions than the others, and hence provide better models for analysis.

The European Community

Efforts in the direction of European integration before World War II were confined to either theoretical speculation or ultimately abortive structures of hegemonic domination by force of a single power. Following the war, the idea of European integration gained popular favor in the form of the European movement.

Postwar Europe provided a particularly fertile field for experimentation with new forms of international organization. The European peoples needed to escape from the destructive nationalism which had led to the devastation of two world wars within a half-century. Furthermore, not only had the wars caused vast economic loss and human suffering on the Continent, but Europe had lost its former role as the hub of international politics. Thus, following the war, the idea of European integration gained a degree of support which it had never enjoyed before from both national elites and the various European peoples.

On April 18, 1951, France, West Germany, Italy, Belgium, the Netherlands, and Luxembourg signed the draft treaty of the European Coal and

Steel Community, thereby establishing the first European organization with a supranational structure. Previous organizations, composed of representatives from member states, had based their decisions on a compromise among national viewpoints and national interests. The Coal and Steel Community created the first common European authority, independent of governments and able to make its own decisions. To this body the governments transferred some of their sovereign power.

Since the launching of European integration by the Coal and Steel Community, the six participating members have formed two other bodies. The first was EURATOM (the European Atomic Energy Community), created to further the use of nuclear energy for peaceful purposes and insure that Europe did not lag behind in the coming atomic revolution. The second was the European Economic Community (the Common Market), formed on January 1, 1958, in order to establish a vast single market for all products, with a broad measure of common economic policies. This would bring into being a powerful productive unit generating steady expansion and providing greater stability and a rapid rise in living standards. Beyond this economic goal, the founders of the EEC hoped that this form of organization would pave the way for further political integration of the member states. These three organizations (ECSC, EURATOM, and EEC) have now been merged into one organization, the European Community.

The driving forces behind European integration have been both political and economic. Individually, the European countries cannot compete as equals in world trade against the United States and the Soviet Union. But were an economic union of 200 million people to be created, Europeans could hope to play a full role in developing their own economies and those of the developing nations which look to them for aid.

The objective is not simply to permit trade in goods between separate economies, but to merge existing markets and establish in their place the conditions and characteristics of a single market. This means abolition of the traditional barriers to trade (e.g., customs duties, quotas) and less obvious hindrances, such as discrimination and private agreements to share markets, control of the conditions under which imports from the rest of the world can enter the new economic area (a common external tariff), and maintenance of free movement of persons, capital, firms, and services. Divergent national policies must gradually be merged into a harmonious whole (particularly in the field of agriculture) while moving toward a common economic policy for the entire Community.

To establish a single market and work out common policies, the European Community has organized an institutional system whose basic structure is federal: a European Commission, independent of the member states, a Council of Ministers, consisting of representatives of the governments, a European Parliament entrusted with democratic control of at least some issues, and a Court of Justice. The activity of these institutions, set up to work out and apply the common rules of the Community, is political in nature though economic in its field of operation. It aims not only at integrating the actions of producers, workers, and businessmen, but also at harmonizing the policies of the national governments and the major role they play in determining the conditions of economic activity.

The Common Market: A Balance Sheet

In economic terms, the success of the European Community has amazed even its most fervent advocates. Trade within the Common Market has been expanding dramatically, and trade with the United States and the rest of Europe has also grown. The Community has enjoyed an economic growth rate higher than the United States or Britain; it has expanded its share of world trade, and steadily built up its monetary reserves.

This prosperity reflects in part the continuation of economic stimuli which have been operating on the Continent for some years, but the Common Market has also had its direct impact. Since its formation, trade between members has increased even more rapidly than before. More recently the Common Market confirmed its credentials as a full-fledged customs union. Industrial tariffs on trade among its members were abolished, and uniform tariffs established on imports from the outside world.

The impact of the economic integration thus far achieved upon the political development of the European Community is more difficult to appraise. The operations of the Community to date are no doubt less supranational than European federalists might wish. However, the European Commission, which acts independently of the member states, has accumulated far more de facto power than it is accorded by the letter of the law. This accretion of Commission authority has occurred partially by default; the Council of Ministers, representing the member states, has often lacked the technical expertise to challenge programs proposed by the Commission. The Commission has also developed a highly successful integrating technique concerning the packaging of proposals, whereby the member states are induced to yield in certain areas in the expectation of benefits in other areas. In spite of its impressive successes, the European Community has not yet begun the final assault on the citadel of national sovereignty, and fundamental differences over the next steps to be taken continue to divide the members of the Common Market. In fact, the very success of the Community in overcoming economic obstacles to integration has accelerated the day when basic political disagreements among the member states can no longer be avoided or postponed.

Political divisions within the six represent two conflicting concepts of how best to coordinate political policies. At one extreme, France has proposed a "Europe of fatherlands," a kind of confederation in which maximum sovereignty can be retained by the participating states. Other Europeans, led principally by the Dutch, have preferred a more supranational solution, in which the European Commission and Parliament would play a greater role. The problem has become more complex with the requests of Great Britain and other members of the European Free Trade Association for admission to the Community.

Britain's desire to affiliate is in many respects the clearest possible evidence of the growing political and economic significance of the European Community, since it represents an historic break with the long tradition of British policy toward the Continent. Britain is not simply motivated by the economic and political disadvantages it sees for itself in standing aloof, but also by the positive gains to be won by combining with the six.

Any great increase in membership will alter the character of the Community. Most of the change will be simply a function of increasing the size and decreasing the homogeneity of the group, although to some extent it will be the result of redistribution of the balance of interest within the Community. The United Kingdom would bring with it a complex of worldwide economic and political commitments, a different legal system, and a host of other institutional and historical differences.

As the Community members continue to merge their economies and develop their capacity for acting as a unit, they approach the role of an equal partner with the United States, sharing equitably in the responsibilities and burdens which have hitherto rested mainly upon the latter. The European Community therefore offers an effective way for the developed countries of the West to join together in discharging some of their common obligations and responsibilities. The Community can work with the United States for the creation of a more viable world order to accommodate the needs and interests of the less developed nations in their effort to modernize. The two groups can also concert more effectively for military defense against aggression and for a common political approach ultimately designed to bring about basic changes in Soviet purposes and objectives.

Fulfillment of this promise by the European Community depends on three conditions. First, members of the Community must develop their readiness and ability to act as a unit, which is implicit in their ultimate goal of European federation or confederation. The Community seems likely to progress gradually to that goal, but in the shorter term the central institutions of the European Community, particularly the Commission, must be given more power, and must develop the capacity to act on behalf of the members in their external relations. The limited progress thus far achieved in this respect will have to be amplified once the United Kingdom and others have joined.

Second, development of an effective and enduring bilateral partnership between the United States and the enlarged European Community is of fundamental importance. This partnership would cover the major economic, political, and military problems confronting the United States and the enlarged Community.

Third, the partnership must face outward toward the rest of the world. The building of their own resources and unity will enable the Atlantic nations to discharge more effectively the crucial tasks facing them. A close partnership must not prevent a broader community of nations, and must allow other interested nations to participate.

Thus the opportunity offered by the European Community obliges both Europe and the United States to see that it does come into being as rapidly as possible, that it grows in strength and influence, and that the United States and the European Community are able to work together effectively in pursuit of common purposes and in the discharge of common tasks.

Common Markets in the Non-West

Modern technology and the new automated or semiautomated methods of industrial production make large producing units more economical and more competitive than smaller producing units. General awareness of this throughout the world, plus the spectacular economic performance of the European Common Market, has encouraged the underdeveloped states to attempt some similar groupings. Two arguments are usually advanced in support of these organizations. First, a Common Market arrangement makes possible a certain rate of industrial growth at lower cost than separate attempts by each state, because the Common Market is able to take advantage of the economies of scale and specialization. Second, since large markets are usually more attractive to foreign investors, the Common Market would induce new investments and therefore encourage industrialization. Three Common Markets are emerging in the less developed areas. The Central American Common Market (CACM) includes Costa Rica, El Salvador, Guatemala, Honduras, and Nicaragua. The initial steps leading to the formation of CACM were the Multilateral Treaty on Free Trade and Central American Integration, signed in June, 1958, at Tegucigalpa, and the General Treaty of Central American Integration, signed in December, 1960, in Managua. The 1960 treaty provided for creation of the Central American Economic Council and a permanent secretariat, and also set the stage for the creation of CACM. The general treaty went into effect in June, 1961, and, among other things, provides for common external tariffs by 1970. CACM is the most successful of the underdeveloped areas' Common Markets. It is estimated that the value of intraregional trade increased seven-fold between 1960 and 1965. The success of CACM is due to the careful studies that were carried out by ECLA (Economic Commission for Latin America) prior to its formation, and to the minimum of politics within its operations.

The East African Common Market (EACM) includes Kenya, Tanzania, and Uganda, and leaves the door open to Zambia and other Central African countries. EACM, a direct by-product of the East African Common Services Organization, is an integral part of the East African Community contained in the Treaty for East African Cooperation, signed in Kampala on June 6, 1967, and going into effect on December 1, 1967.

EACM has been relatively successful despite internal strains among its members. Both Tanzania and Uganda feel that Kenya is gaining most from the Common Market because of its more advanced economy and relatively higher stage of industrialization. This unequal distribution of gains in the Market is at present under study in order to determine its effects and find an equitable solution.

The Arab Common Market includes Iraq, Syria, Jordan, and Egypt. Ever since the creation of the League of Arab States in 1945, efforts had been made toward some kind of economic unity among its members. Nothing cohesive was established until the signing of the Arab Economic Unity Agreement on June 6, 1962, which went into effect on April 30, 1964.

The Economic Unity Council, established as a result of the 1964 agreement, decided to institute an Arab Common Market, as provided for in the 1964 agreement. The Arab Common Market came into being on January 1, 1965, and aimed at gradual elimination of intraregional tariffs by 1975 and establishment of common external tariffs. To become a member of the Arab Common Market, a country had to be a member of the Arab Unity Agreement; in order to be a member of this agreement, the country had to be a member of the League of Arab States. This is obviously an effort to keep non-Arab countries out of the Arab Common Market. Kuwait, a signatory of the June 6, 1962, agreement, decided at the last minute not to join because of internal pressures from its business community, which felt that it would lose more than it would gain by joining. While the Arab Common Market has not met with great success, reductions of internal tariffs and uniformities of external tariffs are proceeding on schedule.

Two basic difficulties account for the limited progress of common markets among the underdeveloped states. First, since almost all of them are primary producing countries, trade among them is limited to these commodities; most of what they need for industrialization, such as capital equipment, has to come from the outside. Second, lack of an enforcing or problem-solving mechanism makes each country its own master with regard to vital decisions. There is no agreement on the choice of industrial locations; each country feels that certain industries should be located on its own territory. This struggle for industrialization makes the smooth operation of a common market very difficult.

The United Nations

The United Nations is composed of six principal organs which operate through a number of committees, commissions, and boards. They are: the General Assembly, the Security Council, the Economic and Social Council, the Trusteeship Council, the International Court of Justice, and the Secretariat.

THE GENERAL ASSEMBLY. The General Assembly, in which all member states are represented, is the largest organ of the United Nations. It meets every year in regular session; special sessions can be called by a majority of the states, the Security Council, or one member with the concurrence of a majority. Every member of the United Nations has one vote in the General Assembly. Recommendations on important issues require a two-thirds majority, while on less substantial issues only a simple majority is required. The General Assembly functions as a world forum to maintain international peace and security, advance international economic and social cooperation, and promote welfare of nonself-governing and trust territories. In addition, the General Assembly regulates budgetary matters.

THE SECURITY COUNCIL. This is composed of five Permanent Members (China, France, United Kingdom, Union of Soviet Socialist Republics, United States of America) and ten members elected by the General Assembly for two-year periods. It functions continuously, and each member has one vote. Resolutions on procedural matters are passed by any nine affirmative votes, and resolutions on "other" (substantive) matters require nine votes including the concurrent votes of the permanent members. This is the famous "veto": a negative vote by a permanent member on a nonprocedural question. The Security Council has primary responsibility for the maintenance of peace and security. It therefore undertakes pacific settlement of disputes, and is also authorized to take preventive or enforcement action in cases of "threats to the peace, breach of the peace, or act of aggression."

THE ECONOMIC AND SOCIAL COUNCIL. This is composed of 27 members elected by the General Assembly for three years. It normally holds at least two sessions a year; each member has one vote, and decisions are arrived at by simple majority. The Economic and Social Council works to improve standards of living everywhere and is concerned with the solution of international economic, social, and health problems. Its operations are also directed to the promotion of cultural and educational cooperation, and the universal respect of human rights and freedoms.

THE TRUSTEESHIP COUNCIL. This is composed of all members holding trust territories, plus China and the Soviet Union (which hold none) and an additional number of members to balance the number of trust-administering states. These additional members are elected by the General Assembly for a period of three years. The Council meets twice a year; each member has one vote, decisions being arrived at by majority voting. The Trusteeship Council carries out the function of the United Nations regarding trust territories, except for those areas designated as strategic.

THE INTERNATIONAL COURT OF JUSTICE. This is composed of 15 judges elected concurrently by the General Assembly and the Security Council for nine-year terms. Except for judicial vacations, the Court is permanently in session at The Hague; nine judges constitute a quorum. It functions as the judicial organ of the United Nations.

THE SECRETARIAT. This consists of a Secretary-General and such staff as the United Nations may require. The Secretary-General is the chief executive officer and administrator of the United Nations and acts in this capacity in meetings of all of its principal organs except the International Court of Justice. He is appointed by the General Assembly on the recommendation of the Security Council for a period of three years. The Secretariat is the administrative agency of the United Nations.

The Changing Role of the United Nations

The United Nations, as its founders realized, is not a world government and has a limited function in the settlement of conflicts of interest between states. Preservation of the peace by the United Nations was postulated upon the hoped-for unanimity of great power interest following World War II. The United Nations emphasized collective security, while the League of Nations had emphasized the necessity of disarmament.

The United Nations was designed to be a balancing force in international politics through maintenance of the status quo and the grand design of the victorious powers. While the UN has failed to balance world politics or maintain the status quo, it has demonstrated a high degree of flexibility in adapting itself to new circumstances. In becoming an institution for change, the UN system has taken on the dual role of institutionalizing new factors in world politics and communicating their impact to the system at large. A result of these developments has been a revision in the operations of the General Assembly and the office of Secretary-General, both of which assumed new roles and functions. These two organs became the main regulatory centers of the process of change, clearinghouses of postwar conflicts and accommodations.

The shift from the early conception of the UN which prevailed at San Francisco—that of an aristocratic organization animated by the dominant spirit of the chief victorious powers—to a diverse and curiously democratized institution reveals some of the difficulties and dangers which the western world in general, and the United States in particular, will encounter in the future. In fact, major contemporary criticisms of the UN have focused on the great differences of aim and purpose among the 51 founder members and many of the 75 newly-independent countries which were later elected to membership.

The founders emphasized organization of peace through collective security, to be achieved by great power cooperation. The great powers were chosen as permanent members of the Security Council in the expectation that they would agree on how to keep international order, and work together through united decision and coordinated action against any breach of the peace by the smaller powers. In the event of disagreement among them, each was armed with a veto on action by others. The optimum results of this system would be successful defense of the status quo; the worst possible outcome would be stalemate.

The supposition was in error. The Soviet Union's decision to subordinate the main purpose of the organization to its own national ends was the first breach in the spirit of the Charter. At the same time, the United States hoped to convert the UN to an instrument of its foreign policy, often attempting to overburden the organization with responsibilities clearly outside its competence. The rise of anticolonialism was another divergent influence. The new countries are placing their campaign for the end of all colonial rule above the "international peace and security" implications of the Charter.

The newly-independent states which were not active participants in international politics during World War II know little of the depth of feeling that brought the UN into being and the reasons for the presence in the Charter of each long-debated article. The Allied states that sent their delegates to San Francisco in 1945 held strong beliefs formed from their experiences in two world wars and their previous attempt to create an effective world organization. They were determined that there must be a new international organization, and knew that it must demand more from its members than the League of Nations in order to be effective.

The majority of the new states of Asia and Africa were spared these experiences, and looked on the Allied nations' actions at San Francisco in their own special way. Their whole history, insofar as it was at all politically conscious, had been completely dominated by the struggle for independence. They are less interested in what often seems to them theoretical formulas for preservation of world peace than with the immediate problems of giving their new independence a stronger economic and social base and helping other colonial peoples to attain independence. They still mistrust all ex-colonial powers, including those now rapidly freeing their colonies. Since the same powers are prominent in the effort to preserve the integrity of the UN, the new states have deep suspicions about their motives and actions.

In addition to these factors influencing the actions of the UN, the impact of the early period of the cold war on the UN can hardly be overstated. When great power harmony was abandoned, the Security Council —the main center of guarantee for maintenance of the status quo—began to lose the prominent role which the framers of the Charter had planned for it. In addition, the cold war era stripped the UN of any effective leadership. Its effect on the structure of the UN was to produce significant changes in the function of both the General Assembly and the Office of the Secretary-General.

In short, no one of the organization's key bodies—the Security Council, the General Assembly, or the Secretariat—is functioning today as was planned at San Francisco.

The Security Council, which was intended to act as the executive organ with primary responsibility for maintenance of international peace and security, is held in a state of chronic stalemate. Because the Security Council has been so completely frustrated, the General Assembly has moved into the gap and taken leadership in political matters. Landmarks in this process include the "Uniting for Peace" resolutions of 1950 which authorized the General Assembly to take jurisdiction of a political-security question on which the Security Council was unable to reach a decision, development of a military action capability under General Assembly control in the 1956 crisis in the Suez Canal Zone and in the Congo affair of 1960–1964, and open assault on colonialism in Africa, launched in 1960 and developed during the following years.

The Secretary-General's office has also developed in response to these trends. Particularly during the tenure of Dag Hammarskjöld, but evidenced under his successor U Thant as well, is a determination to make the Secretary-General a significant political force in his own right. The dominant majority in the General Assembly is sufficiently powerful to provide the Secretary-General with a political base from which to work. He is sometimes referred to as the "foreign minister of the world's fourth great power," as he moves about the political map applying the name, prestige, and influence of the UN to political problems.

The increased responsibility thrust upon the Secretary-General has been reflected in what is perhaps the major innovation of UN operations in the past two decades—the techniques of "peacekeeping," or as Dag Hammarskjöld put it, "preventive diplomacy." Faced with the inability to resolve the cold war conflict, the UN has turned to attempts to prevent the spread of the cold war into uncommitted areas of the world. Ranging from observer teams and fact-finding commissions to the creation of full-blown military forces, UN peacekeeping operations have generally had the same mission—to insert a UN presence in a troubled area before the great powers are tempted to intervene. The concept of preventive diplomacy has captured the imagination of many of the smaller states in the UN, who see in peacekeeping operations a constructive way in which they can bring their influence to bear in the international arena. At the same time, the peacekeeping role has led to some of the major controversies which have beset the UN in the 1960's, including the Article 19 crisis in which the United States abortively attempted to deprive the Soviet Union and other countries of the right to vote in the General Assembly because of their failure to pay their share of the costs of UN peacekeeping operations.

Finally, no clearer proof of the changing character of the organization could be cited than the dramatic erosion which has taken place in the notion of "domestic jurisdiction." Originally written into the Charter as a protection of sovereignty against external inquiry, it remains intact in principle but has been riddled with exceptions in practice. The long-standing principle has been that each state is the judge of what constitutes its domestic jurisdiction, and can reject international intervention into such issues as it chooses to except. Ever since the ex-colonial states have assumed membership, however, the scope of interest of the General Assembly has widened to include many questions once considered clearly out of bounds. Without ever resolving the complex legal questions involved, the organization has simply taken account of whatever questions seemed important to it and has let the protests fall where they may.

This is by no means an unclouded benefit, for trampling on sensitive nationalism always engenders strife; the UN, it is said, has begun more controversies than it has solved. But it is beyond doubt that the vast bulk of its members have conceded, whether happily or gloomily, that the scope of action of the UN has broadened widely. The organization has a good deal more to say about questions of peace or war than was envisioned in 1945.

ORGANIZATION: THE ESCAPE FROM DISASTER?

An implicit assumption in this book, made explicit at many points, is that the political world today is undergoing extensive, rapid, and in some cases violent, change. New forces of far-reaching import have been released on mankind, and statesmen are grappling with the consequences. The structures and patterns of international politics, like those of any social system, were originally developed on the basis of and in response to certain prevailing social conditions. Now that conditions have changed so drastically, serious questions must be asked about the relevance of familiar institutions to unfamiliar circumstances.

The international political system is a relatively loose and underinstitutionalized order, calculated to limit without nullifying the inescapable dynamics of state interaction. The inhibitions on state freedom of choice were long ago set at the precise minimum necessary to preserve the integrity of the system while allowing for a wide range of adjustment and stability. Created in the era of absolute monarchy and the musketeer, the systems and processes of world politics proved capable of adapting to such explosive forces as the rise of nationalism, the development of world empire, and the creation of mass armies. Why then are we suggesting that their viability has been seriously compromised today?

This question has also been repeatedly answered in the preceding pages. Contemporary challenges overtax the competence of the state form, and international conflict constantly threatens to spill over the limit of tolerability and safety. The new means of action open to states are too dangerous to use, while the old techniques are inappropriate to the problems. The great questions of today's international life find no answers within the traditional confines of the state system.

Nor can it suffice merely to regard such insistent problems as the escape from destruction, the demands of the non-West, the challenge of communism, and the implications of nuclear energy as insoluble and therefore not fit matters for concern. So powerful are the new dynamics of international life that either answers will be found for them or they will find their own answers. The issue facing political man is whether he will discover methods and mechanisms to dominate and shape events, or whether he will ultimately be dominated by them.

In these terms the problem of organizing human effort for solution of these long-term problems becomes central. The familiar state form has both legal and mystical underpinnings, but in the last analysis its only rational justification is utilitarian. In other words, it must get the job done; if it fails, other structures and other principles must be found to replace it.

The process of experimentation has already begun. New organizational forms have been developed, new processes initiated, and new solutions attempted. Only a very few of these, however, incorporate a fundamental break with the past; most remain tentative steps that seek to preserve the psychic component of sovereignty while restricting its actual force. It is a tribute to human ingenuity that so many ways have been found to have man's cake of sovereignty and eat it too.

No serious observer feels today that such half measures have proved their effectiveness. Such proof may yet be forthcoming; it is premature to argue flatly for outright abandonment of the sovereign nation-state in favor of an unproved vision of world government. But it is clear that no over-all rationale for international politics yet suggested or attempted meets the requirements of the contemporary era. What has taken place up to now is a massive purchase of time for innovation and—hopefully—hard thought. The era of difficult decision and new techniques of action lies ahead.

Some way must be discovered to cope effectively with the new forces of world politics if man is to win release from the tension of contemporary life and move out from under the mushroom cloud of nuclear destruction. New ways of organizing human effort across national lines must precede any direct attack on the problems. History teaches that success and renown are the rewards of those that most quickly and powerfully respond to the challenges of civilization. Students of international politics can enthusiastically dedicate themselves to this end. The penalty for failure may be disaster; the reward for success may be a better life on this planet for everyone.

REFERENCES

Abraham, Willie E., *The Mind of Africa*. Chicago: University of Chicago Press, 1962.

* Bailey, Sydney D., *General Assembly of the United Nations* (2nd rev. ed.). New York: Frederick A. Praeger, Inc., 1964.

* Indicates paperback edition.

* Camps, Miriam, *European Unification in the Sixties*. New York: McGraw-Hill Book Company, 1966.

* Cassirer, E., *Myth of the State*. New Haven: Yale University Press, 1961.

Clark, W. Hartley, *The Politics of the Common Market*. Englewood Cliffs, N.J.: Prentice-Hall, Inc., 1967.

* Claude, Inis L., Jr., *The Changing United Nations*. New York: Random House, Inc., 1966.

————, *Swords into Plowshares* (3rd rev. ed.). New York: Random House, Inc., 1964.

Cox, Arthur M., *Prospects for Peacekeeping*. Washington, D.C.: The Brookings Institution, 1967.

Curzon, Gerard, *Multilateral Commercial Diplomacy*. New York: Frederick A. Praeger, Inc., 1966.

Eagleton, Clyde, *International Government* (3rd ed.). New York: The Ronald Press Company, 1957.

* Feld, Werner, *The European Common Market and the World*. Englewood Cliffs, N.J.: Prentice-Hall, Inc., 1967.

Goodspeed, Stephen S., *Nature and Function of International Organization* (2nd ed.). New York: Oxford University Press, Inc., 1967.

Green, Reginald H., *Unity or Poverty*. Baltimore: Penguin Books, Inc., 1968.

Haas, Ernest B., *Beyond the Nation-State: Functionalism and International Organization*. Stanford, Calif.: Stanford University Press, 1964.

* ————, *International Political Communities: An Anthology*. Garden City, N.Y.: Doubleday & Company, Inc., Anchor Books, 1966.

* Kay, David A., ed., *U.N. Political Systems*. New York: John Wiley & Sons, Inc., 1967.

MacDonald, Robert, *The League of Arab States: A Study in the Dynamics of Regional Organization*. Princeton, N.J.: Princeton University Press, 1965.

* Mitrany, David, *A Working Peace System*. Chicago: Quadrangle Books, 1966.

Nicholas, Harold G., *The United Nations as a Political Institution* (3rd ed.). London: Oxford University Press, 1967.

Nye, Joseph, *Pan-Africanism and East African Integration*. Cambridge, Mass.: Harvard University Press, 1965.

* ————, ed., *International Regionalism*. Boston: Little, Brown and Company, 1968.

* Padelford, Norman J., and Leland M. Goodrich, eds., *The United Nations in the Balance*. New York: Frederick A. Praeger, Inc., 1965.

Wallerstein, Immanuel M., *Africa: The Politics of Unity*. New York: Random House, Inc., 1967.

* Indicates paperback edition.

Wightman, David, *Toward Economic Cooperation in Asia*. New Haven: Yale University Press, 1964.

Wionczek, Miguel S., ed., *Latin American Economic Integration*. New York: Frederick A. Praeger, Inc., 1966.

Index

Action:
  capability in, 59–76
  definition of theory of, 8
  limitations on, 161–79
  organization for, 40–46
Actors (*see also* Nation-State; States):
  concept of, xi, 8, 13
  as regional, 135–36, 140–41, 273–74
  as universal, 135, 137–40
Adjudication, procedure of, 154, 155
Adjustment:
  conflict and, 143–59
  procedure of, 81
Agreement, technique for, 81 (*see also* Decisions)
Agricultural capacity as capability factor, 68, 71–72
Aid (*see specific types*)
Alliances, use of, 116, 118, 119 (*see also* Bloc actors)
Almond, Gabriel, 10
Alternatives, choice among, 48–49
Ambassadors, functions of, 43–44
Anarchy of international system, 102, 107, 113, 119, 263

Anticolonialist, ideology of, 90, 122, 137, 191–92, 213, 220, 221–23 (*see also* Non-western world)
Antihierarchy, concept of, 218, 219
Apolitical, *definition* of, 22
Approach of this study, 13–16
Apter, David, 10
Arab Common Market, 279
Arab Economic Unity Agreement, 279–80
Arbitration, procedures of, 154–55
Armaments (*see* Military doctrine; Military force; Warfare; Weaponry)
Arms race, 186 (*see also* Warfare; Weaponry)
  disarmament and, 202–6
  logic of, 203–4
Aron, Raymond, 10
Automation, 132, 241 (*see also* Technological revolution, results of)

Balance of payments, 86
Balance of power, 8, 13, 14, 30, 114–19, 124–25, 143, 274 (*see also* Equilibrium theory; Power)